HOW I FOUND FREEDOM IN AN UNFREE WORLD

HARRY BROWNE

AVON BOOKS ◆ NEW YORK

AVON BOOKS
A division of
The Hearst Corporation
105 Madison Avenue
New York, New York 10016

Copyright © 1973 by Harry Browne
Published by arrangement with Macmillan Publishing Company, Inc.
Library of Congress Catalog Card Number: 72-90549
ISBN: 0-380-00423-2

First Avon Books Printing: January 1974

AVON TRADEMARK REG. U.S. PAT. OFF. AND IN OTHER COUNTRIES, MARCA
REGISTRADA, HECHO EN CANADA

Printed in Canada

UNV   29   28   27   26   25   24   23   22   21

To Jeannette

CONTENTS

Prologue

Part III—*A New Life*

Epilogue

Appendix

Prologue

1

Freedom in an Unfree World

FREEDOM is the opportunity to live your life as you want to live it.

The urge for freedom is so much a part of human nature that it can never be suppressed by laws, slogans, or commandments. There is a difference, however, between the urge and the reality. For most people, freedom remains a pleasant fantasy—something to dream of while carrying out daily obligations in the real world.

They spend their lives talking vaguely of what they want in life, what they think they're missing, why they don't have it, and who it is that prevents them from being free.

For most people, freedom is an "if only." "If only it hadn't been for my wife, I would have been a success." Or "If only it hadn't been for Roosevelt (or Nixon or whomever), the country would be free."

The unfree person can never fully repress his urge for freedom—whether he considers his jailer to be his family, his job, society, or the government. And so, from time to time, halfhearted attempts are made to break free from the restrictions.

But unfortunately, those attempts usually depend upon the individual's ability to change the minds of other people—and so optimism ultimately turns into frustration and despair.

11

Hoping to be free, many people engage in continual social combat—joining movements, urging political action, writing letters to editors and Congressmen, trying to educate people. They hope that someday it will all prove to have been worthwhile.

But as the years go by they see little overall change. Small victories are won; defeats set them back. The world seems to continue on its path to wherever it's going. Until they die, the hopeful remain just as enslaved as they've always been.

The plans, the movements, the crusades—none of these things has worked. And so the unfree man continues to dream, to condemn, and to remain where he is.

There must be a better way.

There must be a way to be free without having to wish for a miracle. It must be a way by which an individual can change things without having to rally the rest of the world to his side.

It has to be a way through which he can get rid of exorbitant taxes, have the time to do what he wants to do, enjoy love without tiresome complications, remove irritating social restrictions, and free himself from the hundred and one burdens that others daily hand him.

And it must be a way that doesn't require that he re-educate all of the other people involved.

Fortunately, there is such a way.

It isn't necessary to join a massive campaign to reconstruct the society in which you live, nor do you have to patiently re-educate everyone you deal with.

There's a way that depends entirely upon what *you* choose to do. You can be free without changing the world. You can live your life as you want to live it—no matter what others decide to do with their lives.

IS IT POSSIBLE?

If that doesn't seem possible, I'm not surprised.

After all, how can you live as you want to live when there are so many people who won't let you?

How can you spend your money as you please when the government takes so much of it in taxes? How can you do what you want to do when the government and society have prohibited many of the things you'd like to do?

How could you live your own life when you have responsibilities to your family, your friends, your job? How could you possibly ignore the demands that others make upon you?

I realize that the odds against a free life must seem pretty formidable right now. And yet there are already individuals who live their lives as they choose. Some of them may have begun with greater problems than you face now. But in spite of their problems, they've found freedom without waiting for the world to be free.

To be free in an unfree world isn't nearly as unrealistic as it might seem at first glance. After all, it's commonly assumed that there can be free nations in a world that contains enslaved nations. Why, then, can't there be free states within a nation that isn't free? Or free towns within an unfree state?

Most important, why can't there be free individuals within unfree towns, states, or nations?

Freedom *is* possible, and you can have it—if that's what you really want.

I can't know which specific freedom you crave most— freedom from social restrictions, family problems, high taxes, bad relationships, the treadmill, governmental repression. Whichever one is most important to you, we'll cover it and more. And I think you'll find that the principles to be stated will apply to any type of situation that may be restraining you.

It's not likely that you'll ever gain your freedom by joining, marching, picketing, or complaining—because all those methods rely upon changing the attitudes of others. What I have in mind concerns the use of methods over which you have complete control.

WHY YOU ARE NOT FREE

Freedom is the opportunity to live your life as you want to live it. And that *is* possible, even if others remain as they are.

If you're not free now, it might be because you've been preoccupied with the people or institutions that you feel have restrained your freedom. I don't expect you to stop worrying about them merely because I suggest that you do.

I do hope to show you, though, that those people and institutions are relatively powerless to stop you—once you decide how you will achieve your freedom. There are things you can do to be free, and if you turn your attention to those things, no one will stand in your way. But when you become preoccupied with those who are blocking you, you overlook the many alternatives you could use to bypass them.

The freedom you seek is already available to you, but it has gone unnoticed. There are probably two basic reasons why you haven't taken advantage of that freedom.

One reason is that *you're unaware of the many alternatives available to you.*

You don't have to go to jail to avoid exorbitant taxes. Nor do you have to be a social leper if you refuse to knuckle under to social pressure. You don't have to give up love in order to avoid complicated, restrictive family problems. And you don't have to go without friends to avoid having your life at the disposal of others.

But if you're unaware of additional alternatives, it's easy to see these matters as being either/or questions. There *are* additional alternatives—ways by which you can have what you want without bringing bad consequences upon yourself.

The second reason you're not free is because *you've probably accepted without challenge certain assumptions that restrict your freedom.*

Out culture is saturated with philosophical "truths" that are commonly accepted and acted upon—and are rarely challenged. I think of these truisms as *traps*.

A typical example of a trap is, "It would be selfish to be concerned with your own freedom—you must think of others first." Or "The kind of freedom you want is immoral," or "The government is more powerful than you are," or "You have to accept the will of the majority."

There are probably hundreds of such traps, but I've reduced those that I've seen to fourteen basic types.

It's very easy to get caught in a trap. The truisms are repeated so often they can be taken for granted. And that can lead to acting upon the suggestions implied in them—resulting in wasted time, fighting inappropriate battles, and attempting to do the impossible.

Traps can lead you to accept restrictions upon your life that have nothing to do with you. You can unwittingly pay taxes you don't have to pay, abide by standards that are unsuited to you, put up with problems that aren't really yours.

Traps are assumptions that are accepted without challenge. As long as they go unchallenged, they can keep you enslaved. That's why it's important that we challenge them in the following pages. I think you'll find that most of them have no more substance than ancient clichés such as "The world is flat."

If you're not free now, it's very likely that you've accepted some of these traps. And you probably haven't known of a number of alternatives that could get you out of your restrictions without the pain and effort that you might have assumed would be necessary.

As we look at these traps and alternatives, I hope you'll become aware of the unlimited number of avenues open to you. You possess a tremendous amount of control over your situation—control that's disregarded when you focus attention upon the people who seem to stand in your way.

YOUR FREEDOM

Most books dealing with freedom present an involved plan that depends upon the support of other people. These usually urge you to pass the book on to others, sell the idea to a great many people, and gain the support of the public in order to be free.

This isn't that kind of book. If you were holding the only copy of it, and if no one else could read it or accept its conclusions, the ideas would still be useful to you.

We'll be dealing only with your freedom. Whether the ideas would work for others is unimportant; what you have to decide is whether they can work for you.

You won't have to convince anyone else of anything. Every idea in the book will depend solely upon your own action.

I can assure you that I didn't achieve my freedom through long hours, articulate oratory, or mysterious powers of persuasion. And yet I *am* free.

More than for any other reason, I'm free because I've *chosen* to live that way. I've concentrated upon the things I control, and used that control to remove the restrictions and complications from my life.

As a result, I'm now free to live my life as I want to live it. Despite all-time high taxes, I pay ridiculously few taxes. Despite my irregular life style, I live my own life without interference from society.

Every day of my life is mine to use as I see fit. My time isn't committed to the state, to society, to a treadmill, or to fruitless relationships with people with whom I have nothing in common. I have no fear that the phone will ring any moment to tell me of something new I "must" do with my time.

I hadn't needed to hide my head in the sand to achieve this. I have valuable relationships—personal, professional, and romantic. I make far more money now than I did when I was restricted—and it takes far fewer hours to make it.

I'm involved with people who add to my life, and I'm independent of those who would take from it.

My life is of little importance to you, however, and this book is not an autobiography. The title was chosen to let you know that at least one person has accomplished the freedom you seek, and that it can be done without changing the nature of the world. The attention will be devoted to your freedom—but the principles and ideas presented will be those that brought freedom to me.

In the process, it's important to recognize that you will make all the decisions yourself. I can't tell you how to live, nor can I tell you what you "must" do to be free. Instead, I can suggest dozens of opportunities from which you can choose. And I can point out the various traps that may be enslaving you now.

You will then have to decide for yourself how you'll use these suggestions. If the ultimate decisions aren't made by you, you could never act with the conviction and purpose necessary to achieve your objectives. You have to decide *what* you're going to do and, above all, you have to know *why* you're doing it. Otherwise, plans and hopes are meaningless, temporary resolutions, to be shelved the first time anything happens to interfere.

So please don't gain the impression that I'm telling you how to live. *You* have to decide how you're going to live. There will be scores of suggestions made in this book— and you'll have to decide which ones you can accept and can act upon. If I write with passion and urgency in places, don't assume that I'm demanding a specific course of action from you; the greatest urgency will be in encouraging you to make the decisions for yourself.

LET US BEGIN

In the first section we'll look at the numerous traps that enslave people, the multitude of assumptions that people accept without challenge, the many restrictions upon one's life that need not exist. It's interesting to see how empty are many of those assumptions when looked at closely. At the end of that section, I hope it will be obvious to you why you aren't free now.

The second section will offer specific alternatives—ways of being free of the things that may be enslaving you, whether they be government, bad relationships, social restrictions, the treadmill, family problems, whatever.

The third section will include techniques that can be used to make the changeover from a non-free life to a free life. There are numerous ways to release yourself from the complicated problems that seem to demand that you remain in permanent bondage.

But we must keep things in their proper sequence; otherwise, the techniques will be useless. Until you know why you're enslaved and what you have to work with, the alternatives will offer little help.

It all begins with you, because you're the person who has to make you free. So it would serve little purpose to construct an image of an ideal person and hope to make you conform to that image. My suggestions can only work within the context of who you are and what you're capable of doing.

Freedom is the opportunity to live your life as you want to live it.

Most of the rest of the world will remain unfree during the rest of your life. Most people will continue to lead what Thoreau called "lives of quiet desperation"[1]—paying high taxes, bowing to social pressures, working long hours with little to show for them, never having the time to do what they want to do, resigning themselves to loveless compromises that masquerade as marriages.

Fortunately, that doesn't have to be your life.

Even in an unfree world, you can be free.

[1] Henry David Thoreau, *Walden*, p. 22 (listed in bibliography).

What do you suppose will satisfy the soul, except to
walk free and own no superior?   —WALT WHITMAN

It is not recognized in the full amplitude of the word that
all freedom is essentially self-liberation—that I can have
only so much freedom as I procure for myself by my
owness.   —MAX STIRNER

PART I Why You Are Not Free

2

The Identity Traps

THERE ARE TWO IDENTITY TRAPS: (1) the belief that you should be someone other than yourself; and (2) the assumption that others will do things in the way that you would.

These are the basic traps, of which many others are variations. In the first trap, you necessarily forfeit your freedom by requiring yourself to live in a stereotyped, pre-determined way that doesn't consider your own desires, feeling, and objectives.

The second trap is more subtle but just as harmful to your freedom. When you expect someone to have the same ideas, attitudes, and feelings that you have, you expect him to act in ways that aren't in keeping with *his* nature. As a result, you'll expect and hope that people will do things they're not capable of doing.

WHO ARE YOU?

Let's begin by recognizing what we know about *you*.

We know that *you are different*. You're different from everyone else in the world.

Just as no two persons' fingerprints are identical, no two people are identical in terms of their knowledge, under-standing, attitudes, likes, and dislikes.

Your knowledge is the result of your experiences—what you've done and seen and heard, where you've been, who you've known, and what you've learned from them. No one else has lived that life and experienced all the same things.

Your ways of interpreting what you see are also unique. What you consider to be logic or common sense will vary in some way from another person's logic.

As a result, you see and interpret and react to what goes on around you differently from anyone else.

That's not hard to see. And yet the root of the identity problem is that most individuals are oblivious to these differences. They assume that all people want the same things—or that they *should* want them. They expect everyone to respond in the same way to the same things. They assume that what one person or elite group sees and accepts should be accepted by everyone.

This can range from one person expecting another to enjoy the movie he enjoys to the individual who's upset if everyone doesn't go to church.

All individuals are different. Each one has his own identity—with his own knowledge, understanding, perception, and attitudes. You're in the Identity Trap when you overlook these differences—and that can get in the way of your freedom.

You are you and only you. You live in a world of your own, composed of your own experience. You can't be someone other than who you are.

CONSEQUENCES

What else do we know about you?

We know that you act in ways you think will bring particular consequences to you. You eat a sandwich because you expect it to taste good or to relieve the hunger in your stomach. You work in order to be paid money you can spend, or because you enjoy the work. You turn the ignition key in your car in order to start the engine.

In some cases, you carefully think out your actions. In other cases, you act from habit; you rely upon previous experiences and assume that a given action will produce the desired effect.

In every case, however, you're acting in ways that you think will bring you the *consequences* you want. And you avoid doing things that you think could bring consequences you don't like.

IDENTITIES

As you do this, you recognize the *identity* of each thing you deal with; you use it in a way that's consistent with its nature.

For example, a stone is called a stone because of certain characteristics that distinguish it from what we call a peanut-butter sandwich. You can't *eat* a stone; but, because of what it is, you can use it to build something. In the same way, you can't swim in a tree, but you can use the tree for shade or for firewood.

To get what you want, you determine the nature of the things you must deal with. Certain things can produce certain effects and no others—that's outside your control. What you *do* control is your choice of things that will be the appropriate means to the end you seek.

A human being has characteristics that distinguish him from a stone or a tree or a sandwich. So you don't expect a human being to be a stone or anything else.

And just as each stone is different from every other stone, so are human beings different from one another. You have to recognize those differences in order to be able to deal with people in ways that will bring you the consequences you want.

Each person will act in keeping with his own identity. This means he'll be bound by the limits of his own knowledge and experience—even if he wishes he weren't. To expect him to act otherwise is to fall into the Identity Trap and hope for something that can't be.

You can't entrust your investments to an individual who knows nothing about money. You can't expect a knowledge of chemistry to be used by someone who's never seen a test tube.

Neither can you assume that someone will do what you've decided is right. You've decided it from *your* unique knowledge and interpretations; *he* acts from *his* knowledge and his interpretations.

You're in the Identity Trap when you assume an individual will react to something as *you* would react or as you've seen someone else react.

You could make everyone else be, act, and think in ways of your choosing if you were God. But you aren't. So it's far more useful to recognize and accept each person as he is—and then deal with him accordingly.

You can't control the natures of other people, but you can control how you'll deal with them. And you can also control the extent and manner in which you'll be involved with them.

The paradox is that you have tremendous control over your life, but you give up that control when you try to control others. For the only way you can control others is to recognize their natures and do what is necessary to evoke the desired reactions from those natures. Thus, your actions are dictated by the requirements involved when you attempt to control someone else.

Everything you do will produce an effect or consequence of some kind. The consequences you get will depend upon the identities of things and people and how you deal with them. To be able to predict those consequences depends upon your ability to perceive the true identities of things and people.

TRUTH

So the factor of *truth* becomes important. You want to see things truly so that you can deal with them properly.

Whenever you fail to see something as it is, you'll expect a result from it that's different from what will occur.

Sometimes a thing turns out to be different from what you'd thought it was. A comparison of the first impression with later impressions can show that the earlier view was insufficient and somehow distorted. So in terms of possible later discovery, all current knowledge is *incomplete,* or will be enlarged later.

You can see this easily with regard to people you meet. Your first impression may be generally correct, but it often proves later to have been superficial or incomplete. And as a result of later knowledge, you sometimes change your ways of dealing with them.

In addition, you don't have the time to discover everything that might be relevant about a given situation. You have to make assumptions. And that can lead to reading into things what you expect to find. You can be so sure something is going to be a certain way that you don't notice that it isn't.

For many reasons, your perception won't always be accurate. And as you interpret what you see, your logic may not always be flawless; you might not draw all the proper connections.

This means you view things *subjectively*[1]—colored by your own unique perception and interpretation. And other people view things just as subjectively.

Not surprisingly, arguments develop over the "truth" of a given situation, since each person sees things in his own unique way. Very often, however, those arguments miss the point. Truth isn't an end in itself. It's always a means to an end.

The purpose of knowing "truth" is to be able to make it work for you. You need the truth in order to deal with things as they are and get predictable results from them.

---

[1] In most cases, I use words as they're commonly defined; in a few cases, I've redefined words to make them more explicit. Most key words in this book will be defined as they're introduced. If you're not sure what I mean by a word, check the Glossary on page 389.

The specific application for which you need the truth might be different from another person's. You may want to know the truth of a particular mechanical cause-and-effect relationship so you can fix your car. Another person may want that knowledge in order to build a bomb. And someone else may want it just to maintain his image as a learned man.

The uses may vary, but the principle is always the same: You want the truth so you can use it to produce a consequence that you want.

Truth is information that leads to predictable results. So if your understanding of the truth works for you, it is true enough—so long as you're prepared for the possibility that the addition of other factors may alter the cause-and-effect relationship.

Your ability to get what you want depends upon these considerations: how clearly you recognize the identity of each thing and person you deal with, how well you isolate the relevant factors in any cause-and-effect relationship, and how well you allow for the possibility that other factors might alter the relationship.

HAPPINESS

You act in ways you believe will produce the consequences you want. But *why* do you do that? What is it you're trying to accomplish?

You may decide that your goal in life is a good marriage, fame, wealth, or any number of other things. But each of these things is only a means to a further end.

For example, let's suppose you've decided you want a new car. *Why* do you want it?

It may be that you expect to be free of the mechanical problems that bothered you with the old car. Or you may expect to receive more respect with a new car. Or you may expect driving to be more enjoyable.

Whatever the reason, it's a means to a further end: You believe that getting a new car will lead to a *greater feeling of well-being.* You believe you'll feel better with the new car than you would without it.

Of the many ways you could spend the money, you believe that getting the car will produce more mental well-being for you than any other alternative will produce. You may have to forego some other purchases to do it, but you think that those other things won't provide the well-being that a car would.

In everything you do, with the knowledge and insight at your disposal, you choose what you think will give you the most well-being and the least mental discomfort. The objective is what is usually called *happiness:* the feeling of well-being.

Happiness isn't a new car, fame, a good marriage, wealth, or a warm blanket. Those are *things*. Happiness is what you feel *inside of you as a result* of the things that happen to you.

Happiness might be *produced by* a good marriage, fame, a new car, or a warm blanket. For some people, happiness occurs as a result of doing favors for other people; for others, it results from bringing about social reforms; for still others, it comes from believing they've outsmarted someone. It might come from a big meal, sexual intercourse, music, art, dancing, singing, working, kissing, studying, gardening, resting, etc. These are things that might make an individual feel good.

It's also possible for any of those things to make one feel unhappy—or feel nothing at all.

Whether you will be happy, unhappy, or indifferent at any given moment depends upon who you are and what happens to you. You can't simply decide to be happy and suddenly feel a gust of mental well-being. If you're not happy at any given time, it's because of what is happening to you.

Happiness is an *emotion,* an involuntary reaction to what happens to you. And unhappiness is an involuntary feeling of discomfort as you react to things that don't suit your nature.

To change your mental state from unhappiness to happiness requires that you change your circumstances. And *this is why you do things*—to bring about the circumstances that will make you happier.

Everything you do is motivated by the desire to feel as much happiness as possible and to eliminate mental discomfort—either in the short term or the long term.

For example, you may work hard at your career for many years because you feel "it will all be worth it someday"—meaning it will enable you to do the things that will make you feel good. Or perhaps the pursuit makes you feel better than anything else you've considered.

Or you may do certain things because you're afraid that if you *don't* do them you'll feel bad. You may lend money to your relatives only because you'd feel guilty if you didn't. Or you might go to church each week because you'd feel irreverent if you didn't.

A *positive decision* is one in which you choose among alternatives to maximize your happiness. An example would be deciding whether you'll be happier going to a movie or a football game.

A *negative decision* is one in which you choose among alternatives to minimize your unhappiness. An example would be deciding whether to let your roof leak or to deplete your savings account to get it fixed. Neither choice will increase your happiness; you're trying to decide which choice would be the least unpleasant.

A free man spends most of his time making positive decisions—choosing among attractive alternatives.

Most people, however, spend most of their time making negative decisions—deciding which alternatives would be the least unpleasant, trying to keep things from getting worse. As time passes, such a person settles for less and less, believing that it isn't possible to be free and profoundly happy. When you tell him there are ways to break out of the pattern, all he can see is that to do so would cause more unpleasantness.

There *are* ways to break out of such patterns, however, and many of those ways will be suggested as we proceed.

YOUR IDENTITY

What makes you happy will depend upon your own personal nature—which is different in many ways from that of any other human being. To try to find happiness by doing what seems to make others happy is to fall head first into the Identity Trap.

Others can suggest what you "should" do, or what "ought" to make you happy, but they will often be wrong. You have to determine for yourself who you are, what makes you happy, what you're capable of doing, and what you *want* to do. Be open to suggestions, but never forfeit the power to make the final decision yourself. Only then can you act in ways that will bring you happiness.

You're in the Identity Trap when you let others determine what's right or wrong for you—when you live by unquestioned rules that define how you should act and think.

You're in the Identity Trap when you try to be interested in something because it's expected of you, or when you try to do the things that others have said you should do, or when you try to live up to an image that others say is the only legitimate, valid image you're allowed to have.

You're in the Identity Trap if you allow others to define labels and impose them upon you—such as going to PTA meetings only because that's what a "good parent" is supposed to do, or going to visit your parents every Sunday because a "good child" would never do less, or giving up your career because a "good wife" puts her husband's career first.

You're in the Identity Trap if you feign an interest in ecology to prove your civic interest, or give to the poor to prove you aren't selfish, or study dull subjects to appear to be "intellectual."

You're in the Identity Trap if you buy a Cadillac to prove you're successful, or a small foreign car because your friends are anti-Detroit; or if you shave every day to prove you're respectable, or let your hair grow long to prove you don't conform.

In any of these ways, you allow someone else to determine what you should think and be. You deny your own self when you suppress desires that aren't considered "legitimate," or when you try to appear to be having fun because everyone else is, or when you settle for a certain life because you've been told that's all you should expect in the world.

And you're in the Identity Trap when you allow others to convince you that you don't even have a right to challenge these things.

When you take these various assumptions for granted, you're denying your own identity—an identity that's crying out to be expressed in ways that could bring you a great deal more happiness.

No cosmic judge has declared, "Thou shalt be a good son," or "Thou shalt be a successful businessman," or "Thou shalt be a good wife and mother." *You* have chosen, perhaps carelessly, the identities you try to live up to.

No one can tell you what identity you *should* have. But we can discuss some ways to look inside yourself to discover the identity that's naturally yours. Only then can you act consistently, purposefully, and in ways that will bring happiness to you. And every artificial identity that you cast off will bring more freedom to you.

Instead of taking for granted assumptions about what you "should" be, start from the inside—from inside of *you*. Find out who *you* are—that unique collection of feelings, desires, perceptions, and understanding. Respect what you see in yourself.

Then look at the world and decide what you can have that, combined with *your* nature, could produce real happiness. And then figure out how you can make it happen.

We'll discuss later some techniques of this self-exploration. If done with energy and honesty, it can be one of the most important, rewarding, and exciting tasks you can undertake.

Let it all come from you. Don't try to identify with an

ideal person, a label, or a code that others think is best for you.

They aren't you; they can't make your decisions for you.

THE IDENTITIES OF OTHERS

At the same time, you can waste precious time when you ignore the individual identities of other people. They aren't you; you can't expect them to be.

When you misread someone's identity, you expect from him what he can't provide. You can't make a stone catch fire; neither can you make someone be something he isn't.

You're in this form of the Identity Trap if you expect your wife to act in certain ways because your mother acted that way, or when you assume someone will see the same logic you see, or if you expect an atheist to accept the principles of Christianity.

It's so easy to slip into the Identity Trap when dealing with people. You can meet someone who has qualities you enjoy, but then find it hard to accept his drawbacks when they become evident. You wish that somehow the values could stay and the limitations disappear.

And that can tempt you to try to change him, so that he'll be everything you want. Unfortunately, however, you'll most likely be frustrated in the attempt.

This doesn't mean that no one ever changes. People constantly change as they acquire new knowledge and discover new alternatives. But each person changes in harmony with his own nature, in keeping with his own desires for change and growth, in ways that make sense to *him*.

Recognize each person you deal with as a different, distinct, individual entity, and you won't have identity problems. Try to avoid labeling individuals and then expecting them to live up to your labels.

You can decide for yourself which of the people you meet have the most to offer to you and develop relationships with them, based upon the compatible values between you. The alternative is to throw away your precious life trying to change others, to make them see what you see, to make them into what you want them to be.

Each individual seeks happiness for himself in the way that *his* knowledge and perception indicate to him. He isn't you; don't expect him to be.

AVOIDING THE TRAP

There are four basic principles that I believe can help to avoid the Identity Trap:

1. *You are a unique individual—different from all other human beings.* No one else has the exact same nature that you have; no one else reacts to things in exactly the way you do. No one else sees the world exactly as you do. No one can dictate what your identity *should* be; you are the best qualified person to discover what it *is.*

2. *Each individual is acting from his own knowledge in ways he believes will bring him happiness.* He acts to produce the consequences he thinks will make him feel better.[2]

3. *You have to treat things and people in accordance with their own identities in order to get what you want from them.* You don't expect a stone to be a fish. And it's just as unrealistic to expect one person to act as someone else does. You don't control the identities of people, but you can control how you deal with them.

4. *You view the world subjectively—colored by your own experience, interpretation, and limits of perception.* It isn't essential that you know the final truth about every-

---

[2] I could use up pages answering every possible exception to this principle: suicide, masochism, altruism, etc. In every case, I come to the same conclusion: The individual feels that his actions will provide more mental well-being or less mental discomfort than anything else he can think of. To test this conclusion, just ask yourself how the individual would feel if you were to interfere with his wrist-slashing, getting his daily beating, or doing "good works."

thing in the world; and you don't have the resources to discover it.

Instead, the test to be applied to any idea is: *does it work?* Does your identification of things lead to the consequences you expect? If it does, what you've perceived was true enough for that situation. But recognize the context of the situation and be skeptical when generalizing from that test to draw broader conclusions.

Those observations can help you to keep out of the Identity Trap. You don't have to try to live a life that isn't yours. What others say you should be is based either upon what they are or upon the way they feel you'd be of more value to them. Neither can be a valid basis for determining how you should live your life. They're doing and saying what makes *them* happy, and their conclusions are drawn from their own limited, subjective experience.

You are what you are. And it will be up to you to discover what that is. I'll help you in every way I can in this book, but the decisions will be up to you.

The Identity Traps are the belief that you should live in a way determined by others and the assumption that others will react to things as you would. These two traps are the most basic of all traps.

They might seem terribly obvious to you. If so, good—because the other traps are much less obvious, and many of them are subtle variations of these two.

None of them has to affect your life if you hold to the realization that you're a unique individual, a "first" in the world, one who'll have to determine for himself what will bring him happiness.

If that principle seems far removed from the problem that led you to this book, I hope to show you shortly that this is the foundation necessary to free yourself of any restriction.

Until you discover and accept yourself fully, you won't have the conviction or the courage to be free.

As soon as you trust yourself, you will know how to live.
—JOHANN WOLFGANG VON GOETHE

Nature, to be commanded, must be obeyed.
—FRANCIS BACON

3

The Intellectual
and Emotional Traps

TO BECOME FREE requires a well-conceived plan of action. It can't be achieved by occasional spur-of-the-moment hunches. To be free, you must know *what* you're doing and *why*. Otherwise, slight setbacks can cause you to discard your plans and give up.

The two traps covered in this chapter affect the *what* and *why* of your actions. When you're in the Emotional Trap, you don't know—in any long-term way—*what* you're doing. And when you're in the Intellectual Trap, the *why* is lost.

THE FIRST TRAP

The Intellectual Trap is the belief that your emotions should conform to a preconceived standard. This, of course, is a variation of the Identity Trap, for it's an attempt to make yourself be something you aren't.

You're in the Intellectual Trap when you try to deny your bad feelings—such as hate, fear, jealousy, or guilt. Or when you hold back tears because "crying isn't manly."

You're in the trap when you try to deny *good* feelings—such as infatuation for someone who's "beneath you," or enjoyment of something that's frowned upon, or when you try to make yourself feel good about someone or something that *doesn't* make you feel good.

You're also in the trap when you believe you should be happy simply because you're doing what you've been told will make you happy.

A good example is the businessman who has to keep reminding himself that his $40,000-a-year job and carpeted office are what he's always wanted. Or the woman who keeps telling herself she *must* be happy, now that she finally has a husband, four children, and a home in surburbia. Each of them is living a life he's been told *should* make him happy; and if it doesn't, he attempts to *make* his emotions respond.

The Intellectual Trap is an attempt to regiment your emotions so that they'll react according to an intellectually determined standard.

An *emotion* is an involuntary response to something that happens. It isn't intentional; you can't command yourself to feel something. But when it happens, your body reacts—a warm prickling at the back of your neck, or a twist in your stomach, or a tightening of your chest. And there's usually an urge to express yourself outwardly—through laughter, tears, talk, hitting or hugging someone.

These are *emotions* or *feelings* (I'll use the two words interchangeably), involuntary reactions to something that happens. The two basic emotions are happiness and unhappiness—the feelings of mental well-being and mental discomfort.

Other emotions are variations of those two. Positive emotions include love, affection, self-satisfaction, pride, anticipation of pleasure, any form of the glow we call happiness. Negative emotions include fear, hate, disappointment, sorrow, jealousy, guilt, any kind of mental discomfort.

Happiness is the object of your actions, the consequence you seek when you act. But it's important to remember that *happiness is an emotion.* You can't turn it on at will.

You feel it as an involuntary response to the conditions in your life at a given moment.

Your emotional nature (like almost everything about you) is unique. What makes someone else happy might be interesting, curious, even fascinating to know; but it doesn't tell you what would make *you* happy.

You can't find happiness by telling yourself to "be happy." Nor can you find it by doing the things that others have said make them happy. Nor can you find it by telling yourself that a "good" man or a "moral" woman or a "rational" person would be happy doing a certain list of things.

To find happiness, you must know how your unique emotional nature responds to things. You must observe and *take seriously* your own emotional reactions. For if you attempt to fit your emotions to a preconceived standard, you lose touch with yourself and blind yourself to the most important part of yourself—to what would make you happy.

If you do that, there's no reason to be surprised if doing the "good" things doesn't produce great joy for you. Life will be relatively tasteless, gray, and boring if you deny the very emotions that are telling you what makes life joyous and exciting.

That doesn't mean you have to be a slave to your emotions. You can get into trouble by responding rashly to your feelings. The recognition of a feeling isn't a command to act in a given way. There are alternatives—ways of satisfying the emotion without getting into trouble. But if you refuse to *recognize* emotions, you're acting at cross-purposes with yourself. You're denying *you*.

NEGATIVE EMOTIONS

Negative emotions can act as *signals* to you, letting you know that there's an uncomfortable part of your life that needs attention.

For example, if you feel jealous about someone, it may

mean you're not sure the relationship you have is really right for you, and you're afraid it can be taken from you easily. If you hate, it might mean that you've made yourself vulnerable to someone whose desires are in conflict with yours, and he's using that power in ways that hurt you. And if you're afraid, you may have put yourself in a dangerous position you're not equipped to handle.

To deny those emotions will leave the problem unsolved and make them more likely to recur in the future. You can't wish away negative emotions; but if you recognize them, you can take steps to eliminate them.

To acknowledge your discomfort doesn't obligate you to act on the urge that accompanies it. What you do about the situation is a separate matter; there are usually several alternatives.

To be jealous doesn't mean you must restrict your lover's activities. To hate doesn't mean you have to attack. To be afraid doesn't mean you have to run (although that may sometimes be the best course of action).

Another way of denying your emotions is to convince yourself you won't be afraid in a given situation. You dive into it, "knowing" you should be able to handle it, and create more problems for yourself. Your mind is clouded by the fear you were determined not to feel, and you can't handle the situation effectively.

You can't be something you aren't. Don't tell yourself you can do things if your experience tells you that you can't. First, you'll have to increase your ability to deal with such situations; and that takes more than false confidence.

Don't try to deal coolly with an individual whose presence always infuriates you. Recognize your reaction and find a way to deal with him that doesn't require a confrontation. Or better yet, arrange things so you don't have to deal with him at all.

This applies especially to critical matters—cases where you have a great deal to lose by getting into something you can't handle. Don't try to stand up to your employer if you always go to pieces when you walk into his office.

In smaller matters, you can afford to be more adventurous. You can use easier situations to test and enlarge your capabilities, so long as you recognize and accept the risks involved.

POSITIVE EMOTIONS

It's just as damaging to deny your positive emotions. Certain things that please you may be frowned upon by your friends or associates. But so what? *Your* happiness is the object of your actions; what difference does it make that others happen to have some ideas of what is "correct"?

If you like country music more than symphonies, why deny it or feel self-conscious about it? If you prefer watching TV to reading Shakespeare, so what? Don't be intimidated by common intellectual standards; they're of no importance compared to your own reactions.

I know it can be easy to be frightened by an emotion if it seems to threaten your present way of life. You can even have an emotional reaction to an emotional reaction.

For example, it may bother you if you're attracted to a woman other than your wife. You may feel that since you're married, you're going to stay married, and that you don't want anything to interfere with that. But the recognition that you feel something for another woman isn't a command that you get a divorce or commit adultery. It can be a signal to alert you to deficiencies in your marriage—things you're missing. Make use of the signal; look for ways to fill in what's missing within the context of your marriage.

That a married person must be monogamous in mind as well as in action is simply one more example of an intellectually determined standard. If your best friend says that he never even notices another woman, that's not an indication of what you should expect of yourself.

Your emotions can also be signals that it's time to reexamine your existing values. Perhaps they're alerting you that you've inadvertently moved away from your own best interests.

Your positive emotions are the seeds of a tastier life. They're trying to tell you how you can be happy. If you ignore them, suppress them, or deny them, you lose the vital guidepost that could lead you toward happiness.

Most people are capable of profound, rich emotions; they have the potential for deep and lasting happiness. But they've tuned themselves out in an attempt to be what they've been told they should be. It's not surprising that they can't really imagine lasting happiness.

IN THE TRAP

You're in the Intellectual Trap any time you try to censor your emotions so they'll conform to an intellectually determined standard, no matter how plausible the standard.

You're in the trap when you believe you shouldn't feel warmly toward someone you've been told to dislike. Or when you decide you should admire someone whom "everyone knows" is a great man. Or when you believe you should love your mother—even if there's nothing lovable about her.

You're in the trap when you continue to do something long after you've stopped enjoying it, or if it's something you never enjoyed much to begin with, or if you're bored by most everything you do.

If you find that you don't feel enthusiastic about *anything*, it may be because you've lost touch with your emotions—the source that can tell you what would bring excitement to your life. That's where you must look for the answer.

If you deny your feelings, all the intelligent thinking and planning in the world won't lead to happiness.

THE EMOTIONAL TRAP

The Emotional Trap is the belief that you can make important decisions at a time when you're feeling strong emotions. It's the reverse side of the Intellectual Trap.

Not only do you *feel;* you *think*. Thinking is the conscious, deliberate, volitional attempt to perceive identities and utilize them. You can *think* to observe, to identify, to create, and to establish the conditions necessary for your happiness. Your thinking and action create conditions to which you respond emotionally.

You *think* in order to be able to *feel* happiness.

Thinking is the *means;* feeling is the *end*.

Your emotional responses tell you what things make you happy and unhappy. But at the moments when you feel strong emotions such as hate, infatuation, anger, or excitement, your thinking is usually clouded. The Emotional Trap is the belief that you can make important decisions at such a time. That's the time when you're *least* likely to recognize all the alternatives and consequences.

For example, you're in the Emotional Trap if you decide to propose marriage because of a sudden infatuation. Or if you decide to quit your job while engulfed by anger at your boss or associates. Or if you decide to respond to sexual arousal in ways you've already realized could cause trouble for you.

These emotions are very real and must be recognized. But you can't make the best decision at the moment you're engulfed by them. You're bound to overlook many important considerations.

If you're infatuated with someone, *enjoy* it; revel in the glow for all it's worth. But don't try to make important long-term decisions at such a time. Can you imagine how many disastrous marriages are the result of such passing glows?

If you're enraged about your job, go off by yourself, relax, and wait until your mind clears. Then consider *all* the ramifications. You might still decide to resign if you believe such moments of anger are too high a price to pay for your income. But if so, you'll have decided at a time when you're equipped to do so—and you'll be better able to stick by your decision.

If you've decided that certain types of sexual encounters could cause trouble for you, respect that decision. You can't reopen the case intelligently when you're breathless with excitement and the boss's wife is about to "change into something more comfortable." Tomorrow morning you can re-examine the rules and the possible consequences involved. You might decide then to change your values, but you may also remember a number of good reasons why you made your original decision.

I've found that it's a good rule to *never make an important decision when your emotions are in control*. I try to program myself in advance to remember this rule when I need it. When I'm in an emotional state (either positive or negative), I try to keep just enough intellect[1] working to tell me one thing: *don't decide now*. I wait until I've relaxed and can think more clearly.

THE EXPANDING CYCLE

Unfortunately, many people act upon their emotions the moment they occur. Such a person doesn't want to take the time to recognize all the considerations involved. Afterward, he may have to pay an extremely high price for a brief episode of happiness.

I once knew a woman who was basically quite intelligent, but her blind spot seemed to be this urge to act before recognizing the consequences. She hastily married a man who was exciting but not compatible with her. When

---

[1] The word *intellect* will be used interchangeably with *thinking*, in the same way that *emotion* and *feeling* are being used synonymously.

things went poorly in the marriage, she suddenly "knew" that a baby would bring them closer together.

She stayed in that mood long enough to get pregnant. Needless to say, the baby only complicated matters—creating financial crises to go with their other problems. I'll skip over a few of the other crises and hasty decisions until we get to the third baby.

By that time, she knew she was in the wrong place. When she finally got out of the marriage, she had three children, no income-producing skills, and was dependent for child support on an unreliable man.

That led to another loveless marriage as a "final solution" to her financial problems. That didn't work either, of course, but it was even harder to get out of.

As I said, she was basically intelligent. But she was unable to program herself to avoid important decisions when her emotions were dominant. There were always other alternatives to her actions, but she could never see them at the time of decision. Eventually she came to feel that life itself was cruel, that other people were causing her problems, and that it was unfair to demand a high price of her when she was the one who was being mistreated. To her, freedom was a joke.

She reached the point where there was no way she could support herself and the children, so she finally let her first husband have custody of them. Because she loved them, she paid a terrible price for the rash decisions she'd made in the past. Each time she'd made one of those decisions, she was sure she was escaping a difficult price, while in reality she was only adding to the price she'd have to pay someday.

IN THE TRAP

The Emotional Trap is typified by the assumption that one's feelings of the moment will be permanent. This inspires actions that produce consequences that still have to be dealt with after the feelings have passed.

You're in the Emotional Trap whenever you promise favors to friends or family in a glow of affection but regret your promises later. Or when you lose more money than you can afford in the stock market because it's fun to act on hunches. Or when you buy an $8,000 piano you don't know how to play because the idea suddenly excites you.

Immediate pleasures can turn into permanent pains when you act as if the emotions of the moment are all the information you need to consider. You're ignoring consequences—including the possibility that what you feel now may change.

You're not likely to get entangled in the Emotional Trap if you recognize your emotions, respect them, create plans to satisfy them, and carry out those plans—always allowing for changes in *you,* as well as in the world.

INTELLECT AND EMOTIONS

Your *intellect* and your *emotions* are both essential, real parts of you. Each has a function; neither can be disregarded if you're to get what you want in life. To deny either of them is to fall into one of the traps.

You're in the Intellectual Trap if you let your intellect tell you what you should feel.

You're in the Emotional Trap if you let your emotions make important decisions for you.

Both traps lead to trouble.

You have to know what you're doing and why. The Emotional Trap blinds you to *what* you're doing because you can't see the consequences clearly. And the Intellectual Trap cuts you off from the only important *why* connected with your actions—knowing that what you're doing will lead to what you *know* will create happiness.

To achieve genuine, durable happiness, you have to recognize your emotional nature and intelligently think ahead to create situations that will trigger happy emotions from your unique nature.

Then, when your plans have produced what you wanted, you can disregard your intellect, relax, and just *feel*. You'll be able to act spontaneously within that context because you've eliminated any possibility of bad consequences.

Then you can allow yourself to be engulfed in a flow of genuine positive emotions.

And that's what life is all about.

No one has ever talked himself (or anyone else) out of an undesired emotion by hurling insults or by delivering a moral lecture.   —NATHANIEL BRANDEN

4

The Morality Trap

THE MORALITY TRAP is the belief that you must obey a moral code created by someone else.

This trap is a variation of the Identity Trap in that it leads you to try to be something other than yourself. It's an easy trap to get caught in and an easy way to lose your freedom.

Morality is a powerful word. Perhaps even more powerful is the word *immoral*. In an attempt to avoid being labeled *immoral*, many people allow themselves to be manipulated by others.

WHAT IS MORALITY?

At the same time, the concept of morality is very vague. What is it? Where does it come from? What purpose does it serve? How is it determined?

My dictionary defines *morality* as "Moral quality or character; rightness or wrongness, as of an action." Well then, let's refer to the definition of moral, which is: "Related to, serving to teach, or in accordance with, the principles of right and wrong."

Now we're getting somewhere; all we need is a defini-

tion of *right*. And I suppose you can guess what *that* is:
"in accordance with justice, law, morality, etc."[1]

Unfortunately, this definitional merry-go-round is typical of the common understanding of morality. You should
do something because it's "right" —but *by what standard?*

It seems to me that there are three different kinds of
morality. I call them *personal, universal,* and *absolute.* By
looking at each of them, I think we can get a clearer idea
of what morality is and how it can be useful in helping
you to achieve your freedom.

PERSONAL MORALITY

We've seen that you act in ways that you hope will
bring the best consequences to you. And the "best consequences" are those that bring you happiness.

You always have to consider the consequences of your
actions; they're the point of anything you do. However,
any given act will undoubtedly cause *many* consequences.
You may see that a particular action will produce a consequence you want, but you might also be aware that it
could produce other consequences that you don't want.

For example, suppose you say, "All I want is a million
dollars." Probably the quickest way of getting it would be
to buy a gun and rob the largest bank in town. If getting a
million dollars were *all* that mattered to you, that would
be an obvious choice.

But the million dollars *isn't* all you want. There are
other considerations, such as: You want to *keep* the
money (longer than just until you're arrested); you want
to spend the money on things you *like* (not on hiding
from the FBI); you want to enjoy the things the money
can buy (none of which is possible in jail).

It's unrealistic, then, to say, "All I want is a million dollars." The money is a means to other ends, and *it has to*

---

[1] *Webster's New World Dictionary of the American Language,* 1966 edition; World Publishing Company, New York.

be obtained in a way that won't interfere with those ends.
Otherwise, you might do something (such as robbing a
bank) that would make it impossible to achieve what you
really want.

The original statement would be closer to the truth if it
were phrased, "What I want is enough money to buy the
things I want and to be free to enjoy those things and to
have the respect of people I like and without obtaining the
money in a way that will interfere with other values that
are more important to me."

Since you're always seeking numerous different goals,
you try to foresee the ways in which something immediately desirable might get in the way of other things that
are ultimately more desirable. You try to consider more
than just what's immediately in front of you. You're placing things in a broader context.

Obviously, you can't expect to foresee *all* the consequences of a given act, but you can try to see all the significant ones. In some cases, such as the bank-robbing example, there are obvious consequences that immediately
rule out a proposed course of action.

In other cases, more subtle possibilities will be recognized after a few minutes' thought. But there will also be
cases in which you won't be aware of the specific consequences until *after* you've acted and begun to experience
them.

CODE OF CONDUCT

Because you can't foresee all the specific consequences
of what you do, there's a need to have some generalized
rules available that can help keep you out of situations that could be troublesome. Those rules can be valuable if they do two things: (1) steer you away from potential disasters; and (2) remind you of the things you
must do to satisfy your most important long-term desires.

The basic question is: "How can I get something I want

without hurting my chances for other things that are more
important to me?"

It is this generalized, long-term attitude that underlies an
individual's basic code of conduct. And when we speak of
morality, I can't think of any other sensible reason to be
concerned about the subject. Its purpose is to keep you
aimed in the direction you most want to go.

Personal morality is an attempt to consider all the rele-
vant consequences of your actions.

"Relevant" means those consequences that will affect
you. How your actions affect others is only important in-
sofar as that, in turn, affects you.

A personal morality is basic to your overall view of
how you'll find happiness. It's so important that a later
chapter will be devoted entirely to questions that can help
you form such a morality for yourself.

And it's important that you form it yourself. No one
else (including me) is qualified to tell you how to live. A
realistic morality has to consider many personal factors:
your emotional nature, abilities, strengths, weaknesses,
and, most important, your goals.

Your code of conduct has to be consistent with your
goals so that you don't do anything that would make those
goals unattainable. A code devised by someone else will
necessarily be based upon the goals *he* believes possible
and desirable.

To be useful, a morality shouldn't include rules for every possible situation. It shouldn't be concerned with minor questions involving only immediate consequences. It's
devised to prevent big problems for you and to keep you
aimed toward the ultimate goals that mean the most to
you. Moral questions are concerned only with matters that
involve large consequences.

There's a difference, for instance, between investing
three dollars in a movie that might prove to be a dud and
investing your life savings in a risky business venture.
There's also a difference between tasting a different food
that's commonly eaten (such as snails) and sampling toad-

stools in the forest. The first might cause a stomachache; the second could poison you.

A useful morality will prevent you from doing things that might take years to correct, while keeping you aimed in the direction of the things that are most important to you.

And since such matters are an outgrowth of your own personal values, it's obvious that no one else can create your morality for you.

A *personal morality* is the attempt to consider all the relevant consequences of your actions. This is only one of three common types of moralities, however.

UNIVERSAL MORALITY

The second type is a morality that is meant to apply to everyone in the world. A *universal morality* is one that's supposed to bring happiness to anyone who uses it.

When you're exposed to the ideas of someone who has apparently done well with his own life, it's easy to conclude that he has all the final answers. His reasoning makes sense to you; he has results to show for his ideas. What further proof could you need to demonstrate that he knows how to live?

He probably *does* know how to live—*his* life. It would be foolish not to consider the ideas such a person offers. But it would also be foolish to expect that, as intelligent as he may be, he could have answers that apply to every life in the world.

His ideas have worked for him because he's been wise enough to develop ideas that are consistent with his own nature. He hasn't tried to live by the standards created by others; he's found his own. And that's vitally important.

You must do the same thing, too—if you want your code of conduct to work that well for you. Your rules have to consider everything that's unique about you—your emotions, your aptitudes, your weaknesses, your hopes and fears.

When you try to live by someone else's rules, you can

get yourself into lots and lots of trouble. For example, you can be told that a certain type of action will lead to a certain emotion, and you can suffer a lot of guilt and frustration trying to make your emotions conform to your expectations.

Or you can spend your life living in a way that doesn't evoke happiness from your unique nature. And along the way, you might be encouraged to discard the very things that could have led to genuine happiness for you.

Or you can create problems with others by being sure that they, too, should act by the same code.

I've met dozens of people who knew they were "right" about what they were doing and could cite the authority who told them so. But not one of them seemed to be genuinely comfortable in the life style he had assumed.

The easiest time to fall into the trap is when you're exposed to someone whose ideas *do* make a lot of sense. If what he says is logical to you—more logical than what you've heard before—the temptation can be very great to adopt all his ways. Someone like that should be considered very seriously but not accepted *in toto*.

A universal morality is a code of conduct that is presumed to bring happiness to anyone who uses it. I don't believe there can be such a thing. The differences between individuals are far too great to allow for anything but the most general kinds of rules.

ABSOLUTE MORALITY

There's a third kind of morality. The first two are attempts to help you achieve happiness—one self-directed and the other coming from someone else. The third type is the opposite of this. An *absolute morality* is a set of rules to which an individual is expected to *surrender* his own happiness.

There are two main characteristics of an absolute morality:

1. It comes presumably from *an authority outside of the*

individual. It comes from someone or somewhere more important than the individual himself.

2. It proposes that the individual should be "moral" *regardless of the consequences to himself.* In other words, doing what is "right" is more important than one's own happiness.

These two characteristics intertwine, so we'll consider them together.

Absolute morality is the most common type of morality, and it can be pretty intimidating. You can be made to appear "selfish," "whim-worshiping," "egotistic," "hedonistic," or "ruthless," if you merely assert that your own happiness is the most important thing in your life.

But what could be more important than your happiness? It's said that an authoritarian moral code is necessary to protect society. But who is society? Isn't it just a large group of people, each of whom have differing ideas concerning how one should live?

And if an individual is required to give up his own happiness, of what value is society to him? What does he care if society is protected?

It's also suggested that God commanded that we live by certain rules. But who can be sure he knows exactly when and how and what God said and what he meant? And even if that could be established once and for all, what would be the consequences to the individual if he acted otherwise? How do we know?

And if the code did come from God, it still had to be handled by human beings on its way to you. Whatever the absolute morality may be, you're relying upon someone to vouch for its authority.

Suppose you use a holy book as your guide. I haven't yet seen one that doesn't have some apparent contradictions regarding conduct in it. Those contradictions may disappear with the proper interpretation; but who provides the interpretation? You'll do it yourself or you'll select someone to provide it for you. In either case, *you* have become the authority by making the choice.

There's no way someone else can become your authority; ultimately the decision will be yours in choosing the morality you'll live by—even if you choose to cite some-one else (you've chosen) as the authority for your acts.

And there's no way you can ignore the consequences to yourself; a human being naturally acts in terms of consequences.

What happens, however, is that other people introduce consequences that they hope will influence you. They say that your "immoral" acts will: "prevent you from going to heaven"—or "cause other people to disapprove of you"—or "destroy society and cause chaos, and it will all be your fault."

Once again, however, it will be *you* deciding for yourself whether any of these consequences will result and whether any of them are important to you.

The absolute morality fails on its two important characteristics. Even if you choose to believe there's a higher authority, you are the authority who chooses what it is and what it is telling you to do. And since you'll always be considering consequences, even if you try to fix it so that you aren't, it's important to consciously recognize the consequences and decide which ones are important to you.

MORALITY

No matter how we approach the subject, we always wind up at the same place: No one can decide for you what is moral. So no matter what it may be, you *are* living by a personal morality. The question is whether or not you're acting deliberately to make it the morality that will bring you the kind of life you want for yourself.

I'm not suggesting that there is no right and wrong. There most assuredly is. *Right* is what will bring you happiness. And *wrong* is what will cause you unhappiness. The same definitions apply to the words *good* and *bad*.

And since there are no simple answers that can tell you what will bring you long-term happiness, what is *right* isn't necessarily the temptation in front of you at a given moment. A personal morality is vital because it can keep you aimed in the direction most important to you in the long term.

You can't successfully devise such a morality until you know who you are and what you want. And since no one else can answer those questions, no one else is qualified to tell you how to get what you want.

THE TRAP

I realize that, to some people, the concept of a personal, self-determined morality is revolutionary—possibly even appalling. It is contrary to the absolute moralities most people grew up with. And in addition to other decisions, you'll have to decide if what I've said has made sense to you. Whether or not you agree with me isn't as important to you as knowing *why* you believe as you do—and knowing what consequences your beliefs will produce.

The Morality Trap is the belief that you must obey a moral code created by someone else. If you're acting in ways you hope will satisfy someone else's concept of what is moral, chances are you're using an ill-suited code of conduct—one that won't lead you to what you want and that may trap you in commitments and complications that can only cause you unhappiness. So in terms of the trap, *what* you do isn't as significant as *why* you do it.

You're in the trap if you hand a very important dollar to a beggar because "it's wrong to be selfish." Or if you continue to deal respectfully with someone who's made trouble for you because "to forgive is divine."

You're in the trap if you allow yourself to be drafted because "you have a duty to your country." Or if you prohibit drinking in your home because "it would weaken the moral fibre of society." Or if you send your children to Sunday school even though you aren't religious, because "you should give them a moral upbringing."

You might have very good reasons for any of these actions. But if you do them *only* in obedience to moral clichés, you're in the Morality Trap.

PRESSURE FROM OTHERS

There are plenty of people who will be delighted to tell you how to live. You'll hear the words "moral" and "immoral" often enough.

A person who tells you to act "morally" might have any one of a number of reasons. He may really believe that your moral conduct is essential to the future of the world. Or he may believe that he's God's appointed policeman. Or he may be using morality as a weapon to pressure you to do what's best for *him*. Or he may just have nothing better to do with his time.

Whatever his reason, remember that it's *his* reason. Too often, *morality is used merely as a tool by which one person hopes to manipulate another.*

Your reasons for how you live will necessarily be your own. No one knows you as you can know yourself. And only from that self-understanding can you hope to create a code of conduct that will bring you the freedom and happiness you crave.

A useful morality should recognize that other people think differently from the way you do. And it should provide ways of handling those differences without bowing to the dictates of others. There are ways of eliminating the pressure without giving in—as I'll suggest in Chapter 17.

YOUR MORALITY

You are responsible for what happens to you (even if someone else offers to accept that responsibility), because you're the one who'll experience the consequences of your acts.

You are the one who decides what is right and what is

wrong—no matter what meaning others may attach to those words. You don't have to obey blindly the dictates that you grew up with or that you hear around you now. Everything can be challenged, *should* be challenged, examined to determine its relevance to you and what you want.

As you examine the teachings of others, you may find that some of it is very appropriate to you, but much of it may be meaningless or even harmful. The important thing is to carefully reappraise any moral precept that has been guiding your actions.

As you examine each of the rules you've been living by, ask yourself:

—Is this rule something that *others* have devised on behalf of "society" to restrain individuals? Or have *I* devised it in order to make my life better for myself?

—Am I acting by an old, just-happens-to-be-there morality? Or is it something I've personally determined from the knowledge of who I am and what I want—and by what *I* believe the world is?

—Are the rewards and punishments attached to the rules vague and intangible? Or do the rules point to specific happiness I can achieve or unhappiness I can avoid?

—Is it a morality that's currently "in style" and accepted by all those around me? Or is it a morality specifically tailored to *my* style?

—Is it a morality that's aimed *at* me and *against* my self-interest? Or is it a morality that's *for* me and comes *from* me?

All the answers must come from you—not from a book or a lecture or a sermon. To assume that someone once wrote down the final answers for your morality is to assume that the writer stopped growing the day he wrote the code. Don't treat him unfairly by thinking that he couldn't have discovered more and increased his own understanding after he'd written the code. And don't forget that what he wrote was based upon what *he* saw.

No matter how you approach the matter, *you* are the sovereign authority who makes the final decisions. The more you realize that, the more your decisions will fit realistically with your own life.

Personal morality is an attempt to consider all the relevant consequences of your acts. If you think out your morality for yourself, it should open a better life that will be free from the bad consequences that complicate matters.

And it should lead you more directly to those things that bring you happiness. Along the way, you should be able to act more freely; for once you've looked ahead to recognize potentially troublesome situations, you're free to act more impulsively in pleasant circumstances—knowing there's no danger that bad problems will ensue.

When you decide to take matters into your own hands, someone may ask you, "Who do you think you are? Who are *you* to decide for yourself in the face of society and centuries of moral teachings?"

The answer is simple: You are you, the person who will live with the consequences of what you do. No one else can be responsible, because no one else will experience the consequences of your actions as you will.

If you're wrong, *you* will suffer for it. If you're right, *you* will find happiness. You *have* to be the one to decide.

"Who are you to know?" It's your future at stake. You *have* to know.

Freedom comes only from seeing the ignorance of your critics and discovering the emptiness of their virtue.
                                                        —DAVID SEABURY

Volumes might be written upon the impiety of the pious.
                                                        —HERBERT SPENCER

5

The Unselfishness Trap

THE UNSELFISHNESS TRAP is the belief that you must put the happiness of others ahead of your own.

Unselfishness is a very popular ideal, one that's been honored throughout recorded history. Wherever you turn, you find encouragement to put the happiness of others ahead of your own—to do what's best for the world, not for yourself.

If the ideal is sound, there must be something unworthy in seeking to live your life as you want to live it.

So perhaps we should look more closely at the premise—to see if the ideal *is* sound. For if you attempt to be free, we can assume that someone's going to consider that to be selfish.

We saw in Chapter 2 that each person acts always in ways he believes will make him feel good or will remove discomfort from his life. Because everyone is different from everyone else, each individual goes about it in his own way.

One man devotes his life to helping the poor. Another one lies and steals. Still another person tries to create better products and services for which he hopes to be paid handsomely. One woman devotes herself to her husband and children. Another one seeks a career as a singer.

In every case, the ultimate motivation has been the same. Each person is doing what *he* believes will assure his happiness. What varies between them is the *means* each has chosen to gain his happiness.

We could divide them into two groups labeled "selfish" and "unselfish," but I don't think that would prove anything. For the thief and the humanitarian each have the same motive—to do what he believes will make him feel good.

In fact, we can't avoid a very significant conclusion: *Everyone is selfish.* Selfishness isn't really an issue, because everyone selfishly seeks his own happiness.

What we need to examine, however, are the means various people choose to achieve their unhappiness. Unfortunately, some people oversimplify the matter by assuming that there are only two basic means: sacrifice yourself for others or make them sacrifice for you. Happily, there's a third way that can produce better consequences than either of those two.

A BETTER WORLD

Let's look first, however, at the ideal of living for the benefit of others. It's often said that it would be a better world if everyone were unselfish. But would it be?

If it were somehow possible for everyone to give up his own happiness, what would be the result? Let's carry it to its logical conclusion and see what we find.

To visualize it, let's imagine that happiness is symbolized by a big red rubber ball. I have the ball in my hands—meaning that I hold the ability to be happy. But since I'm not going to be selfish, I quickly pass the ball to you. I've given up my happiness for you.

What will you do? Since you're not selfish either, you won't keep the ball; you'll quickly pass it on to your next-door neighbor. But he doesn't want to be selfish either, so he passes it to his wife, who likewise gives it to her children.

The children have been taught the virtue of unselfishness, so they pass it to playmates, who pass it to parents, who pass it to neighbors, and on and on and on.

I think we can stop the analogy at this point and ask what's been accomplished by all this effort. Who's better off for these demonstrations of pure unselfishness?

How would it be a better world if everyone acted that way? Whom would we be unselfish for? There would have to be a selfish person who would receive, accept, and enjoy the benefits of our unselfishness for there to be any purpose to it. But that selfish person (the object of our generosity) would be living by lower standards than we do.

For a more practical example, what is achieved by the parent who "sacrifices" himself for his children, who in turn are expected to sacrifice themselves for *their* children, etc.? The unselfishness concept is a merry-go-round that has no ultimate purpose. No one's self-interest is enhanced by the continual relaying of gifts from one person to another to another.

Perhaps most people have never carried the concept of unselfishness to this logical conclusion. If they did, they might reconsider their pleas for an unselfish world.

NEGATIVE CHOICES

But, unfortunately, the pleas continue, and they're a very real part of your life. In seeking your own freedom and happiness, you have to deal with those who tell you that you shouldn't put yourself first. That creates a situation in which you're pressured to act negatively—to put aside your plans and desires in order to avoid the condemnation of others.

As I've said before, one of the characteristics of a free man is that he's usually choosing positively—deciding which of several alternatives would make him the happiest; while the average person, most of the time, is choosing which of two or three alternatives will cause him the least discomfort.

When the reason for your actions is to avoid being called "selfish" you're making a negative decision and thereby restricting the possibilities for your own happiness.

You're in the Unselfishness Trap if you regretfully pay for your aunt's surgery with the money you'd saved for a new car, or if you sadly give up the vacation you'd looked forward to in order to help a sick neighbor.

You're in the trap if you feel you're *required* to give part of your income to the poor, or if you think that your country, community, or family has first claim on your time, energy, or money.

You're in the Unselfishness Trap any time you make negative choices that are designed to avoid being called "selfish."

It isn't that no one else is important. You might have a self-interest in someone's well-being, and giving a gift can be a gratifying expression of the affection you feel for him. But you're in the trap if you do such things in order to appear unselfish.

HELPING OTHERS

There *is* an understandable urge to give to those who are important and close to you. However, that leads many people to think that indiscriminate giving is the key to one's own happiness. They say that the way to be happy is to make others happy; get your glow by basking in the glow you've created for someone else.

It's important to identify that as a personal opinion. If someone says that giving is the key to happiness, isn't he saying that's the key to *his* happiness? To assume that his opinions are binding upon you is a common form of the Identity Trap.

I think we can carry the question further, however, and determine how efficient such a policy might be. The suggestion to be a giver presupposes that you're able to judge what will make someone else happy. And experience has taught me to be a bit humble about assuming what makes others happy.

My landlady once brought me a piece of her freshly baked cake because she wanted to do me a favor. Unfortunately, it happened to be a kind of cake that was distasteful to me. I won't try to describe the various ways I tried to get the cake plate back to her without being confronted with a request for my judgement of her cake. It's sufficient to say that her well-intended favor interfered with my own plans.

And now, whenever I'm sure I know what someone else "needs," I remember that incident and back off a little. There's no way that one person can read the mind of another to know all his plans, goals, and tastes.

You may know a great deal about the desires of your intimate friends. But *indiscriminate* gift-giving and favor-doing is usually a waste of resources—or, worse, it can upset the well-laid plans of the receiver.

When you give to someone else, you might provide something he values—but probably not the thing he considers most important. If you expend those resources for *yourself*, you automatically devote them to what you consider to be most important. The time or money you've spent will most likely create more happiness that way.

If your purpose is to make someone happy, you're more apt to succeed if you make yourself the object. You'll never know another person more than a fraction as well as you can know yourself.

Do you want to make someone happy? Go to it—use your talents and your insight and benevolence to bestow riches of happiness upon the one person you understand well enough to do it efficiently—yourself. I guarantee that you'll get more genuine appreciation from yourself than from anyone else.

Give to you.

Support your local self.

ALTERNATIVES

As I indicated earlier in this chapter, it's too often assumed that there are only two alternatives: (1) sacrifice your interests for the benefit of others; or (2) make others sacrifice their interests for you. If nothing else were possible, it would indeed be a grim world.

Fortunately, there's more to the world than that. Because desires vary from person to person, it's possible to create exchanges between individuals in which both parties benefit.

For example, if you buy a house, you do so because you'd rather have the house than the money involved. But the seller's desire is different—he'd rather have the money than the house. When the sale is completed, each of you has received something of greater value than what you gave up—otherwise you wouldn't have entered the exchange. Who, then, has had to sacrifice for the other?

In the same way, your daily life is made up of dozens of such exchanges—small and large transactions in which each party gets something he values more than what he gives up. The exchange doesn't have to involve money; you may be spending time, attention, or effort in exchange for something you value.

Mutually beneficial relationships are possible when desires are compatible. Sometimes the desires are the same—like going to a movie together. Sometimes the desires are different—like trading your money for someone's house. In either case, it's the *compatibility* of the desires that makes the exchange possible.

No sacrifice is necessary when desires are compatible. So it makes sense to seek out people with whom you can have mutually beneficial relationships.

Often the "unselfishness" issue arises only because two people with nothing in common are trying to get along together—such as a man who likes bowling and hates opera married to a woman whose tastes are the opposite. If they're to do things together, one must "sacrifice" his pleasure for the other. So each might try to encourage the other to be "unselfish."

If they were compatible, the issue wouldn't arise because each would be pleasing the other by doing what was his own self-interest.

An efficiently selfish person *is* sensitive to the needs and desires of others. But he doesn't consider those desires to be demands upon him. Rather, he sees them as *opportunities*—potential exchanges that might be beneficial to him. He identifies desires in others so that he can decide if exchanges with them will help them get what he wants.

He doesn't sacrifice himself for others, nor does he expect others to be sacrificed for him. He takes the third alternative—he finds relationships that are mutually beneficial so that no sacrifice is required.

PLEASE YOURSELF

Everyone is selfish; everyone is doing what he believes will make himself happier. The recognition of that can take most of the sting out of accusations that you're being "selfish." Why should you feel guilty for seeking your own happiness when that's what everyone else is doing, too?

The demand that you be unselfish can be motivated by any number of reasons: that you'd help create a better world, that you have a moral obligation to be unselfish, that you give up your happiness to the selfishness of someone else, or that the person demanding it has just never thought it out.

Whatever the reason, you're not likely to convince such a person to stop his demands. But it will create much less pressure on you if you realize that it's *his* selfish reason. And you can eliminate the problem entirely by looking for more compatible companions.

To find constant, profound happiness requires that you be free to seek the gratification of your own desires. It means making positive choices.

If you slip into the Unselfishness Trap, you'll spend a good part of your time making negative choices—trying to avoid the censure of those who tell you not to think of yourself. You won't have time to be free.

If someone finds happiness by doing "good works" for others, let him. That doesn't mean that's the best way for you to find happiness.

And when someone accuses you of being selfish, just remember that he's only upset because you aren't doing what *he* selfishly wants you to do.

Poke any saint deeply enough, and you touch self-interest.   —IRVING WALLACE

6

The Group Trap

THE GROUP TRAP is the belief that you can accomplish more by sharing responsibilities, efforts, and rewards with others than you can by acting on your own.

It's an easy trap to fall into. It's a common expression that "in union there is strength." Just the opposite is true, however. You achieve more for yourself when your rewards are dependent upon your own efforts rather than upon the efforts of other people.

When you join a group effort to achieve freedom, you waste precious resources on an endeavor that has very little chance of success. In the same way, group efforts are common in businesses, marriages, and even friendships, and there too the Group Trap can cause subtle problems.

Groups are not living entities. They don't think or act; *only individuals do*. And yet, any group effort is based upon the assumption of a *group purpose* that overrides the individual differences of its members. It's expected that the group will act as a single unit with a unified purpose.

Only individuals think—and each one thinks differently. Their interests and desires may overlap, but each person will continue to define his own objectives and have his own opinion concerning the best way to achieve those objectives.

Perhaps each person entering a group unconsciously assumes that it will act in unison for *his* objectives and by *his* methods. But every other participant probably has a similar assumption regarding *his* ideas.

What they get instead will inevitably be a compromise. The individual's goals and his concept of the best methods will be automatically compromised *before* anything happens to further his objectives.

It also means a certain amount of time and effort will have to be spent to *arrange* the compromise— again, before anything concrete is done to further the objectives.

On the other hand, the individual who acts alone doesn't have to alter his objectives. He can employ the means he considers best suited to the objective, and he doesn't have to waste time and effort trying to arrange a compromise with partners.

INCENTIVE

Another problem is encountered in group endeavors. When the efforts and rewards are shared, it becomes apparent that the individaul's own efforts will have a less significant effect upon his ultimate reward than if he were acting alone.

Suppose that the group consists of two people—a business partnership, for instance. If the two partners have agreed to work equally hard and share the rewards 50-50, the significance of each person's efforts has been cut by 50 percent. Whatever value the individual provides to the group, he'll receive only half of its reward.

Of course, he expects to get half the value added by the other person, too; but *he doesn't control the other person's effort*. He controls only his own effort. So what *he* controls will produce only a half reward.

The situation is worse if the group is larger. If one hundred people are engaged in a crusade to bring about a social change of some kind, each individual's effort adds only one percent to the whole. It's doubtful that any such endeavor is won or lost by an additional one percent of effort. Consequently, the individual's participation becomes *irrelevant* to the outcome (contrary to "get out and vote" campaigns).

Whether he goes out to work hard or stays home in bed, the outcome will be the same. In such a situation, there's a strong incentive to stay in bed.

The popular answer to such reasoning is "Yes, but what if everyone thought that way?" But he isn't *everyone;* he's only *him.* He isn't deciding for everyone; he's merely evaluating the significance of his own actions—and when he works in a group, his actions don't contribute much.

Sometimes this realization will cause an individual to drop out of a group entirely. More often it will simply cause him to work *less*—to make small decisions here and there in favor of relaxing as opposed to overdoing it.

If the arrangement were such that everything he did had a direct bearing on his own rewards, he would have a continual incentive to extend his efforts. He'd be encouraged to work harder than he would have worked under the group arrangement.

The more directly individual rewards are tied to individual achievements, the greater incentive there is to increase one's individual effort.

JOINT EFFORTS

Joint efforts are possible. In fact, they're necessary to increase standards of living. You can't produce your own automobile from scratch—nor can you really produce much of anything without relying upon the efforts of others. You need tools, materials, and information; and you can't produce all those things yourself.

This problem is solved by what is called the *specialization of labor.* When some individuals spend all their working time producing a single product, while others specialize in producing other products, the result is greater production of all products. The specialization of labor has made it possible for many more things to be available to everyone.

But each person must retain control of his own responsibilities, efforts, and rewards if the maximum incentive is to be maintained. Otherwise, his efforts will be less significant and therefore less productive.

It's necessary to exchange with others to acquire whatever you need along the way, but you don't have to enter into sharing agreements of the kind described earlier. It's more efficient to *separate* responsibilities and rewards, not share them.

The Group Trap is the assumption that greater strength can be achieved by sharing. Just the opposite happens: Individual objectives are watered down, time and effort are wasted in arranging compromises, and individual incentive is reduced.

The individual becomes much less flexible and mobile, because he must deal with others before getting on with the task at hand. As Thoreau said, "The man who goes alone can start today; but he who travels with another must wait till that other is ready."[1]

THE GROUP TRAP

The Group Trap comes packaged in many wrappings. In its broadest form, it is any economic system that separates achievements from rewards. If an individual is required to share what *he* produces but can also have a share of what *others* produce, his obvious incentive will be to produce as little as possible and live off the rewards produced by others. Consequently, total production will be reduced and there will be less to split up.

The Group Trap also applies to a combined effort to clean up the community, lower taxes, end pollution, stop prejudice, accomplish social reforms, promote an idealogy, or stop a war. In each case, the individual's efforts become almost irrelevant to the outcome.

[1] Henry David Thoreau, *Walden*, p. 87.

It's an example of the Group Trap when someone says, "If we all stick together and follow this plan, we'll succeed." You *won't* all stick together; you'll each do things in your own individual way. You'll depend for your success upon others sticking to the plan—and you may wind up spending most of your time futilely trying to herd them into line.

And you'll probably recognize that you could sit at home and not change the outcome one bit—or you could work very hard and still not change the outcome one bit. Your actions are only *your* actions, not those of the group.

Further examples of the Group Trap are business partnerships, profit-sharing plans, pooling resources in marriages, and efforts to set up "communes" that eliminate individual incentives.[2]

A more subtle example of the Group Trap is the labor union. Not all individuals join labor unions enthusiastically, but, of those who do, most assume that they'll be able to make more money through the combined strength of the union membership.

When one recognizes the value of the specialization of labor, it makes sense for an employee to consider hiring someone to negotiate for him. But when negotiations are conducted *collectively*, without regard to individual differences in value, the individual's incentive is sidetracked again.

In a unionized job, your wage is determined by factors other than your individual worth, so the chances are that you'll be paid too much or too little. Either event has its consequences.

If you're underpaid, you're wasting your time in that job. If you're overpaid, you have little incentive to grow into new areas of your job or find out what you're capable of. In addition, you might *lose* your job if you're getting

---

[2] These early chapters are devoted to pointing out the drawbacks in the normal ways of doing things. Later chapters will offer alternatives that I believe are more effective.

more than you're worth to the employer. If your pay exactly matches your worth, it's purely accidental.

Since the pay of each individual in the union is determined by factors other than his own achievement, his incentive to produce deteriorates. Once again, the overall output is bound to be reduced thereby—which means that the overall reward to be shared won't be as high as it could be.

Professional athletes are often represented by agents who negotiate their contracts for them. An agent might represent several athletes to the same employer, but each individual's contract is individually negotiated. No attempt is made to rely on the group for bargaining power. Consequently, individual incentives are maintained fully, value is encouraged, and rewards are greater.

If you have anything to offer the world, you're bound to accomplish more for yourself in a situation where your reward is tied to your own individual effort.

VARIATIONS

In addition to the examples just given, there are numerous variations of the Group Trap.

A typical example is the concept of *democracy*. If the majority vote of the group is binding upon all, the individual forfeits his ability to make decisions for himself.

Politicians love to declare that the "people" have chosen for themselves at the polls." But the "people" don't have a mind; only individuals do. Those who have voted against the winner are now under the jurisdiction of someone who doesn't represent them.

Even the concept of the "majority" is often misleading. In any election, many people vote against the winner, many others abstain from voting because they realize their individual votes are irrelevant to the outcome, and others aren't even allowed to vote (but are bound by the outcome). Those who voted for the winner are usually a minority—and even they may have voted only for the least unpleasant alternative.

Another variation of the Group Trap is the assumption that you're responsible for people who are starving in other parts of the world. You could work for the rest of your life to change that—but your effort would never make a noticeable dent in the problem.

You're in the Group Trap, too, any time you assume that someone can speak on behalf of anyone but himself. When someone tells you that you owe something to your country, to what is he referring? Your "country" consists of more than 200 million individuals with different attitudes, desires, activities, and principles. Do you owe it to every one of them to do as each of them wants you to do? What you "owe to your country" is really what someone wants you to do to please *him,* but for which he's unwilling to make it worth your while.

In the same way, no one can speak on behalf of all Americans, Negroes, Mexicans, women, or students. The attempt to do so is an attempt to create pressure in favor of what the *speaker* wants.

Another typical example of collectivizing is a statement like "We're all to blame for the death of John F. Kennedy." How can we *all* be responsible? Does this mean that you should personally police the world to be sure that no one ever does anything that might be considered wrong?

In the same way, when someone says, "We have the ability to get to the moon, but we can't even get along with each other," whom is he talking about? I don't know about you, but *I* don't have the ability to get to the moon; however, I *can* get along with *some* people. Doesn't he really mean, "While some men have learned how to go to the moon, other men (perhaps himself included) don't know how to get along with people"?

TYPES OF ALTERNATIVES

As you view any situation in which you have a goal, there are basically two types of alternatives available to you. I call them *direct* and *indirect*.

A *direct* alternative is one that requires only direct action *by yourself* to get a desired result. An *indirect* alternative requires that you act to make *someone else* do what is necessary to achieve your objective.

Once you've seen the positions and attitudes of the other people involved, a direct alternative requires only that *you* make a decision; an indirect alternative requires that you *change* the attitude of one or more other persons so that *they* will do what it is you want.

For example, suppose you feel your taxes are too high. An indirect alternative would be to start a campaign to lower the tax rates. A direct alternative would be to look for ways to avoid having to pay them.

Or suppose you belong to a club whose rules and activities have changed to the extent that you no longer enjoy being a member. An indirect alternative would be to try to change the minds of enough members to return the club to the conditions you enjoyed previously. A direct alternative would be to quit the club and find a better one.

Or suppose you're a college student who's dissatisfied with the curriculum offered at your school. Examples of indirect alternatives would be to try to influence the administration to change the curriculum or try to influence higher powers to change the administration. Examples of direct alternatives would be to find a more agreeable school or to study the missing subjects on the side.

The examples of choices I've cited aren't necessarily the only ones available; they were cited to illustrate the two *types* of alternatives from which you can choose. A direct alternative requires only a decision on your part; an indirect alternative requires that you get others to make decisions that would benefit you.

You control only yourself. That doesn't mean that it's impossible to convince someone else to act in a way you'd like him to act. But the process of having to hope for a favorable reaction from someone else makes an indirect alternative less certain than a direct alternative.

When you join a group in hopes of furthering your aims, you're involved in an indirect alternative. You're hoping that the others in the group will act in ways that will further your objectives. But since each of them has his own individual goals and his own methods, the result will invariably be something quite different from a multiplication of your own strength.

This principle applies whether the group consists of you and one other person or you and thousands of others. In every case, your objectives and plans are diluted as they merge with those of the other members of the group.

SELLING OTHERS

One of the greatest encouragements to wasted effort is the concept of positive thinking. To say "You can do it if you'll just believe you can" is to try to wish away reality. In those situations that involve direct alternatives, your own mental attitude can make quite a difference. But in situations involving indirect alternatives, false confidence can induce you to waste your time futilely trying to change others.

It's easy to get involved in a group with the assumption that you'll work hard to persuade others of the rightness of your ideas. But each of those others is an individual human being—with his own knowledge, attitude, goals, and plans. Your mental attitude will have no more effect in changing his nature than his mental attitude could change yours.

A realistic man recognizes the identity of each person he deals with. He knows that he can't change the identity of the other person just by willing it. He takes the identities of others seriously and then decides what direct alternatives exist for him in view of those identities.

That doesn't mean that no one ever changes his ideas or plans. But the changes occur only when they make sense to the individual—when they are harmonious with *his* basic nature.

There are occasions when you must sell something to someone else—possibly even sell for a living. But an efficient salesman doesn't approach the world with the idea that his persuasive powers could change anyone.

Rather, he accepts people as they are and relies upon two talents: (1) his ability to *locate* people whose self-interest would be satisfied by his product or service; and (2) his ability to demonstrate to those people the connection between his product and their self-interest.

I realize that most salesmen waste their time trying futilely to persuade anyone and everyone they meet. But that's why most salesmen make poor livings for the amount of time they spend at it.

The most successful salesmen, consciously or intuitively, recognize and accept the identities of the people they deal with. They take seriously their prospects' attitudes and objections. And they don't waste their time with inappropriate prospects. Because they realize that they can't sell everyone, they're more selective in picking the people they'll try to sell.

A KEY TO FREEDOM

The recognition of the two types of alternatives is one of the most important keys to freedom. Most people automatically think in terms of indirect alternatives—who must be changed, how people must be educated, what others should be doing. Consequently, they spend most of their lives in futile efforts, trying to achieve what can't be achieved—the remaking of others.

In any situation, a free man immediately looks first at the identities of the other people involved and appraises the situation by the simple standard: *Is this what I want for myself?* If it isn't, he looks elsewhere. If it *is*, he relaxes and enjoys the situation to the maximum—without the problems that most people take for granted.

He automatically thinks in terms of direct alternatives. He asks himself, "With things as they are, what can *I* do by myself to make things better for myself?"

Most people usually assume that there aren't many direct alternatives, that the only one available would be to change oneself. But that's because they're not geared to looking for them.

It can also be because they're not free to act upon them—because of other restrictions in their lives.

For example, if you're deep in debt, on a treadmill, and locked in difficult personal situations, you can't take advantage of the alternatives a free man could use to insulate himself from high taxes or repressive government. As a result, you could assume that your only alternative is to join a movement to attempt to lower the general tax rates.

In this way, one kind of freedom often depends upon the existence of other freedoms. Whichever freedom you miss most, it may be out of reach because of a lack of other freedoms.

A free man doesn't need groups, because he's in a position to take advantage of the numerous direct alternatives that require only *his* decision, not the changing of others.

Throughout this book we'll be looking at many traps, issues, and techniques. In every case, I'll be suggesting direct alternatives that are much easier to employ than the normally assumed alternatives that require the cooperation of others.

Those direct alternatives do *not* require that you become a hermit, change yourself, give up things you enjoy, or in any other way sacrifice yourself in order to make things work. The point is simply that there are numerous ways to improve your situation without having to go to the trouble of making others agree with your way of thinking.

It's possible to have relationships with others, contracts with others, business dealings, and every other form of social activity. But those relationships will be far more rewarding for you if you recognize identities, find those that are compatible, and arrange matters in ways that appeal to the self-interest of each person involved.

EASIER WAYS

The Group Trap is the belief that you can accomplish more by sharing responsibilities, efforts, and rewards with others than you can by acting on your own.

You waste precious time, effort, and money when you attempt to achieve freedom through the efforts of a group. You can achieve far more for yourself using direct alternatives to free yourself or government interference, social pressures, and other conditions that restrict you.

If you're not free now, a good deal of your present situation may be the result of restrictive relationships—business partnerships, unsound marital arrangements, misguided allegiances to friends or family. In Chapter 18 through 22 I'll suggest ways that those objectives might be more efficiently achieved.

Group endeavors are inefficient because they neutralize incentives by creating shared responsibilities, efforts, and rewards. You think and decide and act only for yourself. It isn't realistic to believe you can double your thoughts and actions by adding an equal partner, or that you can multiply them a hundred times over by joining a large group.

There are easier ways—ways in which you can go as far as you're willing to and be rewarded accordingly.

Down to Gehenna or up to the Throne,
He travels the fastest who travels alone.
—RUDYARD KIPLING

7

The Government Traps

GOVERNMENTS PLAY a very important part in most people's lives. Well over one-third of one's income is spent for various taxes—income taxes, property taxes, sales taxes, import duties—although some of the taxes are paid indirectly through the costs of products and, thus, not noticed.

The significance of government can be demonstrated by a look at any daily newspaper on any day of the week; the coverage given to news concerning governments is overwhelming.

Because of these things, it's not surprising that most people turn first to government whenever they become concerned about their freedom. They assume either that the government must do something to help them be free, or that the government is obstructing their freedom. But few people have ever considered exactly what a government *is*—so they keep trying through government to increase their freedom without ever understanding their failures.

They waste a great deal of their freedom working to affect the government—through voting, politics, educating others (who are in turn supposed to affect the government), protesting, etc.

Their freedom is wasted because most of the popular assumptions about government won't hold up under close examination. I think there are four basic Government Traps—popular misconceptions about the nature of government:

1. The belief that governments perform socially useful functions that deserve your support.

2. The belief that you have a duty to obey laws.

3. The belief that the government can be counted upon to carry out a social reform you favor.

4. The fear that the government is so powerful that it can prevent you from being free.

Fifteen years ago if anyone had suggested to me that those beliefs were mistaken, I would have been aghast. But today I can't conceive of any other conclusions.

The subject of government is fascinating. For it has to do with how you and I and everyone else gets what he wants in daily intercourse with others—and how that's affected by governments. A close investigation of the subject can produce surprising conclusions. So let's take a closer look.

THE MARKET

As we've seen before, all individuals are different—fortunately. Without such differences there would be very little diversity in what is produced; there'd be no specialization of labor. As it is, there's a wide difference in the kinds of work individuals are willing to do. These differences make many kinds of products and services available.

There are also wide differences in tastes and desires. This, too, is fortunate. For these differences make the world orderly. If everyone wanted the same things, we would all be struggling *against each other* to acquire what little was available.

Diversity is the source of harmony in human relationships. Because our tastes are different, we can exchange with each other in a way that is mutually beneficial. If you and I have *exactly* the same values, there is no way we can trade. One of us will have what each of us wants most—and he won't give it up.

With our difference in values, I can trade something to you for something I value more. You, on the other hand, will be getting something you want more than what you're giving up. Each of us improves his situation without hurting the other.

This is a *market*—a compatibility of values that makes an exchange possible. Literally billions of such markets operate every day—as exchanges are made all over the world. For example, an employee trades his time and effort for something he wants more—money. An employer, meanwhile, trades his money for something *he* values more—the time and effort of the employee.

These markets provide the only way to know exactly what individuals really want. Only when an individual gives up something he has in an exchange can you know how much he values the thing he says he desires.

Human wants are limitless. We each want a multitude of things—far more than we could ever obtain with our limited resources. So to state a desire for something doesn't specify *how much* that thing is desired by the individual. Only when he offers to *give up* something in order to get it do we know how much he values it.

Will the man who says he wants a yacht be willing to give up his car, his food budget for a year, his clothes and furniture—in order to have the money to buy a yacht? Will the man who wants the poor to be fed be willing to go without entertainment for six months—in order to raise money to give to the poor? Will the woman who wishes she had more time to spend with her children be willing to give up the women's club, cocktail parties, and bridge—in order to have the time to spend at home?

Desires are limitless; resources are limited. These two conditions are the reasons that individuals must make choices. Individuals decide how they'll use their limited resources to satisfy their strongest desires. In doing so, they develop *value scales,* which we can see only by looking at the exchanges they're willing to make.

Perhaps an individual can't tell you exactly what's on his value scale, but he chooses in accordance with it when faced with a decision. And he chooses that which he believes will bring him the most happiness.

MEETING PLACE

Billions of exchanges take place daily, and they're expressions of the desires of billions of human beings. If we could somehow add up all the desires of all individuals in a given area (or the whole world) and compare that with the products and services available, we would have the *General Market.*

Not only is it impossible to make such a calculation, but even if we could, it would be outdated by the time we added up the figures. For the market is constantly changing. Each individual's values change constantly as he acquires new knowledge and new resources. And the availability of things to buy is constantly changing as producers make changes in what they offer to the public.

So the General Market constantly changes. But to whatever extent we can observe it, it represents an accurate expression of what people, in general, are choosing to do with their available resources.

Within the General Market we find a multitude of differences in motivations. In the car market, for example, one man buys a big car that satisfies his desires for comfort, prestige, and mobility. At the same time, another man buys a small car that gets him where he wants to go with a minimum of expense.

What we see as the General Market is the net effect, or *trend,* created by these many different purchases. But no matter what the overall trend, it contains within it numerous *different* desires, availabilities, and purchases.

TYPES OF TRANSACTIONS

Within the General Market there are two basic kinds of exchanges. The most common is a *two-sided transaction*—one in which each party participates because he wants to.

The possible reasons for entering a two-sided exchange are endless, of course. They include positive decisions made in order to increase one's happiness (such as buying a better car to drive) and negative decisions that are made because things would get worse without them (such as getting the roof fixed to avoid being flooded by rain).

In each case, the individual enters the relationship because what is offered is better than what he had before. He *could* have left things as they were, but he prefers not to.

In a *one*-sided transaction, one of the participants *forces* the other to choose between two new alternatives. He introduces violence (or the threat of it) as a way of making the unwilling participant a part of the relationship.

A common example is a hold-up. A man points a gun at you and forces you to choose between violence and losing your money. You would prefer not to have to make *any* choice, but you're forced to; you can't leave things as they were.

If you have to choose between paying to have your roof fixed and letting it leak, you're in a similar position (you can't leave things as they were before the roof started leaking), but your quarrel is with *nature*. In a hold-up, it's another human being who's inflicted the negative decision upon you.

If your wife confronts you with the choice of changing your ways or losing her, there too you must make a negative decision. But your participation in the relationship itself was a voluntary decision (unless it was a shotgun wedding).

Only the first example of the three was a one-sided

transaction—a relationship between two human beings where one party has used violence to force the other to participate.

It should be noted, however, that the thief isn't getting "something for nothing." He still has to work for what he gets. He gives up his time, takes risks, pays for his gun, and works in other ways. No matter what you want, or how you intend to get it, you have to pay a price for it.

EXCHANGES

When we talk of government we're talking of something that exists in the General Market I've just described. So let's sum up what we've seen of the ways people get what they want through the market:

1. Nothing is free. To acquire anything requires an expenditure of time, energy, or money. (Not even natural resources can be used without an application of effort—whether that be cutting down a tree or picking up an apple.)

2. Anything you want that you can't provide entirely for yourself requires an exchange with someone else.

3. A one-sided transaction doesn't provide a gain for the unwilling participant—even if he receives something in return. It wouldn't be one-sided if *he* valued what he receives more than what he must give up, for then he'd have entered the transaction willingly.

4. Whatever an individual does is the highest-valued alternative that he believes is available to him.

5. At any given time the General Market reflects the consensus of the highest values the people therein believe possible. As individuals go about their business, they're getting the best they know how in the world as it is.

SPEEDING UP HISTORY

But some people are impatient. They look about them and get the impression that things aren't moving as fast as they could be. They want to improve upon the natural, automatic processes of the market.

And so they form *governments*.

They hope thereby to make things available to more people more quickly. In addition, they hope to have their lives and property protected for a smaller price than they think it would cost without government.

The basic mistake is the assumption that with a government they will have *more* than what they would have had in the marketplace. The truth is that they wind up with *less*. For the government can only give you something by taking away something you wanted *more*.

It's easy to think that government programs *add* to what's available. But they don't; they *replace* what was available. And we've already seen that at any given time the General Market expresses the highest-valued desires of the people within it. So the government can only act by replacing a desire with something valued less.

People seek government action because they don't approve of what other people choose to do with their lives. They want to overrule the decisions others have made concerning the uses of their own time and money.

It generally works this way: The individuals in Group A want something that requires the cooperation of Group B. But they can't (or won't) convince Group B that it's to the advantage of Group B. So Group A calls upon the government to pass a law that compels Group B to cooperate.

For example, a few critics want American car manufacturers to build automobiles with more safety accessories than the car makers have chosen to include. The car makers have decided (wisely or not) that potential car buyers *don't* want those accessories enough to pay the extra price required.

If Group A (the critics) can't convince either Group B (the manufacturers) or Group C (the buyers) of the importance of the safety additions, they still have some alternatives available. They could refuse to continue buying what they consider to be unsatisfactory cars, or they could publish their findings (if there's enough interest to create a market.)

Instead, they choose to go to the government. They believe they must coercively impose their safety standards upon all car makers and car buyers—regardless of those individuals' values.

If the laws are passed, some buyers may approve, even though they might not buy the new cars when the prices go up. Far more car buyers will be unhappy, because they would have preferred less stringent standards and lower prices—which is why the car makers resisted the higher standards in the first place. Obviously, if they'd thought most car buyers wanted to pay more for safer cars, they'd have offered just that, in order to sell more cars.

ENFORCED CONFORMITY

Many people think we're protected against dishonesty or inefficiency through government licensing and inspection requirements. But different individuals want different kinds and amounts of protection, For example, you might decide not to buy something until you're assured that it's what you expect—by *your* standards. I, on the other hand, might hire someone else to protect my interests. A third man might prefer to risk his money rather than pay the expense of having a product guaranteed.

These differences between us pose no problem. Each of us can do as he chooses—trusting or not trusting the people we deal with, paying for as much or as little protection as we want.

When the government intervenes, however, *all* of us are required to adhere to standards set by the government—and at a cost dictated by the government. Almost all of us are deprived of the choices we would have preferred.

In a world of vastly different tastes, the government imposes one way upon us and forces everyone to adhere to that one way.

Despite our differing tastes, the government decides

which products we're allowed to buy. Federal agencies rule products out of the market, import quotas prevent other products from being available, and legal monopolies (such as the postal service or public utilities) prevent us from choosing between alternative ways of obtaining services.

Again, our preferences are overruled and we're forced to take what the government has decreed to be "best"—leaving us without the things we could have had without government intervention.

Government regulation always overrules the consumers. What consumers *don't* want, they don't have to buy; what governments don't want, consumers *can't* buy. What consumers want (protection, inspection, etc.), they can get; what the government thinks they should have, consumers are *forced* to take and forced to pay for.

It's important to recognize that these government decisions are *not* benevolent, kindly forms of advice and help. No, they are enforced by violence. If you should ever decide that your business will continue to provide what consumers want, despite government regulations, you'll be met with violence.

You'll be fined. If you refuse to pay the fine, your bank accounts will be seized. If you continue to provide what consumers prefer, you'll be ordered to close your business. If you resist, gentlemen with guns will take you to jail.

Absolutely *every* government regulation is enforced by violence. If you've never seen that violence, it's because you've been careful, obedient, or lucky. Would regulations still be obeyed if the police, courts, and jails were dissolved?

GOVERNMENT BUSINESSES

The same principles apply when governments set up businesses—schools, lending institutions, insurance companies, or foreign-aid programs, etc. It's claimed that "society needs them" and the free market won't, or can't, provide them.

But who is "society" if not the same people who are already expressing their needs and preferences in the marketplace? *If they aren't willing to pay for the service in the free market* (the General Market apart from the government), *who can say they're willing to pay for it through government?*

Who will provide the resources (time, energy, and money) to pay for the services? Obviously, the cost will be borne by the same people who've already chosen to do *other* things with their resources. The government can't create resources out of thin air any more than you or I could. The resources will have to come from people who'd rather use them for something else.

Since there's no justification for that, various arguments are presented to demonstrate the value of various government enterprises.

For example, it's often said that a government business will "pay its own way"—meaning that consumers will buy its services at prices sufficient to pay its expenses. Why, then, bother to call upon the government? If the service were truly able to pay its own way, it would be profitable for someone to offer it in the marketplace. If no one has, it only means that no one really believes it *can* pay its own way.

The next argument claims that the government can offer the service without "making a profit." But what is a profit? It's simply a net gain a person receives for the time, energy, and money he's expended. Will the workers in a government business donate their time and energies without pay? Obviously not.

Perhaps what's meant is that there won't be any profit earned on the money invested. But that means someone's going to have his money confiscated and invested in a government business without getting the profit he could have made investing it in the free market.

It's also claimed there will be no "entrepreneurial profit"—meaning no one will be paid for appraising the market to determine the desire for the service, putting the organization together, and making sure it will run right. But who will make sure the business is sound?

If the government claims it can do away with profit, it means either that (1) there has been no appraisal of the market potential for the service; or that (2) the appraisal has been done by someone who's grossly underpaid and thus not to be relied upon; or that (3) the necessary appraisal has been stolen from someone else; or that (4) the appraisal is being paid for with other government funds that won't show up on the ledgers of the enterprise.

In any case, the "non-profit" claim is of no benefit to the public.

No matter what the argument, the conclusion is the same: *The government has no mysterious ability to do things that can't be done in the free market.* It can't command resources that don't already exist.

It can only overrule the decisions of its citizens—eliminating their alternatives and replacing those alternatives with activities they've desired less. It takes money from the General Market and spends it on less-valued choices, adding the cost of itself in the process, and leaving people with less than they would have if there were no government.

Any individual in the General Market can give to the poor, pay for someone else's schooling, donate money to foreign governments, or hire protection. It isn't *his* choice he's concerned about when he wants the government to do those things. It's *someone else's* choice that he's trying to overrule.

All government actions depend upon one-sided transactions, in which an attempt is made to force an individual to choose between paying for what he doesn't want and going to jail.

These principles apply to *any* government—from the local school board to the federal government.

Governments don't rule; they overrule.

WHY GOVERNMENTS?

Why, then, do governments have such widespread acceptance?

I can think of three reasons:

1. Most people believe that governments add to the general well-being, rather than reduce it. They haven't recognized the simple economic truths we've covered here.

2. Many individuals believe they're getting more benefits from the government than they give up. They pay a price in taxes and reduced alternatives (many of which they may not have recognized), but feel that they get back more in subsidies and special privileges.

In other words, they don't think that "society" benefits but believe that they, individually, come out ahead. As Frederic Bastiat put it, "The State is the great fictitious entity by which everyone expects to live at the expense of everyone else."[1]

The same attitude can apply in non-financial matters. A person may be pleased with laws that keep others from smoking marijuana or buying what they want or associating with whomever they choose. He's glad to see the government imposing his tastes upon everyone else.

3. The last-ditch argument for government is that it's necessary for the protection of life and property. It's easy to assume that without government we'd be at the mercy of thieves, rapists, and murderers. How would you protect yourself if there were no government?

Chances are you'd protect yourself by locking your doors, staying out of dangerous areas, keeping your children away from situations where they can't protect themselves, and choosing whom you'll allow in your home.

Sound familiar?

It should, for that's probably what you're doing already.

[1] From the essay *"The State"*—included in *Selected Essays on Political Economy*, p. 144.

Governments don't protect you. They can't. All they can do is promise to make the person who hurts you pay for his crime—if they can catch him. The criminal won't pay *you* back, of course, so they punish him only as a deterrent to future crime. If you think the deterrent is working, why is crime always such a public issue?

Occasionally, a government policeman actually prevents a specific crime from taking place or from being completed. The odds against that are tremendous, however. If you want to eliminate *all* risk of violence, your only recourse is to pay for a guard to watch over you and your property day and night. And if that's what you want, you can hire a guard to do it—but the price you already pay to the government won't purchase him.

Small wonder that the Los Angeles Chief of Police advised residents to "bar their doors, buy a police dog, call us when we're available, and pray" as the best methods of protecting themselves from crime.[2]

ENTER THE SYNDICATE

There's no way an individual can escape having to protect himself—with or without a government. But it's assumed that no one person can protect himself against what's called "organized crime"—the "Mafia" or other syndicates. How can an individual cope with a problem so large?

Why not? No individual could build a shopping center by himself, since the materials must be obtained from hundreds of remote places around the world and thousands of operations are required to build the buildings. Somehow, though, the job gets done through the voluntary actions of literally millions of people throughout the world. And no one has to be coerced to make it possible.

If governments didn't coercively monopolize the market for protection, there'd undoubtedly be more forms of pro-

[2] Los Angeles *Times*, June 4, 1971.

tection offered on a *voluntary* basis to those who feel threatened by organized crime.

But let's assume for the moment that individuals *would* be helpless against organized crime if the government didn't protect them. We could paint a pretty grim picture of the Mafia's effect upon our lives.

What is it we fear would happen if the Mafia were unrestrained by the government? Here are some of the problems that it's assumed we'd face:

1. So-called "protection rackets" would flourish. Businessmen would have to pay tribute to the Mafia or be violently put out of business.

2. Extortion would run rampant. You might have to pay off the Mafia in order to prevent being pushed around, or for the privilege of getting a job.

3. If worst came to worst, you might even have to pay off the syndicate just to be allowed to remain on your own property. If so, you'd never own anything outright; you'd always have to pay someone for the privilege of keeping what you thought was yours.

4. The syndicate might even tell you where you could work, or where you'd *have* to work, or how to run your business, or what kind of services they'd let you offer, or perhaps they'd even prevent you from competing with their businesses. Who could stop them?

5. And they might take the profits from their rackets and use them to compete with your business—using your own money to cut into your market.

That's a pretty grim picture. Would you want to live in such an environment? You'd have to pay for the privilege of working, going into business, staying on your own property. You'd be told what you couldn't do in your relationships with customers and friends. And you might even have to finance your own competitors.

AND SO ...

To prevent that nightmare from becoming a reality, we have a government. And what does the government do?

1. It imposes corporation taxes, license fees, and sales taxes upon businessmen—coercively shutting down any business that doesn't pay.

2. It seizes income taxes as payment for the privilege of working.

3. It gives you the one-sided choice of paying property taxes or losing your property. So, as economist F. A. Harper has pointed out, you don't actually *own* anything; you *rent* from the government. Sales between individuals are only exchanges of the privilege of renting property from the government. He who doesn't pay the annual rental is forcibly evicted from his property.

4. The government decrees what products you can offer to your customers (through the Federal Trade Commission and other agencies) and how much you can charge for your services (setting both minimum and maximum limits for wages and prices), requires massive bookkeeping, and imposes many other rules upon your business or your employment. And if it gets into trouble with other governments, it can even enslave you in its army to fight, and possibly die, on its behalf.

The government delegates some of its coercive powers to labor unions which, in turn, prevent many people from working at jobs where they'd otherwise be employed on a mutually profitable basis.

The government will prevent you from going into the business of delivering first-class mail—even though prior to that law private postal companies delivered the mail for a lower price, gave faster service, and made profits for themselves.[3]

[3] A thorough review of the development of the U.S. Postal Service into a legal monopoly is given in Chodorov, *One Is a Crowd.*

And if that weren't enough, try starting your own phone company.

5. On top of all this, the government uses the money it takes from you to operate businesses that may be in competition with your own. It has mortgage companies, ladies' underwear factories, charities, print shops, laundries, and hundreds more. Since it can always come back to you to cover its losses, it usually charges less for its products than you have to charge to stay in business.[4]

So to protect you from the syndicates, the government makes you pay tribute for the privileges of working, going into business, or staying on your own property. It dictates the terms of your relationships with customers and friends. It finances your competitors with your money. And it can even enslave you in its army.

What could the Mafia do that would be worse?

It's important to realize that a two-sided transaction is no threat to you. If someone *offers* you something, you can turn it down. And, surprisingly, most of the "crime" the government presumes to protect us against are two-sided transactions the government doesn't approve of.

For example, the *U.S. News & World Report* claims that the total yearly take from organized crime is $19.7 billion.[5] But a closer look at the figures indicates that less than a billion dollars of that is in crimes of violence. Over 90 percent of the total is in two-sided transactions like gambling, loan-sharking, alcohol, prostitution, and drugs. You can simply decline to participate in any of that.

In addition, much of the government's "law enforcement" is devoted to preventing free market transactions between willing participants—enforcement of "fair competition" laws, licensing laws, etc.

And to do this, the government imposes a one-sided transaction upon you. Surprisingly, you can avoid most of what is labeled "crime" by a simple choice not to participate. But you're not given the choice to avoid participating with the protector.

[4] Many of the U.S. government's business enterprises are detailed in Stone, *Fact Sheet.*
[5] *U.S. News & World Report*, October 26, 1970, p. 30.

Since you already pay separately for the things that actually protect you (locks, alarm systems, insurance, watch dogs, etc.), would protection be much more expensive if there were no government?

NATIONAL DEFENSE

What about national defense? Isn't the nation safe from foreign enemies only because of the government?

What *is* a nation? In common usage, a nation is considered to be a geographical area under the jurisdiction of a single government that isn't a subdivision of a larger government. The government assumes responsibility for the defense of the geographical area and makes all decisions regarding armed conflict with outsiders.

If there were no government, there'd be no nation. And if there were no nation, there'd be nothing to defend.

If that sounds too simple, think about it. No aggressor conquers a nation by overcoming every single inhabitant and occupying every part of the geographical area. It would be far too expensive to do so.

Instead, the aggressor applies force against the country until the *government* of that nation surrenders. Then the aggressor takes over the existing governmental machinery to enforce the occupation. If no such machinery existed, how could it enforce the occupation?

Hitler couldn't have conquered Europe without the help provided by the governments of the occupied nations. Would he have sent every one of his Nazis into Norway to police all the Norwegians? If he had, who would have been left at home to police the Germans?

That doesn't mean that aggression would stop if there were no governments. But the aggression would be no more formidable than the examples of crime we've already covered.

Hydrogen bombs and other modern tools of war are effective only when they can be used to pressure governments. Enemy rulers have nothing to gain by destroying

U.S. property and people—except as a means of pressuring the government to surrender. Otherwise, the more they destroy, the less value to them in conquering the nation.

If there were no federal government in the U.S., the Communists would have to conquer fifty different state governments—which would be far more difficult. But what if there were no state governments? Then they'd have to conquer every town separately.

But what if there were no town governments—no governments at all? Then they'd have to make over 200 million separate conquests—and use millions of their own policemen to set up new governments.

Obviously the answer to the threat of communism (or any other enemy) is *not* a stronger government to defend us but just the opposite. We'd be far safer if there were no government to conquer.

It's surprising how many "national issues," problems that "cry out" for government intervention, wouldn't even exist if there were no governments.

The dictators of the world have always operated in countries where there was a strong respect for government. The prevailing European awe of the state has produced an endless number of tyrants, wars, and low standards of living.

And now that generations of Americans have been taught that governments are vital to their well-being, present-day Americans are afflicted with all the problems that invariably result from big government.

Such a trend has developed over many lifetimes; it won't be reversed within ours.

Governments grow naturally because individuals see them as ways of increasing their rewards at lower expense. It's an oversimplification to say that people want "something for nothing." All people want to obtain as much as possible for as little effort as possible; that's why labor-saving devices are valuable.

Unfortunately, however, government *isn't* the labor-saving device it appears to be. It always gives back less than it takes. But because it *does* appear to be a giver of good things, its appeal is almost universal and there isn't much likelihood that the trend will be reversed.

THE GOVERNMENT TRAPS

Let's take another look now at the four Government Traps:

Trap #1: *The belief that governments perform socially useful functions that deserve your support.* If all the individual gains or losses caused by an act could be totaled, the net total would be the *social effect.* While this could never be tabulated, we've seen logically that any governmental activity will provide *less* than what the General Market has already made available—when *everyone's* values are taken into consideration. The government's "services" replace services that had been valued more highly by the General Market.

Trap #2: *The belief that you have a duty to obey laws.* The "obligation to obey laws" is a good example of one person trying to manipulate another through the use of moral dictums. Your obedience doesn't even perform a socially useful function; it only enhances coercion and disorder.

The only relevant consideration is the personal consequence to you: what you will gain if you break a law versus the loss imposed upon you if you're caught, together with the degree of risk that you'll be caught. If you choose to obey a law, it should be because of the consequences to you—not because you have an "obligation."

Trap #3: *The belief that the government can be counted upon to carry out a social reform you favor.* Even if you're willing to try to use the government for your own purposes, it isn't likely to bring about the changes you seek.

Any government program can be made to sound promising at the time it's introduced, but just look back over the past twenty years or so to see what the actual results have been.

The foreign aid that was going to save the world from communism has actually been used to enrich various nations *before* they fell to the Communists—Cuba, China, Eastern Europe, etc. And it's been used to finance both sides of the wars in Vietnam, the Dominican Republic, and other places.

Back in 1964, the government started promising an "early end" to the Vietnam War, but the promises and realities were far, far apart.

At home, look at the many housing projects that were going to do away with slums. Where can a government point to a slumfree big city as proof of its effectiveness?

Remember the War on Poverty? The Alliance for Progress? The Full Employment Act of 1946? Grand dreams, lots of money spent, no success.

Governments have a consistent record of failure in their endeavors. Even if you're willing to force others to pay for what you want, no government is going to solve the ecology problems, make women professional equals, prevent monopolies, or fulfill any other objective you may have in mind.

Working through government to get what you want is a classic example of an indirect alternative. The success of your plans depends far more upon what other people do than upon your own decisions. First you have to rally public support so that Congress will act; then you must hope that the President and the bureaucracy will carry out the plan as you intended it. You have to go through thousands of people to get to your objective.

Whatever it is you want, there's bound to be a direct alternative available that requires only your own decision. If there are people you want to aid, for example, you can accomplish far more by keeping the taxes and paying the money directly to those people.

The government can't carry out your plans for you, but *you* can.

Trap #4: *The fear that the government is so powerful that it can prevent you from being free.* We've seen in this

chapter the principles upon which a government is organized. It attempts to overrule the General Market and inflict its way upon individuals.

Fortunately, the government is subject to the same market principles that we are. Its resources are limited, so it
can't hope to enforce its laws adequately by policing every
person individually.

The government's method of organization is a perfect
example of the Group Trap. Since it can't escape the consequences of a mistaken policy (any more than we can),
it operates very ineffectively.

Many people think things would be better if the government were only more efficient. Happily, it isn't. For collectively, we are free to the extent that the government is
inefficient and unable to carry out its coercive programs.
And individually, you are free to the extent that you *take
advantage* of the government's inefficiency.[6]

WHAT IS GOVERNMENT?

The Government Traps ensnare many people because
they never stop to recognize what a government is. *It's an
agency of coercion that's accepted as necessary by most
people within its area of influence.* It differs from the
Mafia only in that the Mafia isn't usually considered necessary by the people in the communities it "serves."

Governments usually *do* enjoy that respect. Even those
people who want the "ins" relaced by the "outs" consider
the institution itself to be necessary.

I don't expect to see a world in which there would be
no theft, aggression, or coercion. But it would be refreshing to live in one in which no agency of coercion had the
acceptance of most of the people around me. Dealing with
an agency of coercion would be much easier if you didn't
have to cope also with "law-abiding" neighbors who act as
unpaid functionaries of the state.

[6] We'll look at the techniques for doing that in Chapter 16.

I believe a world without "government" would be a better place to live. However, that doesn't tell me how to deal with the world in which I *do* live.

But a realistic understanding of government keeps you out of the Government Traps. You won't waste precious time and energy trying to work through the government to become free. Nor will you allow blind allegiance or patriotism to keep you from living your life as you want to live it. Nor will you be deterred by the government's apparent powers.

There's nothing to be gained by trying to make the government more efficient, by trying to get the "bad guys" out and the "good guys" in. The government has nothing to offer you.

And therein lies the answer to the famous cliché, "The government should do for the people only what they cannot do for themselves."

There's nothing the government can do for you that you can't do for yourself—far less expensively, far more easily, and far more securely. And you can do it for yourself without first having to obtain the approval of the electorate, the establishment, or anyone else.

. . . the art of government consists in taking as much money as possible from one class of citizens to give to the other.
                                                        —VOLTAIRE

8

The Despair Trap

THE DESPAIR TRAP is the belief that other people can prevent you from being free.

Despair isn't hard to come by. If you've been trying to create a freer climate in the nation, you've probably accumulated plenty of reasons to be despondent. Or if you've been trying to convince your friends and family to accept your way of life, you probably feel very misunderstood and unappreciated by now. Or if you've been trying to smooth out difficult relationships with your lover, business associates, or relatives, you may be about ready to throw in the towel.

There are many things that can make you feel that you're an alien in the world, one who will never be understood.

Siegmund, a character in Richard Wagner's opera *Die Walküre*, summed it up well: "Whatever I thought right, to others seemed wrong; what I held to be bad, others approved of."

Despite these kinds of problems, the goals of freedom and happiness are totally realistic. If they aren't being achieved, it's the method that's wrong, not the objective.

You have to accept the world as it is. But that doesn't mean you should look at the people who oppose your ways and conclude that there's no chance to be free. The world includes much more than just the people you've been dealing with.

There are undoubtedly many, many people with whom you have nothing in common. But there are also plenty of people who see things in much the same way you do. If you haven't come in contact with them, it may be because you've unnecessarily confined yourself to those with whom you've been associating.

And it may be that you haven't discovered ways of *finding* the kinds of people who could add to your life, instead of detract from it.

There's no one in this world exactly like you. But there are undoubtedly people who want many of the same things you do, people who look at things in much the same way you do, and people who want what you have to offer.

The popular conventions of society might discourage you from breaking out of uncomfortable situations to find those people. Such hallowed traditions as one marriage, one career, one employer, staying in one place, etc., can cause you to feel that you must make the best of whatever situation you're already in.

But "making the best" frequently means either giving up your own happiness or trying to change others. Neither way makes any sense.

You don't have to stay where you are. You can look for someone who doesn't have to be forced to love you, someone who will be enthusiastic about what you have to offer, someone who will help you get what you want because it will be in *his* self-interest to do so.

THE DESPAIR TRAP

You're in the Despair Trap if you believe that you have to stay where you are and work things out somehow. Or if you believe that you couldn't be any better off if you were to change your situation. Or if you think that the government or society can stop you from being free.

You're in the Despair Trap if you think that you'll always be poor because you come from a family that's always been that way. Or when you feel that love relationships must always deteriorate into uneasy compromises. Or when you believe that "people" don't appreciate good products, good ideas, or good individuals.

You're in the trap when you think there are too many complications in your life to be able to break out from where you are. Or when you think that freedom and happiness are overrated myths.

A MARKET FOR YOU

The General Market embraces personal relationships as well as commercial ones. All relationships are governed by market principles as individuals come together, exchange or share as appropriate, and work toward the advancement of their own happiness. The same principles apply to finding a friend that apply to finding a buyer for your product.

Within the General Market there's a whole world of potential relationships for you if you realize that you don't have to please everyone.

If you want a marriage partner who's compatible with your way of life, you don't have to prove to everyone that your way is right. You need to find only *one* person who meets your needs and who wants you as you are.

You don't need millions of friends; you only need enough to provide the companionship and shared interests you'd like to have. So it isn't important what the other people are like.

Let me illustrate this with a commercial example. General Motors is the acknowledged giant of the automobile industry; its success is often discussed. Its name has become a symbol of bigness and domination. Some people think it controls the market; others think it must be doing everything right and pleasing everyone.

How big and successful is it?

In a typical year General Motors will sell around four million new cars. With over 200 million individuals in the U.S., it sells new cars to about 2 percent of the population. Some individuals will buy new GMC cars, others will buy other brands, others will buy used cars, and most of them won't buy any cars at all.

Only 2 percent! Yet by tapping such a small percentage of the market, General Motors pays a dividend every year to its stockholders and high salaries to the men who run it. With such a small share of the market, its profits are enormous. It *is* a success.

But what if GMC's executives decided they should be able to sell cars to *everyone*? Suppose they increased their advertising budget and flooded the market with sales appeals designed to get everyone to buy a new car. Suppose they made impassioned sales appeals to widows on Social Security, desert prospectors, little children, and invalids.

Obviously, the company would be broke in no time. And probably one of the executives would go home and grumble over his martini, "The world is no damn good; people don't appreciate what we're trying to do for them."

It's just as foolish to feel that *you* must make everyone understand that you're right, that your desires are legitimate, that you should be able to do as you want. You don't have to. Just concentrate your attention (as General Motors does) on finding those people who are appropriate for you. You can ignore the others.

In Chapter 17 I'll suggest ways that you can find the people who represent your best market.

In the meantime, recognize that the market you're dealing with now is only a small part of the whole. Out there in the world are many different kinds of people. And among them are people you can work with, love with, associate with, make friends with. They are people to whom your ideas and ways and desires are the best possible.

In addition, there are people who don't want you to be free. They may not approve of your going your own way. They may want to censure you, attack you, tax you. But there are ways of handling them, too, as we'll see.

Don't focus on indirect alternatives and think that you get what you want only by changing those around you. There are numerous opportunities that require only *your* decision. There are plenty of compatible, attractive people who will gladly offer you what you want.

Don't be depressed by what others say about your freedom and happiness. They aren't the whole world, and they don't have all the answers.

There is a better world to find when you're free to look for it.

Little souls wish you to be unhappy. It aggravates them to have you joyous, efficient and free. They like to feel that fate is disciplining you. It gives their egos wings if yours are clipped. You can ruin your life in an hour by listening to their puerile opinions.   —DAVID SEABURY

9

The Rights Trap

THE RIGHTS TRAP is the belief that your rights will make you free.

It's not hard to fall into this trap and become preoccupied with your rights as a way of getting what you want. You've probably heard since childhood that you have certain rights—to life, liberty, property, the freedom to pursue your happiness.

In addition, it's easy to feel that someone owes you certain things in a relationship—such as respect, honesty, or fair play.

Unfortunately, rights exist only in theory. In practice, they don't accomplish much—no matter how much people may discuss them.

By implication, a right to something means that someone else must provide that something, whether or not he wants to. A right to your property, for instance, means that you should be allowed to keep your property—even if others want to take it. A right to a job means that someone must provide a job for you even if he prefers not to.

Rights are invoked only when there's a conflict of interest. Otherwise, there's no need for them.

One reason it's so easy to walk into the Rights Trap is that it sometimes seems to be the only way to deal with a conflict. But that's only one of three methods of handling such situations. You can:

1. Rely upon your rights to get you what you want.

2. Find a way to make it in the other person's self-interest to provide what you want.

3. Find a way of getting what you want without his being involved.

In my experience, I've been involved in many situations in which the second or the third method has worked for me. But I've never found a situation in which the first method has been useful.

We've seen that an individual acts in ways that he believes will provide the most happiness for himself, based upon his own knowledge of the alternatives available. He'll do what *you* want him to do only when he thinks that's the best alternative for *him*. If he thinks there are better alternatives for him, he won't do what you want.

It's as simple as that.

USING YOUR RIGHTS

Let's see how the alternatives apply to various matters in which rights are often invoked.

It's popularly assumed that you have a right to your life. Unfortunately however, if someone kills you, your right is of little value. The police may investigate, may even find the killer, may even take him to court and convict him, may even execute him. But none of that will change the fact that you're dead.

Obviously, it's more effective to see to it that no one has both the intention and the opportunity to kill you.

Another right that's often discussed is your right to your property. But once again, what use is that right if your property is stolen? Stolen property is rarely recovered by the police and returned intact to its owner.

Whether or not you have a right, you still have to protect your property or risk losing it. It's more effective to make it difficult for a thief to steal it—so that it will be in his self-interest to go elsewhere.

It's often said that everyone has a right to a job or to a

"decent" standard of living. But who will gladly give up his own happiness to make that possible? If it's in an employer's self-interest to hire you, he'll do so; if not, your right won't get you a job.

The fact that governments claim to protect these rights is insignificant. There are still murders, thefts, and unemployed people—as well as arsons, rapes, and uneducated people who had a "right to an education."

Whether or not there are *fewer* problems as a result of laws isn't relevant. They still happen—and if they happen to *you*, it's no comfort that they happen less often to others.

In the same way, your rights offer little protection against the government itself. You can feel that the government doesn't have a right to tax you more than a certain amount. But unfortunately, the government probably *does* tax you more than you think is fair.

Many people believe the Constitution should protect their rights. But has it done so?

I've heard it said that the Constitution is perfect but that the politicians create problems by ignoring it. But if the Constitution can't make the politicians repsect it, of what value is it? It's interesting to talk about, but not really useful to your freedom. For, in practice, the Constitution is whatever the President, the Congress, and the Supreme Court choose to think it is—and that may be considerably different from what you think it is.

If a law is passed to protect your rights, it's an uncertain, temporary safeguard at best. Laws are broken, amended, repealed, overruled, ignored, and ill-enforced. They're not very effective protectors.

PERSONAL RELATIONSHIPS

In personal relationships, it's easy to fall into the habit of expecting others to treat you as you think you should be treated. But that's a form of the Identity Trap.

Each person you deal with will treat you as *his* knowl-ledge and understanding guide him—whether he be a friend or stranger.

It's worthless to insist upon moral conduct, respect, or courtesy. The other person won't forsake his own way in order to accommodate you. Even if you can prove by argument that he "should," he'll respond only reluctantly and your "victory" will be of little practical value.

Sometimes, you can feel that you're merely trying to point out that it's in *his* self-interest to act as you suggest. But again, he won't necessarily agree—even if you're right.

It's more realistic, and far less trying, simply to allow each person to be what he wants to be, while you look for people who already *are* what you want them to be.

A great burden was lifted from my shoulders the day I realized that *no one owes me anything.* For as long as I'd thought that there were certain things I was entitled to, I'd been wearing myself out trying to collect them.

No one owes me moral conduct, respect, friendship, love, courtesy, or intelligence. And since I've recognized that, all my relationships have been far more satisfying. I've made it a point to be involved with people who *want* to do the very things I want them to do.

That understanding has served me well in dealings with friends, business associates, lovers, sales prospects, and strangers. It constantly reminds me that I can get what I want only if I'm willing to enter the other person's world. I have to try to understand how *he* thinks, what *he* believes to be important, what *he* wants. Only then can I appeal to him in ways that will bring me what *I* want.

And only then can I tell whether I really want to be involved with him. That makes it much easier to save the important relationships for those with whom I have the most in common.

THE RIGHTS TRAP

The Rights Trap is the belief that your rights can get you what you want. You're in the trap any time you count on anything other than an individual's self-interest to cause him to give you what you want.

You're in the Rights Trap if you assume that an effective statement of your rights will bring you lower taxes, more personal freedom, or an end to injustice. Those objectives are realistic—but you're much more likely to get them if you forget about your rights and utilize other tools.

You can also fall backward into the Rights Trap by letting someone else pressure you by invoking *his* rights. His rights are as theoretical as yours. And you will look for ways to circumvent them, just as he would. But it's possible to be affected emotionally by his demands if you don't recognize that they're pointless.

It's in *your* self-interest to be aware of the consequences of your actions. If you've made a promise, you can expect bad consequences if you break it. But you should focus your attention on those consequences, not on his concern with his rights.

In fact, this is where confusion can develop. If such things as lying, stealing, or killing would bring you bad consequences, your reasons can be confused with questions of rights.

For example, suppose you've decided that stealing would bring you bad consequences. If someone tells you that by not stealing you're "recognizing property rights," you might also react to someone's claim of a "right to a decent living" as if the context were similar—and you might think you have a duty to satisfy that right.

The consequences to you, not someone's conception of rights, must always be the deciding standard of your actions.

VULNERABILITY

Perhaps there are times when you feel that your rights are the only weapon you have in a dispute. If so, it usually indicates that you've made yourself vulnerable to someone whose self-interest conflicts with yours.

It helps to remember that you are the one who put yourself in the vulnerable position. You have chosen to associate with those who cause you problems—whether they be your family, your business associates, your employer, your employees, or your friends.

If you're not being treated as you want to be treated, it's your vulnerability that must be changed. You could spend the rest of your life trying to educate the others, to change their natures and values, to get them to respect your rights. But you probably wouldn't succeed.

It always makes more sense to concentrate on the direct alternatives—the things you *do* control. What others do is up to them, but there's always a great deal *you* can do. Choose from the alternatives that require only your decision—not from among the many hopes that someone will be something other than what he is.

To rely on your rights or on your ability to change others is far less promising than to rely upon yourself.

THE GREAT MILK ROBBERY

To illustrate this, let's suppose that I walk out to my front porch one morning, expecting to pick up my milk. But lo and behold, I find that it's been stolen. What do I do next?

I can be bitter and feel that the thief had no right to steal from me. But would that get my milk back?

I could stand on the front porch and deliver an eloquent speech, cursing the disgraceful fact that there are thieves in the world. But what would that get me—aside from a few angry neighbors?

To say that there are thieves in the world is only to repeat what I've known all along. To say that it's disgraceful is to say that if I were God, I'd have made the world differently. But since I'm not God, that point is irrelevant, too.

To say that *I* would never steal someone's milk is to acknowledge that I'm different from many of the people in the world—and that I have my own way of trying to achieve happiness. But why should I expect someone else to use *my* way?

The only area of interest is that which *I* control. I've decided to risk theft by having the milk bottles left on the front porch. And I can decide to continue that risk or have the milk handled in some other way.

If I concentrate on the thief's immorality or on my rights, I'm probably leaving myself vulnerable to another theft. But if I use what *I* control to make new arrangements, I can see to it that the theft isn't repeated—and *that* should be my major concern.[1]

YOUR CONTROL

You have so much control over your life, it would be a shame to throw it away. But you do just that if you hope to get what you want by invoking your rights or by trying to change others.

By using the control you do have, you can reduce your taxes, adopt the life style you want, and establish valuable relationships that won't bring problems. There are numerous direct alternatives available to you—many of which will be suggested as we go along.

No one owes you anything; everyone you deal with will choose the best alternatives for himself.

Try forgetting about your rights. They haven't made you free. They didn't bring you the good things you've achieved in your life. Why count on them in the future?

There are far easier ways to get what you want.

[1] And I can think about that while I'm pouring water on my Wheaties.

We are much beholden to Machiavel and others, that
write what men do, and not what they ought to do.
                                        —FRANCIS BACON

Might is a fine thing, and useful for many purposes; for
"one goes further with a handful of might than with a
bagful of right."   —MAX STIRNER

10

The Utopia Trap

THE UTOPIA TRAP is the belief that you must create better conditions in society before you can be free.

It's a very basic, very understandable belief. It's easy to see that other people are arranging things incorrectly—passing the wrong laws, misinterpreting things, even maliciously arranging things to the detriment of others. You can see poverty, repression, prejudice, and other conditions that stifle creativity and happiness.

It's easy to feel that society needs an overhaul (major or minor) before you'll be able to live freely. As a result, you can devote a great deal of effort to attempts to make others understand what you see, to the passing of laws, to a quest for a better society.

While you're doing this, you obviously give up a great deal of time and other resources that could have been used to enjoy life. But it's assumed that once the proper overhaul of society is completed, you'll be able to live more freely.

There are two basic reasons why I don't get involved in the quest to change society: (1) it's an indirect alternative, and so it's a much harder, more permanent job than most people realize; and (2) it isn't necessary. An individual doesn't need to live in a free society in order to free himself—and when he tries to change the world, he's in for a lot more trouble than he may have bargained for.

Let's look first at the scope of the job involved in bringing about social change.

SEPARATE WORLDS

If you think you know the truth about a given situation, it's very easy to assume that all you have to do is point it out to another person. So naturally you're amazed when he doesn't quickly agree with you and do what you want. But here we are back in the Identity Trap again.

It's hard to realize that *you live in a world of your own*—bounded by your own knowledge, your own perception, your own ways of reasoning, your own set of standards. And that other person doesn't reside there. He lives in his own world.

Sometimes your worlds will overlap; with some people, they'll overlap often. But most of each person's world is different from yours. What is obvious to you may seem very strange to him. You can base a plan on making him see the light, but the plan can very easily go astray.

And if it's difficult to influence just one person, think what you're up against when you hope to change the prevailing views of a whole society of people.

Do you know what you face? Do you understand each of the individual natures of the thousands or millions of people you'd have to convert to make your ideal society possible? Will your statement of the truth be sufficient to make each of them give up his own way of seeking happiness and follow your way?

This doesn't mean that the world never changes—for better or for worse. It changes constantly. But what we see as a changing world is the result of millions of individual changes that add up to a net change in the General Market. The general change is a result of many specific individual changes.

You can look through history and see examples where it appears that one man has brought about great social change. And that can lead you to think that you can do the same if you work hard enough or if you're smart enough. But it doesn't work that way.

Large social changes take place only when the market is ready—meaning, when millions of individuals are ready for such change. No matter who was leading the movement, great social changes have occurred only when the market was ready for them. If it was, the social changers succeeded if they acted wisely. If the market wasn't ready, they couldn't move it.

DIFFERENCES AGAIN

We've seen that we live in a world of different people—with different values, tastes, knowledge, moralities, ideas, and beliefs.

The range of diversity among moralities, religions, and philosophies is as great as it is among tastes in clothing and TV entertainment. Everyone is different from his neighbors in some way. There are no unified blocks of people who share a philosophy without deviation. Witness the arguments *among* Catholics and among Socialists.

Every individual seeks his own happiness. You or I might think a man misguided in the way he seeks it, but he seeks it avidly nonetheless. And even if he relies on someone else to tell him how to get it, he won't necessarily choose you or me as the one to tell him.

What we view as a social injustice is merely someone's method of seeking happiness. If you think that someone or some group of people is unjustly poor, your opinion implies that someone else should be giving them more money—through jobs or charity. That "someone else" is the person whose happiness-seeking methods disturb you.

In the same way, if you feel that certain people are being repressed politically, it implies that someone has the power to keep them from doing what they want to do. Again, you disapprove of the way in which that someone is seeking his happiness.

The desire to change social conditions is the desire to

change or prevent the happiness-seeking methods of the individuals you don't approve of.

It's easy to feel that an overhaul of some kind can set things right: laws passed to guarantee income to the poor, political leaders removed, regulations enforced to prevent racial prejudice, tax rates reduced or abolished, etc. Once the overhaul is done, the problems will cease. But will they?

Probably not. It's a mistake to assume that the "villains" will no longer cause trouble. That's highly unlikely. They will continue to seek *their* happiness (as all human beings do), and each of them will do it in the way *he* knows best.

The way he knows best isn't going to be overhauled by the changes you engineer. He'll still believe he was doing the right thing (for him).

THE NEW ORDER

No matter what social changes are made, human beings will continue to be different from one another. Any new order of things will be opposed by many dissidents—just as you might oppose the old order now. The opponents of the new way will work to change it, and they'll be joined by others (previously unaffected and unnoticed) who are bothered by the new conditions.

You'll have to work just as hard to defend your changes as you did to bring them about. There won't be a stopping point where you can say the job is done and you can return to your personal life to enjoy the blessings of freedom.

There's no way you could alter society so that every individual in it will have the opportunity to live his life as he wants to. There are too many conflicts of interest. Someone will have to be dissatisfied; in fact, a great many people will have to be dissatisfied—just as you may be now.

You can believe that once the changes are made, the general benefits will be obvious and people will be glad the changes were made; but don't count on it. That's falling into the Identity Trap—expecting someone else to react to things as *you* would.

You can take the attitude that your way is the *right* way and that those who disagree are simply *wrong*. But that doesn't make any difference. Those "wrong" people will still be upset and create problems for you.

There will always be disputes, conflicts, and problems to deal with. No system can be established that would be completely peaceful, irrevocable, or permanent.

Let's look at a couple of examples to illustrate this.

Suppose that you wish to see property rights respected. That standard appears to be simple, straightforward, unambiguous, and reasonable. It wouldn't seem difficult to establish that as a basic principle of a society.

But there are plenty of people who believe that freedom includes taking what they need from others—usually through political action. Many of them consider inequalities in wealth to be conditions of slavery. They would continue to fight for the social conditions they want.

Even if somehow everyone agreed with the basic principle of "property rights," and it were implemented by law or custom, there would still be many disputes. What *is* property? How can boundaries be defined? Who trespassed first? What constitutes interference? Who makes the final, binding decision to resolve a dispute? You may have answers to those questions, but that doesn't mean that others will accept your answers.

Or suppose your objective is a society in which "everyone has at least a minimum standard of living." What happens if someone can't obtain that minimum through normal market exchanges? Who will be required to give up some of his wealth to bring the first man up to par? Will those who have to provide it be free? Will they refrain from trying to evade your laws? Will they continue to produce wealth that they can't keep?

No matter what standard governs a society, there will be disputes and unfree people. And those people will fight for what they believe to be right for them. You'll be living in basically the same kind of society in which you live today—complete with pressure groups, arguments, subjective interpretations of the rules, and opponents who are trying to change the system to their advantage.

Any governing principle presupposes a method for resolving disputes within the terms of that principle. That requires an agency (such as a court) that can enforce its decision—by violence, if necessary—to be effective.

That means that someone somewhere will ultimately make a decision to be imposed upon someone else who won't like it. The judge's decision will be based upon his own personal perception, interpretation, and sense of justice.

Even if you bring about the general social change you want, the way the change is carried out by leaders, judges, or others may be vastly different from what you expected.

Those who rule will always do so by their own subjective standards—whether their authority is hereditary succession, a military takeover, or a vote of "the people." There will be those within a society who approve, those who disapprove, and those who go their own ways and pay little attention to the rulers.

In many ways, a social structure that appears at a distance to be governed *objectively* by certain clear and fair principles will, in reality, be composed of human beings who'll apply those principles *subjectively*. And that, of course, is what we have already. In fact, that kind of system has always existed—no matter what name it may bear at any given time.

THE PRICE OF LIVING

"Free societies" are usually dreams in which the dreamer hopes to be able to escape the simple prices required to live happily in the real world. He may feel that he'll no longer have to fear economic changes that hurt his way of life, or that he'll no longer have to worry about protecting his property, or that he won't have to deal with the social conflicts he sees today.

The irony is that you pay a *lesser* price when you accept the existence of the social disorders and deal with them individually. You pay a *higher* price when you work to create a better society (through education, politics, etc.).

Even so, you can be encouraged to attack a social disorder by thinking that it's something "abnormal," out of the ordinary, a simple flaw that can be easily corrected to restore things to normal.

As I look at history, however, I become more and more convinced that what we live in *is* "normal"—that things have never been basically any different from what they are now. Many things *have* changed, but the essence of social structures has remained quite the same.

In Florence during the Renaissance, in America during the 1970s, even in a hoped-for free society, the facts remain the same: No matter where or when you live, you'll still have to deal with people different from you. You'll have to cope with people who don't want you to have what you want, and who'll try to take from you what you have. Changing the social structure won't change the prices you'll have to pay to get and keep what you want.

That doesn't mean that one society can't be a happier place for you to live than another. There *are* differences, and it makes sense to consider living in the society whose rules most nearly coincide with the way you want to live. That's a *direct* alternative. It takes far less effort to find and move to the society that has what you want than it does to try to reconstruct an existing society to match your standards.

In the same way, if the society in which you live seems to be heading in a direction you don't like, it makes sense to get out before you're hurt by it. I like to think, for instance, that I would have moved out of Nazi Germany before it was too late.

There are some who would say I should have stayed

and fought the tyrants, or that I might not have seen the danger in time to get out. But no one could realistically believe that my presence there would have made a difference in the national outcome. And if I hadn't seen the danger soon enough to avoid it, I certainly wouldn't have seen it soon enough to stop it.

You can't change the fate of a nation, but you can do a great deal to make sure you're not affected adversely by it. What you have to do is simply part of the price you pay to get what you want in life. And it's always a far less expensive price than you'd have to pay to undertake a social change of any kind.

No matter how difficult the task of changing society, the Utopia Trap is still compelling. And it appeals mainly, I think, because few individuals see any other alternatives.

So one can be induced to write letters, try to educate others, help get the right man elected, throw the tyrants out, and engage in numerous other activities. But these are all indirect alternatives. Your success will depend upon a whole series of "ifs": *if* other people see the light, *if* other people do what you suggest, if, if, if. No wonder such movements are so frustrating.

And as we saw in the Group-Trap chapter, your individual participation in those activities probably won't affect the outcome one way or the other.

USING YOUR POWER

If the prospects for social change are pretty bleak, the prospects for individual freedom aren't.

If you're not free now, it isn't because you haven't done enough to change the world. Quite the contrary, it may be that you've been doing *too much* to try to change the world. The effort you've expended in that direction could have been used to provide freedom for yourself.

There are probably dozens of direct alternatives available to you that would eliminate the effects of social injustice from your own life. And that's ultimately the object, isn't it?

Are taxes too high? You waste precious attention when you try to change the tax structure. There are always ways to avoid paying those high taxes; all you have to do is find them.

Is the government getting too repressive? You could spend the rest of your life fighting it, but your actions won't change the fate of the nation. However, you *can* make sure the repression doesn't get in your way.

The only clear path to freedom is through direct alternatives—decisions that don't require that you influence others. Direct alternatives always exist, and they're almost always far more effective than indirect alternatives.

There are hundreds—thousands!—of ways to be free when you concentrate upon the power you have. But you can't see them if you're occupied trying to change others.

Further ahead, we'll devote eleven chapters to specific methods you can use to free yourself of the chains that may be binding you. All of the methods employ direct alternatives. None of them requires that you change others or change yourself.

AN EXCITING WORLD

The Identity Trap is the assumption that someone else will react as you would. The Utopia Trap is that assumption carried to its ultimate conclusion—the expectation that you can make the rest of the world correspond to your dreams.

You can't. And when you try to do so, you only succeed in throwing away the very real opportunities for freedom that you already possess.

The world is an exciting and beautiful place. It might not seem so if you're bogged down with restrictions on every side. But those who have recognized their own powers and used them to be free see little need to change the world.

The world-changers are powerless. They dream of remaking the world; but they can't, and so they've placed their emphasis where they have no power at all.

Free men recognize that they can't change the world, and so they concentrate on the power they *do* have—which is enormous. They realize that they can choose not to be involved in situations that don't suit them.

So they look for those situations that *do* suit them. And they discover far more opportunities for such situations than most people imagine exist.

A free person doesn't try to remake the world or his friends or his family. He merely appraises every situation by the simple standard: *Is this what I want for myself?* If it isn't, he looks elsewhere. If it is, he relaxes and enjoys it—without the problems most other people take for granted.

A free man uses his tremendous power of choice to make a comfortable life for himself.

The power of choice. You have it. But you forfeit it when you imagine that you can choose for others. You can't.

But you *can* choose for yourself—from hundreds of exciting, happiness-producing alternatives.

Why not *use* that power?

When I remember how many of my private schemes
have miscarried; how speculations have failed, agents
proved dishonest, marriage been a disappointment; how
I did but pauperize the relative I sought to help; how
my carefully-governed son has turned out worse than
most children; how the thing I desperately strove against
as a misfortune did me immense good; how while the
objects I ardently pursued brought me little happiness
when gained, most of my pleasures have come from
unexpected sources; when I recall these and hosts of
like facts, I am stuck with the incompetence of my
intellect to prescribe for society.   —HERBERT SPENCER

Don't worry about the whole world: If you do it will
overwhelm you. Worry about one wave at a time.
Please yourself. Do something for you, and the rest will
fall in line.   —DAVID SEABURY

11

The Burning-Issue Trap

THE BURNING-ISSUE TRAP is the belief that there are compelling social issues that require your participation.

There are always numerous issues before the public—competing for your attention, your concern, your time, and energy. When you view an issue by itself, it can seem very compelling; you can feel that it can't be ignored and that you *must* do something about it. If you become aware of something evil and dangerous, it can seem that you're compelled to work socially to correct it and eliminate the evil.

But if you stand back and look at the whole spectrum of social issues that clamor for your attention, you get a different perspective. Let's identify some of the many issues that writers, politicians, and crusaders have told us are do-or-die, must-be-taken-care-of-right-now matters.

During recent years they've included such things as pollution, civil rights, overpopulation, drugs, conservation, communism, consumerism, women's liberation, poverty, organized crime, law and order, disappearance of animal species, the sexual revolution, government solvency, pornography, educational problems, mental illness, privacy, high taxes, the Vietnam war, campus riots, the military-industrial complex, police brutality, and disarmament. Plus perhaps a dozen more I've overlooked, plus a few more that have become issues since I wrote this.

126

All these issues are presented as matters commanding your attention and participation. But how could you possibly become involved in all of them? And if you could, what would become of your freedom? How can you be free when you're burdened with a responsibility to right the world's wrongs?

You can enslave yourself by assuming a responsibility to observe, judge, and correct any social problems. For the problems will continue indefinitely. They'll never be resolved to everyone's satisfaction. The demands upon your time, energy, and money can never cease.

Look back over the past twenty-five years. Can you think of a single social issue of the magnitude and popularity of those just listed that has been successfully resolved? Has any desperate social need been satisfied? And has the world stopped because of the failures?

At the outset of most campaigns, the organizers assume that a given effort will solve the problem once and for all; just educate enough people, get enough petitions signed, pass a certain law, and the issue will be resolved and we can go back to our private lives.

But once people are educated, they have to be re-educated; new ideas from other sources may turn those you've educated away from the direction in which you'd thought you'd steered them. And once laws are passed, they can be amended or repealed or ignored; so the passing of a law doesn't end anything.

Campaigns for social change are excellent examples of the indirect alternative—working through others to get what you want. Your success depends on the responses of literally thousands of people. Your control over the situation is minute.

And if the issue *is* important, you're enlisting for life. If you do achieve any short-term goal, you'll have to safeguard your victory for the rest of your life.

The existence of evil isn't a claim upon you. "Evil" will always exist in the world. To accept as a principle that you must fight something *because* it's evil is to believe you must fight *anything* that's evil. There's no end to the number of evils that could command your attention. Is that all your life is for—to spend it fighting evil?

Somehow the world goes on—evils, issues, and all. During this century people have coped with world wars, depressions, prejudice, organized crime, and most of the other issues mentioned before. None of them has been resolved; they occur and reoccur.

But through them all, free men in any country have found ways of living their lives freely and happily without feeling a responsibility to be involved. Their lack of participation hasn't changed the outcome of any social issue, but it *has* enabled them to be free.

QUESTIONS

When you're asked to participate in a crusade to deal with any social issue, the matter can seem very compelling. But you may get a better perspective on the issue if you ask yourself a few questions:

1. How much do you really know about the issue in which you're about to get involved? Do you recognize that you're hearing only one side of the problem? Is the person providing the "facts" to you qualified to determine the extent of the problem?

Once an issue gets started, a lot of people in the press, politics, and perhaps in your neighborhood will jump on the bandwagon. Most of them simply repeat what they've heard. The quantity of repetition can be pretty impressive, but that doesn't tell you how true or significant their statements are.

I don't have unquestioning faith in scientists or specialists; I don't believe they necessarily have all the answers—even though they may spend many years in a particular field. But I have even *less* faith that the answers to social problems will be forthcoming from broadcasters, politicians, crusaders, picket lines, or TV personalities. Do their sound and fury constitute factual evidence upon which you should act?

2. How do you know the solutions sought will end the problem? They might even cause greater problems.

For example, there's a great demand that the government outlaw pesticides that are supposedly hurting crops. The government is being asked to protect us. But it was the U.S. Department of Agriculture that pressured farmers into using the pesticides in the first place. The government's original "solution" to a problem has brought about a new problem.

3. Is the issue really of significance to *you*? If the standard to be applied is the existence of injustice, evil or hardship, then there are millions of issues you must deal with, regardless of whether they affect your life. But there are also plenty of matters that apply directly to you. Isn't *that* where your time can be best spent?

4. Is it possible that you're responding to social pressure rather than genuine concern over the issue? Perhaps you're becoming involved in order not to appear "unconcerned," "selfish," or ignorant.

If you get involved for those reasons, you're walking into the Unselfishness Trap or the Morality Trap. What others choose to do with their lives is up to them, but you have no obligation to cooperate.

SOLVING ISSUES

If an issue concerns you, there are both direct and indirect alternatives available to you. The indirect alternative is to try to change the prevailing social trend—which involves changing others. The direct alternatives are the ways by which you can handle the problem so that it doesn't affect you personally.

The second way is by far the easier. Let's look at some examples:

Are you being discriminated against because you're a woman? How long would it take to reorient society so that most businesses would offer better job opportunities to women? Probably a very, very long time.

On the other hand, what do you really need? You obviously don't need to have fifty million new jobs available for females; *you* couldn't fill them all.

Perhaps you resent men treating women as "sex objects." Does it really matter if millions of men continue to do so? What do *you* really need?

Chances are you only need *one* job and *one* man (or maybe two or three). Do you need to overhaul *all* of society just to get one good job? Do you need to re-educate *all* men just to be able to enjoy one good one?

Why not, instead, use some selectivity in trying to meet men who treat women the way you want to be treated? I'm sure such men exist—no matter what your tastes.

And why not pass by the job where you know women will be treated as inferiors? Look instead for employers or customers who are concerned only with value. They're likely to be those who are the most intensely profit-seeking. Those people want quality for their money, not gender.

You need only one man, one job, one place to live, one set of friends. To find them, is it really necessary to become involved in a social movement to change the thinking of millions of people?

OTHER ISSUES

Are you afraid that the drug culture will destroy society? Why? Alcohol hasn't—even though it's created reckless drivers, alcoholics who steal to support their habits, and all the other problems attributed to drugs.

If you think drugs are dangerous, don't use them. If you're afraid for your children, then concentrate your attention on *them,* not on a problem you'll never solve. I can't guarantee that you'll insulate your children from drugs; but if you can't, how could you hope to insulate society at large from drugs?

Are you appalled by protest and violence on college campuses? Then don't send your child to a college where such things hapen. Don't expect to change the attitudes of students; their motives are their own.

Are you afraid that consumers are cheated by manufacturers? Then don't buy from sellers who can't prove the worth of their products. If goods are generally of low quality, it's because sellers have found that buyers prefer not to pay more for better goods.

But that doesn't have to affect you. You can always find, within the General Market, sellers who cater to your minority tastes.

You could crusade for government-enforced quality standards. But history demonstrates that government interference produces worse products, not better. Government standards create red tape, contradictory laws, dictatorial agencies, payoffs, and the loss of your opportunity to buy the products *you* want but which don't please bureaucrats.

If you're afraid there won't be enough food to go around someday, stock up in advance. Wouldn't that be easier than trying to get the whole world to limit population? (With farmers paid *not* to grow crops, it isn't surprising that food output isn't increasing faster.)

The demands that you limit your family to one child are based upon an average of what some people think is the total amount of food and space available. But how is that relevant to you? Acting on such considerations is an example of the Group Trap—treating things collectively instead of individually.

By the same reasoning, you shouldn't drive a car or eat steak or have more than a one-room house for your family—based upon an average of how much is available for the whole world.

The appropriate question is, "How much food and space do *you* have?" Do you have enough to support the family you want, taking into consideration possible changes of circumstances? What will be the consequence to *you*?

If you're concerned about the depletion of natural resources, move to an area where they still exist and buy property that you can preserve the way you want it. If you don't want to live there, are you sure the issue is important to you? And if you *do* want to live there, the cost of property would be less than the cost of trying to change the thinking of the whole country regarding such things.

The entire issue of conservation has always seemed to be a strange one for me. I've never been able to figure out for *whom* we're saving the irreplaceable resources. If *we* aren't allowed to use them, then the next generation shouldn't use them either, nor the one after that.

As certain resources are depleted, others are brought into use. Profit-seeking innovators look for ways to solve such problems because the rewards they receive are worth it. When attempts are made to hold back that evolution, people can wind up paying more for what they value less.

For example, conservationists say that trees should be saved by using recycled paper. A UPI news item reports that Bank of America, American Telephone, Coca-Cola, and McGraw-Hill are among the companies using recycled "ecology bond" paper. The cost at the mill is $20 to $40 *more* per ton than new paper of comparable grade.[1]

That higher cost is an indication that the resources required to recycle paper are *more* precious to the General Market than the cost of new paper. If people truly valued timber in its uncut form, the cost of *it* would be higher than the cost of recycling paper. The price of anything is an indication of its attractiveness and scarcity, compared with other things. When attempts are made to overrule the natural expressions of the General Market, higher prices are inevitable.

SLOGANS

My few brief remarks concerning these social issues are by no means final answers to any of the questions. But, then, neither are the popular slogans uttered on behalf of "ecology," "liberation," "consumerism," and "conservation."

[1] Los Angeles *Herald-Examiner*, August 12, 1971.

There's always a great deal more involved than is popularly discussed. And there's always something you can do for yourself that doesn't require changing other people.

Ask yourself what you'd do if you were *sure* you couldn't change the attitudes of others. What then would you do by yourself to keep the problem from affecting you? If you approach it on that basis, you usually find that there are many more direct alternatives available than you'd noticed while you were busy trying to change others.

Even if you could make big changes in the world, the cost would be gigantic. It's always simpler and less costly to look for direct alternatives—as opposed to those that depend upon getting other people to act as you want them to act. That principle applies in *any* area of life.

Change will take place as a result of broad changes of interests in the General Market. Some changes you'll like; some you won't. But those changes will occur whether or not you participate in these matters.

So you have a choice: should you involve yourself in efforts to advance or retard the change—where your efforts will make little difference—or should you simply make any personal adjustments necessary as the changes take place?

Participation in burning-issue movements might be a good way to meet like-minded people, or it might be that you enjoy the challenges involved. But if you jump into them because you think your participation will change the course of the world, you're probably making a grave mistake.

MY PREJUDICES

These remarks weren't intended to sell *my* side of any of these social issues. As a matter of fact, I more often fit naturally on the same side as the crusaders. I don't care for low-quality products that might hurt me; I don't use drugs; I don't believe I harbor any racial prejudices; I love women for their minds and their emotions, as well as their sexiness. And I don't intend to have children (but not because I think the earth is overpopulated).

But these are matters I can handle on my own. I moved to Vancouver, Canada, from Los Angeles because I was tired of the smog, noise, and traffic. I enjoy seeing beautiful trees around my home; the owners of those trees won't cut them down, because they prefer the beauty to the timber value.

I'd feel foolish, however, trying to tell other people that *they* should reorient their lives to eliminate smog, noise, and traffic. Many people *do* prefer to live in Los Angeles as it is; that's why they're there.

I take the various demands that I join causes with a grain of salt. I realize that the people who lead these movements have their own personal objectives. Many of them would be lost without their causes; that's how they find their happiness. Where would the consumer advocates be without General Motors? Or the employees of the cancer organizations without smokers? Or the politicians without those "pressing, critical, burning" issues?

All that is *their* business, but not necessarily yours or mine.

Burning issues are always presented in terms that make it appear that your freedom is at stake. Well, it is. If you're lured into devoting your precious life to the resolution of social problems, that can end your freedom. You'll carry the burden of responsibility for all the problems of the world.

Is it possible that you're assuming that once the various social issues are resolved, you'll be able to relax and enjoy your own life? If so, the lessons of history indicate that those issues will always be with us in one form or another.

You're not going to live forever. With the years ahead of you, why not start *now* to concentrate on making your life as meaningful, free, exciting, and joyous as possible?

You are the most important issue in the world. What happens in the social issues is only incidental; to concentrate on them is to approach the matter much too indirectly. What you do directly for yourself will have a far

greater impact on your life than what you do in response
to the burning issues of society.

Make *your life* the issue.

Diary: How to Improve the World (You will only make
matters worse).   —JOHN CAGE

In brief, sir, study what you most affect.—SHAKESPEARE

12

The Previous-Investment Trap

THE PREVIOUS-INVESTMENT TRAP is the belief that time, effort, and money spent in the past must be considered when making a decision in the present.

For example, a woman decides not to divorce an incompatible husband because she's already invested twelve years in the marriage. Or a man refuses to quit an unpleasant job because he's had it for fifteen years. Or an investor hangs on to a losing stock because he believes he shouldn't sell it until it rises to the price he paid for it. Or a man continues to fight for a losing cause because he's already invested ten years in the movement.

In each case, the individual feels that to change the situation would mean wasting the previous investment. It's as if he were saying, "If I change now, those years were wasted; but if I stay where I am, those years (somehow) were good." But what difference does it make? The years are gone, irretrievable.

What matters now is what the future offers. And that will depend upon what you do *now* with whatever you have available to you.

The expenditure of resources is only important *before* you spend them. Once spent, they're insignificant. What *is* significant is what you've received in exchange for them.

If you've put twelve years into a losing marriage, what's the best you can get from this point forward? If it would

136

take another twelve years to establish as good a marriage with someone else, you may decide not to make that new investment. But if it would take only twelve *days* to develop the same rapport with someone else, you'd be throwing away an opportunity by letting the past twelve years influence you.

When a financial investment (such as a stock) drops in price, its original cost is irrelevant because you don't have that money anymore. All you have is the *present value* of the investment.

In what way can you use *that* to make the most in the future? If you think the stock you're holding is going straight up from here, you'll want to hold onto it (but not because of what you paid for it). If you think there are other stocks that will rise faster, then you should sell the present stock and buy something with a better future.

In every case, the question is: With what you have now, what is the best way to use that to get the most in the future? What you've paid to get to where you are now is irrelevant; those resources are gone and can't be retrieved, no matter what you do.

The Previous-Investment Trap can sometimes be very subtle. I knew a woman who paid $150 for a fifteen-lesson course. After sitting through the first three lessons, bored stiff, she decided it was a mistake. I suggested she spend her Wednesday evenings in a more profitable way (such as with me).

"I can't do that," she said. "I have a hundred and fifty dollars tied up in it; I *have* to see it through."

She was saying, in effect, "Since I've already wasted my money on this, I'm going to waste my time, too."

Money spent in the past is gone. You can never get it back. You may get the equivalent of it again. But to do so, you must choose the most profitable alternative to you now. Where you spent the money in the past has nothing to do with the question.

THE TRAP

You're in the Previous-Investment Trap whenever you allow what you've expended in the past to be a determining factor when deciding what to do in the future. Learn from the past, but never feel you have to justify a past investment by hanging on to it.

The mark of a good financial investor is his ability to recognize when he's made a mistake, sell out, and prevent his losses from getting worse. Most investors become emotionally attached to the decisions they've made, so they hang on in hopes of recouping the investment later—and they usually wind up losing more.

The same thing applies to any area of your life. Recognize your losses. Don't assume that you can lead a mistake-free life. You can't. But you can recognize your mistakes early and thereby prevent them from compounding into gigantic losses.

If a relationship is wrong, end it and look for a better one. If you've spent your money unwisely, accept it, and determine the best action for the future with what you have left. If you've devoted yourself to a cause that now appears fruitless, get out of it and move on to something that will bring you happiness.

Don't try to justify past mistakes by perpetuating them. For when you do, you throw away the future you could have had.

There is a bright, glorious, free future ahead—if you keep looking forward.

A man should never be ashamed to own he has been in the wrong, which is but saying, in other words, that he is wiser today than he was yesterday.—ALEXANDER POPE

13

The Box Trap

MANY PEOPLE COMPLAIN that freedom isn't possible in the real world. Often the person complaining is an individual who has accepted restrictions upon his life that make it seem impossible to be free. In effect, he's in a box.

A box is any uncomfortable situation that restricts an individual's freedom.

And the Box Trap is the assumption that the cost of getting out of a bad situation is too great to consider.

It's easy to slip into a box and just as easy to stay there. You can come to believe that a difficult situation is just part of living and must be accepted. Let's look at some examples of boxes.

A young doctor might decide, after ten years in medicine, that he really doesn't like it. But he stays where he is, assuming there's no way out. If you ask him why he doesn't change, he may not have a clear, precise reason.

It may be that he's unwilling to acknowledge that he's chosen the wrong profession, or that he doesn't want to disappoint his proud mother. Or maybe he's in the Previous-Investment Trap—thinking that he can't "throw away" the more than ten years of his life he's put into medicine.

A box can be a minor irritant—like a boring monthly family dinner at your relatives' home. Or a pain in the shoulder that continues daily but which you do nothing about.

Or a box can be a big thing—such as the situation of a woman who realizes that her marriage is nothing like her conception of what a marriage should be. She remains in the box because she feels it is unthinkable to try to get out of it.

The Box Trap is the vague feeling that the box must be accepted because there's no way out.

PRICE

Everything you want in life has a price connected to it. There's a price to pay if you want to make things better, a price to pay just for leaving things as they are, a price for everything.

The price may be in time, effort, money, emotional turmoil, or physical discomfort. Ultimately, however, it always comes back to time. You aren't going to live forever, so time is a limited resource. Whatever you do with your time, you pay a price by foregoing other alternatives—other things you could have done with that time. That's why you choose; you hope to satisfy your highest values and let the others go.

A key to good decision-making is the ability to recognize what you're giving up when you choose something. It's obvious that you can't have everything you desire. But often, when choosing to do something, you can overlook the desirable things that you'll have to forego because of the choice you're making.

So it's important to recognize what you're giving up and to make sure that what you're getting is more valuable to you than what you're foregoing. If you do that, you're less likely to have mixed emotions later when the other things appear desirable to you.

BOXES

In effect, a box is any situation that restrains your freedom. As long as you stay in it, you suffer a discomfort of some kind and you forego other alternatives that are more desirable to you.

The box could be a bad marriage, an unpleasant occupation, a debt for something of no value to you, or a social obligation of some kind. A box can also be the problems involved in maintaining an image or reputation that isn't genuinely yours—such as having to watch what you say.

You're in the Box Trap if you tolerate any such situation by assuming that there's no way out of it.

The first thing to recognize is that you're paying a price every day that you remain in the box. You're foregoing more attractive alternatives. And you suffer discomfort just from knowing that you don't like the situation, plus the discomfort of whatever you have to do to keep from rocking the boat.

The second thing to recognize is that there *is* a way out. To get out, you have to pay a price. The price may be in emotional upheaval, in money, in time spent to make things right. Whatever it is, there *is* a price you can pay to get out.

Part of the problem is usually the vagueness of the situation. It's easy to assume that the cost of getting out is too horrible to contemplate, and so you don't even think about it directly. As a result, you can go on living daily in a box without ever knowing exactly what it would require to get out.

If you could know specifically what you're paying by staying where you are and what you would have to pay to get out, you could make a definite choice. You'd know which alternative was truly best for you.

GETTING OUT OF BOXES

If there's a box in your life (big or little), let me suggest a simple method of putting it in focus.

Take a few minutes away from everything else. Find a comfortable chair in a quiet room where you can consider the problem without interruption.

First, identify the box. What is it that's causing you the discomfort?

For example, suppose you've lied to someone and now find it difficult to maintain the lie. You're no longer able to express yourself freely for fear of saying something that would contradict the lie.

Or perhaps your weekends are continually interrupted by relatives who drop in and monopolize your only free time. Or maybe you've made a commitment to contribute money to a particular cause but you now wish you were free to spend the money elsewhere.

Whatever it is, identify the discomfort the box causes.

Next, think of what you would do if you *weren't* in the box. At first, the only advantage you can think of might be the *absence* of the discomfort. But in some way the box is preventing you from doing something you'd prefer to do. And if it were removed, you'd be free to take advantage of desirable alternatives.

Imagine the box gone. And then imagine what you'd do once you were free of it. As you do, it's possible that the thought of one free activity might lead to another. And before long you may be able to think of many desirable possibilities that hadn't occurred to you before.

The next step is to identify the price it would take to get out of the box. As I said earlier, it may not have even occurred to you that there *is* a price that would get you out.

But there's always a way out. If you were to walk out of the box right now, what would it cost you? What would happen that you've been dreading?

The price could be fearful or it could be trivial. But there *is* a price that could get you out of the situation.

If you've lied to someone, you may have to admit that you lied to get out of the box. If so, the price might be the shame of admitting the lie, or the loss of the person's friendship, or the time involved to re-establish a reputation for honesty—or possibly all those things.

The price might be a confrontation with someone—such as telling your spouse you don't want to remain married, telling your boss you want a better arrangement if you're going to continue to work for him, or breaking off a relationship with a friend or relative who brings you only grief.

Identify what you'd have to do in order to end your present discomfort.

Then picture yourself paying that price. It may be painful just to think about it. But try.

If a confrontation is involved, imagine yourself going through the necessary scene. Construct an imaginary conversation with the other people involved. Don't skip over it; mentally live through every word spoken by each person.

As you do, try to think of unexpected things that might come up. Try to foresee the side of a person's character that hasn't been shown to you before. What if he gets mad? What if he starts to cry? What if he becomes abusive?

Go through the entire experience in your mind. If it's the least bit painful, go through it a second time. When you do, it should be less painful. Keep doing this—as many times as are necessary until you can go through the whole thing mentally without it bothering you.

With this, you will have identified clearly the three elements of your situation: (1) what you're paying by remaining where you are; (2) what it would cost you to get out; and (3) what you could do once you're out.

As long as the situation is just a hazy problem with no solution, it can always seem easier to let things continue unchanged—as uncomfortable as it may be. But when you recognize what it's costing you to stay in the box and what you could do if you were out of it, you gain new incentive to do something about it.

The price of getting out might have seemed horrendous when viewed vaguely from a distance. But now that you've identified it clearly, it may lose its power to frighten you. That won't necessarily be the case, but it is likely enough to be worth checking.

In most cases, a half hour spent in this way will lead to the conclusion that it's easier to pay the price and get out than to stay locked in the box.

MAKING TESTS

I don't suggest that you grab this technique and run out to break up a marriage or tell your mother goodbye.

It's a common example of the Intellectual Trap to think that your emotions will automatically adjust to a good idea. And many people have learned by sad experience that they aren't emotionally ready to carry off the ideas they've intellectually accepted.

It's far better to test such ideas in smaller matters and cautiously lead up to the bigger ones.

Take a minor irritant in your life as a first test. Decide what it's costing you, what it will cost to be rid of it, and what you'll do with the freedom you'll acquire when you're rid of it. Then pay the price.

If you have a friend or relative who has been a constant drain on your time, try telling him that you're going to be involved with other things and will no longer have the time to spend with him.

You might not look forward to the confrontation, but if you experience it mentally first, it will be easier to approach. Be prepared for surprises—reactions you didn't anticipate—so that they don't throw you off balance when they happen.

If the conversation becomes difficult and you're tempted to give in, remind yourself of the rewards awaiting you when you get through this. Keep remembering all the good things you'll be able to do with the time you're rescuing.

The confrontation may be difficult, but the next morning you might wake up to a brighter day. You may be surprised at the sense of weightlessness you feel for having removed a burden from your shoulders—a burden you had always assumed you were stuck with.

No matter what the discomfort, there's always a price you can pay to get rid of it.

Suppose you've acquired a debt for something you bought that you really don't care for anymore. Each month you have to write out a check for money you'd much rather use elsewhere. It can be a monthly torment—a symbol that you've made a costly mistake.

Why put up with it? There's always a way out.

Maybe you have twenty payments left. If so, don't take the attitude that you *have* to endure this discomfort for twenty more months. There's a price available that will end it now.

See what you can sell the item for. Don't fall into the Previous-Investment Trap by thinking you can't take a loss on it. You only increase your losses—in money and emotional distress—by hanging onto it.

The outstanding debt may be more than the amount you could sell it for. If so, why not pay the difference in cash and get rid of the problem? Or sell something else you don't need to make up the difference.

You don't gain anything by waiting the twenty months. By then the item will be worth even less, so you'll only lose more money by hanging onto it. Sell it now, pay the difference, and end the problem. Then you won't have to write those monthly checks anymore.

However you handle an irritant, there's no reason to assume you have to endure it just because you've made a mistake. There's always a price you can pay to clear the record and start fresh.

PAY THE PRICE

Cultivate the art of looking for prices any time you notice a discomfort. Find out what it would take to be rid of it; there's always a way. If the first price you discover seems to big to be worth it, think about it some more; perhaps there's an easier way.

Once you get into the habit of looking for prices, you'll realize that *any* irritant in your life can be handled. You'll no longer tolerate that slow, chronic discomfort that eats away at you daily—destroying your incentive, making you think less of yourself, darkening your attitude toward the world.

As you develop this talent, you can move up gradually to the bigger boxes in your life, dealing with them in the same way. Later, we'll spend three chapters discussing the techniques of handling major changes.

And one day you might wake up to realize that there isn't *anything* hanging over your head. You're free!—free to approach the day as *you* want to live it, not restricted by the chronic problems that other people take for granted.

I've never found an exception to the rule that the sooner you pay a price, the less it costs you. As long as a situation continues, you pay a price just knowing that the situation is unresolved. And the longer a situation continues, the firmer other people become in their attitude that you have no right to initiate a change.

No matter how long a situation continues, there's always a way to get out. But the sooner you handle it, the easier it is.

Whenever I can, I choose to pay in advance. But if I become aware of a mistake, I want to pay the price as fast as possible and clear the record. I've become fanatically intolerant of permanent irritants.

Even so, I occasionally carry a burden around with me awhile before I recognize it. It's usually a small discomfort that just seems to hang over me, never quite painful enough to make me fully aware of it but always taking the edge off something I could be enjoying.

Then, suddenly, it dawns on me what's happening. The first thing I want to determine is exactly what the discomfort is. Then I want to know what I might be afraid of that's allowed the discomfort to perpetuate. And I want to know what I'd have to do to be rid of it, once and for all.

Then I want to get to it as fast as I can, pay it, and be free to go onto better things.

If the price is higher than I'd anticipated, the point is still the same. I still have to pay it. There's no point in complaining, blaming someone else, or trying to stand up for my "rights." The sooner I pay the price, the sooner I'm free of whatever the trouble has been.

As always, it's important to concentrate on the direct alternatives. You may feel that someone else is partly or wholly to blame for the problems. But so what? You only waste precious time and attention when you try to make *him* pay the price. You chose wrongly, or you wouldn't be in the situation; that's why *you* have a price to pay.

What happens to him from now on is *his* problem. He'll have to continue living with whatever it is that bothers you about him. But all *you* have to do is pay the price, and he won't be a problem to you anymore.

FREEDOM

So many people live in chains of their own making. They cry out for freedom from political policies they don't like; they complain about the villains who prevent them from being free. And all the time they voluntarily tolerate boxes that reduce their freedom of action by 20 to 50 percent or more.

Getting out of boxes may not get the politicians off their backs. But if freedom is so important to them, why don't they remove the chains that *are* within reach?

Take a look at your own life. What could you do today that would give you more freedom tomorrow morning?

If the dollars you lose in taxes are important to you, then what about the dollars you may be spending to perpetuate boxes you could get out of?

If the hours required to earn the money to pay taxes are vital to you, then what about the hours you spend in uncomfortable relationships?

Every dollar or hour you stop spending to preserve a box is one you could be using for better things. Every day outside of a box is another day added to your free life.

In addition, when you get out of those boxes, you'll be much freer to take advantage of opportunities that will free you in other areas—such as removing the political chains from your back.

As I mentioned in Chapter 10, you're often prevented from using an attractive alternative in one area because you're restricted in another. When you're no longer deep in debt or stifled for time by bad relationships, you can take advantage of the many alternatives available to get rid of high taxes and political repression.

The Box Trap is the assumption that there's no way out of a box. There's *always* a way, always a price you can pay to be rid of it once and for all. Find it and pay it.

The nice part of it all is that you can get out of boxes just by exercising your own initiative. It's a direct alternative that doesn't involve influencing others. All you have to do is to pay the price.

Instead of worrying endlessly about a vague, ominous threat, face it mentally. Get off by yourself, relax, recognize what you're paying already, discover what you could pay to be rid of it, picture yourself paying it. And when it no longer frightens you, pay it and be free.

There are always prices. You pay them whether you change things or leave them alone. The price that gets you out of a bad situation is by far the least expensive one. It's usually far less terrifying than it was when you let it scare you from a distance.

Pay it. You have nothing to lose but your boxes.

When people won't let you alone, it's because you haven't learned how to make them do it.   —DAVID SEABURY

14

The Certainty Trap

THE CERTAINTY TRAP is the urge to act as if your information were totally certain. You're in the trap if you make decisions without recognizing the uncertainty of your assumptions and the risk that goes with that.

It's a normal urge to want to believe that one has the final answers to things. Certainty is a more comfortable feeling than uncertainty.

Unfortunately, a feeling of absolute certainty is usually unrealistic. At any given time, you have at your disposal only a small fraction of the information you would need to make a decision with complete foresight.

When you buy a house, you have no way of being sure the government won't condemn it next year to make way for a new road. When you plan a marketing campaign, you have no assurance that your makret surveys accurately reflect all the conditions that will affect your success. You can never know for sure the thoughts or plans or motivations of other people.

Uncertainty isn't a curse, however. You can still act; you can still make decisions. You use the best information and reasoning you can muster. The important thing is to recognize the *limits* of the information you're using. There are variables you can't possibly predict, there's knowledge that's less than certain, and there's the ever-present possibility that you haven't drawn the best conclusions from what you've seen.

None of these things need stop you from acting. But they must be recognized. They constitute the *risk* involved in what you do. And for every risk there's an accompanying *liability*—a price you'll have to pay if things don't go as you want them to.

You're in the Certainty Trap when you ignore that risk. In everything you do, *there's always a risk*. Sometimes the risk is negligible; often the liability that goes with it is minor. But it exists and must be accepted in order to know what you're doing. Otherwise, you might walk overconfidently into a situation where your loss could be overwhelming.

LOSS OF FREEDOM

The individual who ignores these risks can lose his freedom in three important ways:

1. He's likely to take risks that would be unacceptable if he were to recognize them; and by acting rashly he can get himself into boxes that restrict his freedom.

2. When things don't go his way, his previous certainty can turn quickly to despair and depression; after all, he was "so sure." Now that he's discouraged, his emotions can tempt him to run from his bad consequences into a worse situation. In other words, he's fallen into the Emotional Trap.

3. By accepting opinions as absolute fact, he can allow his freedom to be restricted by information that may not be true.

Let's explore this trap in more detail.

UNCERTAINTY

The desire for certainty can cause you to try to have an explanation for everything that happens.

Many things that happen seem to defy explanation—at least at the time they happen. If so, accept that. If you think you *have* to have an explanation, you can devote a great deal of time and attention to finding the answer to something that may not be that important. Or, worse yet, you could be tempted to accept a rash explanation that isn't true—and which could cause you to act foolishly in a later situation.

For example, a man says, "I was fired from my job because the boss doesn't like Jews; so I'll never work for a Gentile again." Or a woman says, "I was out dancing when my mother had a heart attack; so as long as she lives, I'll never go dancing again."

Or "The Communists wanted that legislation and it passed; so there *must* be a conspiracy that I must devote my life to stopping." Or "That no-talent actress became a star—she must have slept with the producers; so I have to choose between being promiscuous or not acting."

The same thing can apply to more mystical matters. For example, "I dreamt of that accident before it happened; therefore I can predict the future." Or in reverse, "I can't explain the feelings I have, so it must be proof that I've lived a former life." Or "I can't explain how the universe was created; so there must be a God."

There's nothing shameful in acknowledging that you don't have the answers to every question about life. Just accept the fact that you know only a fraction of what's going on in the world. You don't have to attach explanations in terms of a special revelation of God's will, a glimpse at the supernatural, evidence of a conspiracy, or anything else.

I was pleased to read a newspaper interview that demonstrated a calm, reasonable approach to a very controversial subject. Perhaps you remember the best-selling book *The Search for Bridey Murphy*. In it, a hypnotist told how his patient recalled a previous life as Bridey Murphy in Ireland from 1798 to 1864.

For many people, the story was absolute proof of reincarnation. Others scoffed that it was fraudulent or inaccurate.

Virginia Tighe (called Ruth Simmons in the book) was the patient who had the strange experience. You'd suppose that she would be the most certain of what it meant. However, she treats the experience as something very unusual but not necessarily proof of anything. In the newspaper interview in 1971 she said:

> I accepted the hypnotic experience as only that. An experience. I know that something happened, something unusual that was completely honest. I've kept my mind open on anything beyond that.
> I thought all kinds of things might explain what had happened: perhaps a genetic memory or something I had read or something someone had told me. But I've never found a satisfactory explanation.
> Certainly, I still have doubts. I have come to accept the fact that it is possible that reincarnation was not impossible. But I would never sit here and tell anyone that I am the reincarnation of Bridey Murphy.[1]

I see this as a very reasonable reaction to an amazing experience—unusually reasonable coming from the person who experienced it.

You don't need an explanation for everything. Recognize that there are such things as miracles—events for which there are no ready explanations. Later knowledge may explain those events quite easily. But at this date in history, you can't expect to know everything that might be known eventually.

THE QUALITY OF INFORMATION

It's easy to forget that what we accept as certain knowledge from others is subject to the human limitations of perception and logic. No one can be expected to know ev-

[1] Los Angeles *Times*, May 5, 1971.

erything, to see everything with unfailing accuracy, and to interpret what he sees with perfect judgment. And yet, it's easy to accept verbatim the information that's handed us.

To do so, however, is to fall into the Certainty Trap.

Scientific books usually represent the best judgment of their writers, but what they see can easily be superseded later. Holy books claim to reveal "God's word," but they, too, were written by fallible human beings expressing what they believed to be true. "How to do it" books tell what the authors believe are the techniques that worked for them; but they may be misinterpreting the causes of their success—and their techniques may not produce the same effects when you use them.

Any book *might* contain useful ideas, suggestions, alternatives. They can be sources of inspiration to help stimulate your search for answers. But to accept any of them as absolute, final answers to the problems and mysteries of life is to walk into the Certainty Trap.

THE EXPERTS

In the same way, it's easy to overrespect the judgment of someone who appears to have mastered a given field. These are the "experts"—the individuals who apparently have access to information that's outside your sphere of experience. They can range from your successful brother-in-law who has a hot stockmarket tip to the respected Ph.D. who heads a vast research foundation.

Because your resources are limited, you rely upon other people for many things. That's the specialization of labor. You acquire products built by other people, and you pay for them by producing things in your own field of competence.

Information is one of the things you acquire from others. But just as you may have once bought a car that turned out to be a lemon, you can also acquire information that goes sour. Information-providers can make mistakes, too.

There may be many people who know much more than you do about some things. But it's wise to exercise some caution when acting upon the information you get from them.

For example, a man who's been through years of medical school probably knows a great deal more than you about the workings of your body. But don't be surprised if another doctor disagrees with his diagnosis. Years of schooling and experience can't provide either of them with infallibility.

After all, *you're* probably a specialist at something. Are you always right? There are plenty of day-to-day events that can get in the way of your being totally objective and impartial. Why shouldn't you expect the same limitations to apply to other specialists?

Experts are human beings; they're fallible. An expert's research and judgment can be sidetracked by telephone calls, interoffice politics, emotional problems, political objectives, hopes for promotion, and vested interests in previously stated opinions. There's nothing shameful about that; it's normal and to be expected.

Sometimes, truth and objectivity surmount all of those obstacles. But you can't know when and where they have—so it's best to accept all judgments with reservations.

Too often what "everybody knows" may have been originally the outburst of a man who ran out of research time—or one who was bothered by a liver ailment—or it may have been a satirical comment that was intended as a joke.

There was a time, you know, when "everybody knew" the earth was flat and the sun revolved around it. Now, "everybody knows" better. But what we think we know today may be superseded by even more realistic findings tomorrow.

There is no source you can look to for the ultimate truth and final answers to everything, or even anything. You won't find them in the nation's capital, the churches, the courts, the universities, or from the "insiders."

What you hear from these sources are simply statements of opinion by human beings. If you accept them as such, you'll be aware of the risks you take when you act on information, and you'll be less likely to jump into trouble you can't handle.

THE TRAP

The essence of the Certainty Trap is to disregard risks by overestimating the certainty of the information upon which you base your decisions. Taking risks is an inherent part of life; it's only dangerous when you act as if you're *not* taking a risk.

Risks are forms of prices. You gamble with time when you choose to take a risk instead of taking the time to be sure of what you're doing. If you win, you'll have saved time; if you lose, you'll probably spend more time paying off the loss than you would have had to spend checking things out in advance.

There's nothing wrong with taking a risk. The danger occurs when you don't recognize that you're taking one.

You're in the Certainty Trap if you base your life on what someone has told you is the way to live—or on what someone has told you that God has commanded. Or any time you think that a course of action will produce absolutely certain results.

You're in the trap if you let your stockbroker's confidence induce you to withdraw your savings and bet them on one stock. Or if you reorient your way of life because of a new medical discovery published in the newspaper. Or when you allow a flash of inspiration to convince you that you have the final answer to something and let it cause you to take an unreasonable risk.

It's just as foolish to expect *someone else* to act on the basis of *your* knowledge. When you've decided *you* are sure enough of something to act upon it, it doesn't make sense to expect someone else to act with the same assurance. That's a variation of the Identity Trap—expecting others to act as you would, using the same knowledge and premises you use.

AVOIDING THE TRAP

Here are some suggestions that may help you to avoid the Certainty Trap:

1. *Popularity isn't proof*. What "everybody knows" has been so obviously wrong so many times that I don't need to fill this book with evidence of it.

If all your friends are about to embark upon a dangerous adventure and they scoff at your caution, that isn't a reason for you to go against your own judgment.

If everyone in your church or neighborhood is sure he knows exactly who and what God is, how to reach him, and what his rules for human behavior are, that isn't evidence of anything—except evidence that a lot of people say they hold that opinion.

Or if everyone you know is buying real estate in a new development that's "sure" to skyrocket in price, that's not proof of anything. The crowd is wrong at least as often as it's right.

Remember, "everybody knew" the nation was solvent in 1928.

2. *Be skeptical about new information*. Be open to new possibilities, but accept them as possibilities, not as final truth. Be alert to new alternatives and new explanations of things important to you, but don't lose sight of the fact that what you hear and discover may not be correct.

3. *Don't expect to have an explanation for everything*. You may come across a cause-and-effect relationship that seems to work for you. You do something and it seems to produce the result you want. Good. Use it, take advantage of it—but never lose sight of the possibility that the system may not be exactly as you see it now. In other words, don't bet your life on it.

Don't let your guard down and plunge into situations where the risks are too great. Realize that in another situation, other factors may cause the system to work in a different way. By overlooking that, you might lose in one mistake all that you've gained by using the system in the past.

If you find that prayer brings the results you want, good. But don't place yourself in a situation where prayer is the only defense you have against trouble. It may not always work for you in the same way.

If you discover a gambling system that seems to make money for you, use it. But consider banking your profits as you go—just in case the miracle suddenly evaporates.

4. *Recognize that you're seeing only part of what's involved; you can't see everything.* You just don't have the time and opportunity to check out everything. So accept the existence of other possibilities that may not be apparent at this moment. Act on what you see, but with due respect for the existence of other things you can't see.

5. *Recognize the risks and liabilities.* And that's the most important point. There are *always* risks, and risks mean liabilities—prices to be paid if things don't go as you want them to. When you recognize them, you can handle things in ways that make your losses less frequent and less critical.

The individual who plows ahead unswervingly because he "knows" he's right is usually wrong. And when he runs head on into the brick wall he was so sure wouldn't be there, his losses are greater than those of the man who was more cautious.

REACTIONS

When you're aware of risks, you can relax and accept the world. You lose the sense of pressure that commands you to have an answer for everything. Consequently, you're less likely to react emotionally if things go wrong.

For example, whenever you cross a busy street you're taking a risk—even if only a slight one. Anything might happen. You could fail to see a car coming, even if you make it a point to look. You could be hit by an object dropped or thrown from a nearby building. You could trip on a bump, turn your ankle, and be unable to get out of the path of oncoming cars.

Such things don't happen often, but their rarity (combined with an overconfident air) can cause people to react badly in various ways when they *do* happen. One person will direct all his attention to blaming the "villain" who caused the accident. Another will be sure it was "God's will" punishing him for his sins. Another will decide he's been a fool for crossing streets, and now he "knows" he should never do it again (a vow he'll probably keep until his leg heals and he needs to cross a street again).

I think a reasonable man would most likely react by recognizing that he takes risks all the time and that now one of them has gone against him. Maybe the truck driver shouldn't have driven so fast, or the city should have fixed the bump. But he's always known that such things were possible and outside his control, so he automatically assumed a risk when he crossed the street.

His only concern now is to pay the price, repair his damages as quickly as possible, and get onto better things. He won't waste his time blaming people, fearing God's wrath, or making foolish resolutions. He knows that what happened is part of being alive.

The overconfident man approaches things as if he were acting with absolute certainty. But because he's being unrealistic, he wastes his resources by taking foolish risks. He throws away his freedom by rashly jumping into boxes. He often follows a code of conduct that's inappropriate to his nature because he's so sure he's received some absolute word on the subject.

When he runs into trouble, it's such a contradiction to his attitude that it usually causes emotional problems. He often reacts to his disaster by leaping to conclusions opposite to what he held before. Either he was "all wrong" before, but "absolutely right" now—or he declares that the world is malevolent or incoherent.

Meanwhile, the reasonable man recognizes the gamble

in everything he does. He's quite willing to take risks, but only when he's prepared to pay the liability if the risk goes against him. Mistakes, disappointments, losses don't sidetrack him; he keeps moving toward the things he wants.

He refuses to act rashly upon assumptions, no matter how certain others may be that the assumptions are correct.

ACCEPTING THINGS AS THEY ARE

When you accept the presence of uncertainty, you can usually relax and enjoy life more. You don't feel that you have to have a final answer for everything. You accept what you know and act upon it, without expecting to know everything else—past, present, or future.

For example, there's nothing wrong with being in love with someone. There's nothing wrong with enjoying that and making the most of it. What's wrong is to assume that you know at this minute everything you'd need to know to decide to commit the rest of your life to such a relationship.

For another example, if your income suddenly goes up, there's no sensible reason not to enjoy your new wealth. But it would be foolish to assume that you *know* that the income level will continue permanently and thereby commit yourself to future expenditures that depend upon that income.

If you've found an eager market for your product or service, don't let that convince you that *everyone* will want that service. For that might lead you to make investments in your business that are based upon unrealistic projections.

Don't let uncertainty prevent you from enjoying what you have. But don't let overconfidence lead you to act upon what you don't have yet.

THE FINAL AUTHORITY

Many people go through life with the feeling that what they think and know are sort of summations of what they've absorbed from those who "really" know things. This attitude is encouraged, of course, by those who are supposed to be the ones who "really" know—moral authorities, experts, people who are "older and wiser," people who are on the "inside." They speak with convincing authority.

But they, too, act and speak from incomplete information—just as we all do. No one can hope to have *all* the information necessary to speak with final authority. To expect that is to fall into the Certainty Trap.

The experts don't know everything, or even everything about anything. And one thing they know very little about is *you*. The people who tell you how to live have very little knowledge of who you are and what you're capable of doing.

But *you* can know those things—if not totally, then far better than anyone else can. This is why you have to filter information before taking it into your system of doing things.

You have to judge how sensibly the information fits with the way you see the world, how compatibly the action suggested fits with your nature and capabilities, how happy you might be if you lived in the way suggested.

It's easy to think that there has to be an authority outside yourself to judge what is true or false, what is correct and incorrect, what will work and what won't. But there isn't. Even if you'd like to delegate that responsibility to someone else, you can't. You still have to decide *who* will be the judge, and sometime in the future *you* may change that decision.

So you're deciding even when you try not to decide.

It's important to recognize that you *are* the final authority—whether or not you choose to be, whether or not you have the confidence to assume the role. The role is yours, regardless.

You are the sovereign authority for your life. You are the ruler who makes the decisions regarding how you will act, what information you will accept. You do it anyway—but if you *recognize* that you do it, you can gain much greater control over your future.

Once you know that the responsibility begins and ends with you, you start treating information more carefully, you act more deliberately, and you get results that more directly bring you what you need to be happy.

You live in a world of your own, bounded by your own knowledge and experience. It's a wonderful world—full of the power to do things to bring freedom and happiness.

Recognize your sovereign authority. You won't ever be the totalitarian ruler of someone else's life. But you do rule your own.

When you no longer count on other people to be "right," to be certain, to be moral, to be intelligent, you'll turn to the one source of genuine power that exists for you—yourself.

You'll find numerous alternatives that can get you what you want without having to go through other people to do so. You'll discover how much of your freedom and happiness you've forfeited in the past by delegating to other people the power that can be used effectively only by yourself.

Who rules the world?

You do. *Your* world, that is.

If a man will begin with certainties, he shall end in doubts; but if he will be content to begin with doubts he shall end in certainties.   —FRANCIS BACON

The devil can cite Scripture for his purpose.
  —SHAKESPEARE

The best laid schemes o' mice and men Gang aft a-gley.
  —ROBERT BURNS

15

You Can Be Free

IT'S EASY TO BELIEVE that you came into the world with a prearranged program you must follow. After all, long before you arrived, other people figured out how you should live, what laws you should obey, what your obligations are, the whole structure for a "proper" life.

Most people accept that program. They try to find the proper rules and hope to follow them faithfully. They do everything possible to live up to the images that others declare to be "moral," "rational," "in," or acceptable.

The tragedy is that each of them has only one life and he throws that life away trying to live it as someone else has dictated. He accepts the traps without question. He allows the world to act upon him—instead of creating a joyous world for himself.

As a result, he comes to accept as part of life many discomforts, problems, and aggravations. When he gets into a box, he accepts it as his lot.

It *is* tragic.

As you consider the prearranged programs that others hand you, remind yourself that you have only one life. Ask yourself if you're willing to trust it to someone else's information, ideas, or plans. Are you willing to give up the one life you have in order to conform to the way others think you should live?

Your life is all you have. What could possibly be important enough to warrant throwing that life away?

Of what importance is society if you must give up your happiness for it? Of what value is your country if you must sacrifice your life to protect the nation from its problems? Of what value is *anything* if to preserve it you must bend your identity?

Nations, societies, communities, families, marriages, jobs, relationships—these things are all means to an end. And the end is your happiness. You can achieve genuine, durable happiness only when your own identity is preserved. How, then can any institution be more important than yourself in your considerations?

By bending yourself to fit the institutions, you turn things inside out. The institutions must be created and utilized as they serve you—not vice versa. When they don't add anything to your well-being, you have no logical reason to support them.

If I were totally convinced that "society's rules" were well founded, sensible, and truly furthered *society's* interests, I would still refuse to give up my identity and my happiness for them. For of what value to me is society if I must sacrifice myself for it?

As it is, however, the rules *aren't* well founded. They're usually senseless clichés. Misguided attempts to follow them have resulted in wars, poverty, tyranny, violence, and despair. But despite the evidence, plenty of people still place their faith in their society, in their government, and in other institutions.

The moral codes, the legal structure, the social customs, the assumed obligations, the "norm"—all those things are products of limited, subjective human perception. In some cases, they might coincide with good sense, but it would be foolish to accept them without challenge.

These traditions and customs have been informally codified in the clichés, assumptions, and standard practices that I've referred to as traps. In the past chapters, we've looked at fourteen basic types of traps (there are probably more that I haven't identified).

By dismantling the traps, I've been attempting to demonstrate that freedom is more often lost by false assumptions than by the power of one's enemies.

It's quite understandable that the traps carry so much influence. But they are paper chains. And the individual who sees them for what they are will know that it was *his* choice to be enslaved; he hasn't been overpowered.

He'll know that he's been acting on poor information. But more than anything else, he'll see that he has the power to step out of them and into a better life for himself.

He doesn't have to use misguided methods to try to find freedom—such as are suggested by the Government Traps, the Rights Trap, the Utopia Trap, the Burning-Issue Trap, and the Group Trap.

He doesn't have to use inefficient decision-making methods—as seen in the Previous-Investment Trap, the Certainty Trap, the Box Trap, and the Emotional Trap.

He doesn't have to forsake his own nature to get along—as dictated by the Identity Trap, the Morality Trap, the Intellectual Trap, and the Unselfishness Trap.

And if he avoids these traps, he has no reason to fall into the Despair Trap—the belief that he can't be free.

LIFE IS UNDERSTANDABLE

The traps can make the world seem too big and complicated for an individual to act on his own. And that reinforces the individual's sense of helplessness, his feeling that his life isn't in his own hands.

Through it all, however, the world is quite simple.

I find that when I integrate everything I see around two basic principles, it all makes perfect sense: (1) Each person seeks his own mental well-being (happiness); and (2) Everything that happens is the effect of a prior cause.

When you don't understand a situation, it helps to stand back for a minute, think of each person involved, and ask yourself, "What is he trying to do? How does he believe he's furthering his own well-being?" That can make his actions much more understandable and predictable.

It doesn't matter whether his conduct is right or wrong. That's what he's doing. And you're not going to be able to re-educate him instantly.

As you view the identities of others, you make it far easier on yourself if you accept them as they are. Attempts to change others are rarely successful, and even then probably not completely satisfying.

To accept others as they are doesn't mean you have to give into them or put up with them. You are sovereign. You own your own world. You can choose.

In any situation, ask yourself: *Is this what I want for myself?* If it isn't, you don't have to remain there. There are millions of people out there in the world; you have a lot more to choose from than just what you see in front of you now.

YOUR SOVEREIGNTY

You've probably heard all your life that there are things in this world more important than yourself. If so, it can take time to accept the fact of your own sovereignty. It can seem natural to assume that your future will be decided by others, that your purpose in life is to serve society, your country, or the world—as determined by others.

But whether or not you accept it, you *are* sovereign. You rule one life—and you rule it totally.

You decide which information you will accept or reject. *You* decide what your next action will be. *You* decide what moral code you'll live by.

What has happened to you up to now in your life is far more the result of *your* choices than of anything else. Others have affected you, but *you* are the one who decided whether or not you'd associate with them.

If you've acted upon information that later proved to

be false, it was you who decided to accept that information. If you've become involved in relationships with people who later proved to be difficult, it was you who chose to become vulnerable to them. But it was also you who made all the choices that led to the good things you've enjoyed in your life.

You are the sovereign ruler who has chosen which city to live in, which job to take, which people to associate with, which rules to live by. Others may have made requests—even demands—but it was you who made the ultimate choices regarding your action.

But what is most important, it is also you who will make the choices in the future. Whatever you did in the past, you did for the best reasons you knew at the time. But today, you have more alternatives to choose from. And tomorrow, you'll have even more. There's no reason why you have to repeat your choices of the past—unless they proved to be best for you.

What you do from here on will be entirely up to you. *You* will decide—whether or not you decide to think of it in those terms.

If you decide to think that you have no control over your own life, then you'll probably choose to do as others demand—whether that be the government, society, friends, or family. And you might choose to place the blame for your misfortunes upon them.

But if you choose to recognize your own sovereignty, you'll probably think it ridiculous to grant others the responsibility for your success or failure.

A free man would never consider it sensible to allocate the credit or blame for his life to others. If the market for his services should change, it isn't a disaster to him. He's been mentally prepared for that possibility—and he immediately looks for something new, while others might sulk over their poor luck.

If the product he sells goes out of fashion, he looks for something that *is* in demand. If he finds that the city in which he lives no longer pleases him, he looks for one that does. If the government raises taxes, he looks for a way to avoid them. If someone tries to take his property from him, he takes steps to protect it; he doesn't rely upon the police and then blame *them* for his unhappiness if they fail.

He would never consider the possibility that his life is only what others decide to make of it.

He recognizes that others will seek their own happiness—and in their own ways. And he knows that what they do may not be in his self-interest sometimes. He accepts that, without bitterness or accusations, and he relies upon himself.

He recognizes his own sovereignty, he values his own life above all, and he refuses to waste that life—or any part of it—by making others responsible for his future.

YOUR FUTURE

That free man has no advantages that you don't have. His freedom didn't result from an accident of birth. His good fortune hasn't been a matter of luck.

He's free because he recognizes his most priceless asset, the same asset that *you* possess—sovereignty.

Every person is the sovereign ruler of his own life. But few people ever recognize that fact. Those who do will make it their business to find freedom. Those who don't will invariably resign themselves to whatever "society" makes available to them.

Yes, you are the ruler of your life. You choose what you'll believe, what you'll accept, what you'll do.

You've chosen the path you've followed up until now. And you'll make the choices that will take you from where you are now.

What are you going to do with that power?

Are you going to delegate it to someone else to write the rules for you? Or are you going to create rules that will make your life as free and happy as possible?

Are you going to stay in the boxes that confine you? Or are you going to make it a point to free yourself of anything that's uncomfortable for you?

Are you going to be free?

In the first chapter I defined freedom as "the opportunity to live your life as you want to live it." Most people visualize the fight for freedom as an attempt to break out of a physical or cultural prison in which they're held captives.

It's easy to feel that you lack the opportunity to be free because someone has the power to enslave you and is using it. And so you try to reconstruct the social order or your family's understanding in order to have the *opportunity* to be free.

But those prison walls exist only because *you* have chosen to allow them to stand. They have no substance, no restrictive power—except as you choose to accept them.

You don't have to reconstruct the social order; you don't have to overpower the villains; you don't have to re-educate the world; you don't need a miracle. All you have to do is to use your sovereign power of choice to release yourself from those who would keep you in bondage.

The *opportunity* has always been there. You just haven't taken advantage of it.

So we can drop the word *opportunity* from the definition of freedom, because the opportunity already exists—and always has.

Freedom is living your life as you want to live it.

And you can do that by choosing to do so. You can be free. No one can stop you.

The gigantic myth called "society" that rules so many lives doesn't even exist. "Society" is merely a collection of *different* people, tastes, and judgments. It can't enforce its rules upon you. You don't have to uphold causes you don't believe in, go to cocktail parties that bore you, dress and act as you've been told to.

You don't have to be married to someone who wants you to be something other than what you are. You don't have to work for a company that doesn't recognize your talent. And you don't have to stay in a profession that drains your time and prevents you from living as you want to.

You don't have to reject your own interests and live by someone else's code. You don't have to forsake your own happiness for the benefit of anyone. You don't have to obey the laws that the "majority" has decided are "right." You don't have to follow the leadership of politicians, prophets, or philosophers.

You don't have to distort your emotions, tastes, and values to conform to the "norms" others think are best for you.

You are free to live your life as you want to live it. You could get into your car right now and drive to anywhere you choose. There's nothing stopping you. The only reason *not* to do that is if there is something better for you where you are now.

The demands and wishes of others don't control your life. You do. You make the decisions. And the only standard should be to make the decisions that will bring you the greatest happiness.

There are thousands of people who *wouldn't* demand that you bend yourself out of shape to please them. There are people who will *want* you to be yourself, people who see things as you do, people who want the same things you want.

Why should you have to waste your life in a futile effort to please those with whom you *aren't* compatible?

To be free, you have only to make the decision to be free. Freedom is waiting for you—anytime you're ready for it.

GETTING THERE

There's still work to be done—perhaps a lot of it. You'll need specific techniques to get you out of the traps and boxes without sacrificing your future to do it.

You'll need alternatives so that you can avoid taxes without going to jail, live your own life without having to be lonely, dissolve uncomfortable relationships with a minimum of emotional upheaval.

Most of the rest of the book will be devoted to those techniques. All of them deal with direct alternatives—choices you can make that don't involve changing other people. The next section will provide alternatives to free yourself from the restrictions that are binding you now. And the following section will include techniques that will help you to make the transition to a free life.

The goal is in sight. There *are* ways to retrieve the freedom you've disregarded. There are ways to spend more time feeling good and less time trying to ward off problems, to spend more of your life choosing between exciting alternatives and less time trying to keep things from getting worse.

You'll never be 100 percent free, because your limited imagination can always envision more good things than you could have in a lifetime. So you'll always have to make choices, recognize consequences, and keep your most important values uppermost in your mind.

But I'd guess that the average person is no more than 10-30 percent free, and I believe it's possible for almost anyone to raise that to as much as 80-90 percent freedom.

That's a considerable change—and you can make the change if you direct your effort where it will have the greatest effect—on the direct alternatives that *you* control.

The most wonderful part of it all is that it's entirely up to you. You don't have to depend upon circumstances; you can create the circumstances that please you. Your success depends only upon your willingness to assert your freedom and to implement it.

Everyone begins life as a free person. But as time passes, most people accept the prearranged programs and never stop to realize the freedom they possess. They accept standards and situations that are unsuitable to them.

But that doesn't have to apply to you. You can have your freedom back any time you choose to take it.

You can be free.

And nothing, not God, is greater to one than one's self is.   —WALT WHITMAN

Self-reverence, self-knowledge, self-control,
These three alone lead to sovereign power.
                                    —ALFRED LORD TENNYSON

PART II How You Can Be Free

16

Freedom from
Government

MOST PEOPLE seem to think of the government as an all-powerful giant with unlimited resources, super powers of control and surveillance, and the ability to keep every citizen in line.

Such impressions are reinforced by movies and TV dramas that picture government agents calling upon vast resources of information and manpower to bring any criminal or dissenter to bay. And the impression is probably enhanced by newspaper accounts of crackdowns on narcotics rings, smuggling activities, and tax frauds, in which the government has used large numbers of agents to break a case.

All of this can be pretty intimidating. But it has very little to do with your relationship to the government.

For one thing, the government has *limited* resources—just as you and I do. When a large number of agents are utilized to break a narcotics ring, that leaves fewer men to police the average marijuana smoker. And when they marshal their resources to crack a million-dollar tax fraud, that leaves less manpower to look after the normal individual tax returns.

If the government *were* as powerful as people seem to think it is, the war in Vietnam would have been won long ago, crime wouldn't be such a national issue, and the government's grandiose social reforms would be successful. As it is, however, none of those things is true because the government *can't* force many people at once to act in ways they don't want to.

The government is one big Group Trap. To be efficient, it depends upon millions of bureaucrats whose incomes and careers don't depend upon efficient action.

The men who operate the super-secret spy agencies are simply human beings—with ulcers, family problems, interoffice memos to answer, staff meetings to attend, girl friends to see when they can sneak away from the office, office opponents to outmaneuver, and the constant interferences inherent in any bureaucracy.

The government is an inefficient, bureaucratic mess. It isn't surprising that its programs always turn out to cost more than expected, that it almost never successfully completes a project, that bombers bomb the wrong cities in Vietnam, that it's usually rallying its citizens to be patriotic and sacrifice to compensate for the government's mistakes.

In the book *1984*, George Orwell pictured a totalitarian society that has become the standard view of the total state of the future. Everyone's life was controlled by computers, and there was a TV camera in every room to monitor everyone's activities.

Fortunately, such dramas overlook the fundamentals of economics. The larger the government, the less efficient and productive is the economy. Slaves don't produce with the enthusiasm, incentive, and imagination that free people do. Bureaucratic programs just don't work as intended.

So while the totalitarian state may include a TV camera in every room, I doubt that the camera will work.

THREE PRINCIPLES

The first principle in dealing with government, then, is: *Don't be awed by it*. What little the government accomplishes is almost always due to the voluntary participation of its citizens. Those who don't want to help the government can go their own ways without running into much trouble.

The second principle is: *Don't confront the government.* A sure way to make your life miserable is to attack the government head on. Its resources are limited, and it can't waste them tracking down every possible violator of every law. But it will certainly aim its power at anyone who *publicly* defies it. So keep to yourself, do what you have to do.

The third rule in dealing with governments is: *Don't organize.* Don't get a large group of people together to defy tax laws, promote ways of circumventing the government, or openly violate regulations.

By joining protests, you might wind up in jail. And you won't have much freedom there.

And mass campaigns are easy targets. That's where the government is likely to devote its limited resources. When many people are doing the same thing, it's easy to stop them by passing laws or by applying existing laws against them.

When you act alone, however, you're usually not worth the trouble.

YOUR POWER

And when you act alone, you can easily and flexibly do whatever is necessary to stay ahead of the government. If new laws are passed, you can easily change your methods to continue doing what you want to do.

No cumbersome, bureaucratic government can be as agile as an individual who's determined to stay ahead of it.

There are limitless possibilities for avoiding government—without crises, court battles, or fear of being jailed.

Start by listing the governmental restrictions that inhibit your freedom. Determine the possible consequences of ignoring them. It may be that no more than a warning is involved if you're caught. And you might also find that there are legal ways of avoiding the restrictions—if they're important enough to be worth the time to investigate.

In many cases, you can just ignore the law without incurring dangerous consequences. In others, you may have to go to more trouble—such as consulting an attorney or tax accountant.

But act for yourself. Don't organize, and don't look to leaders to help you. Any activity big enough to require a leader is big enough to be noticed and attacked.

LEGAL EVASIONS

For most people, there are more than enough loopholes available to be able to operate freely without running afoul of the law. More than anything else, it simply requires the determination to do so.

For example, I know of a company that operates successfully in spite of governmental regulations. The state in which it's located has been trying to license it for five years, and a federal agency has been trying to shut it down for violating a regulation. The state legislature even passed a special law to bring the company under its jurisdiction.

But to this day, the company still operates in its own way, pleasing its customers, and making profits for its owners. They've moved flexibly and easily into a different method of operation every time a ruling has been made against them. They've had to pay attorneys' fees, but those are insignificant compared to the profits they would have lost had they given in to the bureaucrats.

I once had a similar experience. I was operating a small business in California—burdened with payroll taxes, bookkeeping requirements, and other regulations imposed by the government. There were Social Security taxes, unemployment insurance taxes, disability insurance taxes, and income taxes to be paid or withheld. They cost me money and time, and they reduced the take home pay of my employees.

I regularly received notices from an organization whose purpose was to end payroll taxes. They requested funds, of course, and they also wanted me to join a protest movement to quit withholding taxes once the membership was large enough to be intimidating.

Naturally, I didn't get involved. Instead, I fired all the employees (including myself) and made contracts with each person for his services. Since I no longer had any employees, I no longer paid or withheld payroll taxes.

No bureaucrat called on me to find out why the revenue to the state had been lost.

Meanwhile, the protest movement died its inevitable death, and other employers continued paying payroll taxes.

The "employees" of my company received an additional benefit. They were now independent businessmen, selling their services to me, so they could designate their homes as their offices, coming to my office to perform services for me.

As a result, each of them had far more tax deductions. He could claim as business deductions part of his household expenses, telephone bills, utility bills, car expenses, and other things that are normally considered to be personal expenses. Even with no income tax withheld, very few of them owed anything in taxes at the end of the year.

None of them bothered to file quarterly tax estimates, and none of them ran into trouble from the Internal Revenue Service.

The simple change from employee status to that of independent contractor resulted in lower taxes for everyone concerned. It's a small and common example—but there are probably millions of people who could use that loophole and don't.

It's well known that there are thousands of millionaires who don't pay income taxes. Some of them avoid property taxes as well. Occasionally, there's a hue and cry about it in Congress, but no effective changes are made. No tax law could be written (short of 100 percent confiscation) that wouldn't have numerous loopholes. As one loophole is closed, another opens up. Part of the reason may be that Congressmen don't like to pay taxes, either.

Some people evade taxes by changing their citizenship and/or by operating personal holding corporations through taxfree countries. If you make $25,000 or more per year, it's probably worth looking into. Others move to countries with more favorable tax structures. Did you know, for example, that writers, artists, and other creative people are exempt from income taxes in Ireland?[1]

The laws provide loopholes that allow individuals to establish personal taxfree foundations that receive all their income and pay their personal expenses—without the money being taxable to anyone involved. Unfortunately, a group of people tried to organize this method into a mass movement about five years ago, which resulted in offsetting legislation. But the loophole is still used.

Inheritance taxes can be legally avoided, too. Sometimes it requires only that property be co-owned or transferred prior to death. The important thing is to avoid the normal post-mortem legal processing of an estate.

There are a multitude of ways to legally avoid taxes. I can't list them here or that would defeat their purpose. And you won't find them in magazine articles about taxes. Much of the information in those articles comes straight from the booklet that accompanies your tax return. But once you're determined to cut your taxes, you should be able to find the best ways for yourself.

---

[1] *How to Keep Your Money and Freedom* by Harry D. Schultz (listed in the bibliography) contains a good deal of information, country by country, on matters of banking, citizenship, passports, corporations, and taxes.

OTHER RESTRICTIONS

The same principles apply to other governmental restrictions. If you just stay out of the normal channels of doing things, you can avoid conflicts with the government.

Licenses and regulations can be avoided by using a little imagination. There are plenty of psychologists who are unlicensed and unregulated because they don't call themselves psychologists. And there are plenty of people who do the same things that teachers, doctors, architects, lawyers, beauticians, engineers, bankers, investment counselors, and psychiatrists do, but avoid all the legal requirements by not using the legal titles.

Such things as courtroom battles, jury duty, and the draft are ways by which the state can drain your time and money. But there are always way to avoid each of them.

Many people avoid court procedures, for example, by having separate arbitration contracts with business associates, private marital agreements (without getting legally married or divorced), or appointing third parties to hold funds or arbitrate disputes without the normal legal expenses.

Jury duty is typical of the impositions the state can make upon an individual. Many people avoid it by simply not registering to vote. Since the jury lists are called from voter lists, those people are never bothered. If voting is important to you, that may not be the way to do it—but I quit voting ten years ago and haven't missed it in the slightest.

There are numerous legal ways to resist the draft. There are even many organizations that provide that assistance. If I were vulnerable to the draft, I would check with those organizations for techniques—but then I'd consult an attorney to be sure that the loopholes hadn't been closed by the organization's own activities.

If you want to avoid taxes or regulations, there are always ways to do so without being vulnerable to bad consequences—no matter where you are, no matter what government you're dealing with.

LEGALLY OR ILLEGALLY?

Sooner or later you'll have to make a decision regarding your willingness to obey laws.

There's a normal reluctance to break laws. You can easily feel that you're contributing to the decay of your country, or that you're making yourself vulnerable.

However, there are thousands of once-rich Cubans who wish today that they'd been willing to commit the crime of sending their funds out of Cuba before the government confiscated them. They either thought they were helping their country by keeping their funds at home, or they counted on laws they thought would prevent confiscation, or they didn't want to take the risks involved in smuggling their funds out.

Their views have been shared by people in countries all over the world—people who always thought, "It's different here." They failed to realize that no government obeys laws. It will change, overrule, ignore, or defy them whenever they get in its way. To count on the law to protect you is a grave mistake.

Recognize, also, that you undoubtedly break laws continually. It's almost impossible to drive a car without breaking traffic laws. And most other kinds of laws are filled with contradictions that make nearly everyone a lawbreaker just by going about his own business.

To determine whether or not to break a law, the only consideration should be the consequences to yourself. What is the risk involved? What would happen if you're caught? How much are you gaining by breaking the law?

As you evaluate those consequences, don't overlook your own emotional nature. Don't do something that will make it impossible for you to sleep nights. The money saved may not be worth the anxiety.

But don't be swayed by considerations of patriotism,

"law and order," or national solidarity. Those things are only slogans designed to further the government's interests at the expense of yours.

In my own case, I've *had* to handle things legally. By writing books like this one, I forego the anonymity that would allow me more flexibility. I've chosen to write the books and obey the laws because the books increase my income enough to make the choice profitable.

As it is, however, I've always managed to pay little or no income tax—just by using the government's own laws to my advantage. There are more than enough loopholes to reduce my tax bill to a minimum.

Your decision will be based upon considerations appropriate to you.

Even if you do things legally, it's still best *not* to advertise what you're doing. Often the legality of a technique is determined arbitrarily by a tax collector or a judge. If you flaunt your activities, that could influence a decision against you. And when a loophole is publicized enough, the government may move to close it.

ILLEGAL METHODS

If you're considering breaking a law, check first to determine the legal consequences. It may be something that involves no fines or penalties—but it could also be something very costly. You should have that information *before* you act.

For most things you might want to do there's probably little danger. All you need to do is check the consequences and then go ahead and do it.

A typical example of this is the regulation that prohibits American citizens from owning gold. Many people are upset about it, and movements have been organized to pressure Congress to legalize gold ownership.

Meanwhile, plenty of Americans go ahead and buy gold anyway. Some of them do it legally by taking advantage of the loophole that permits ownership of gold coins. But others buy gold bullion without making a fuss about it.

Several foreign bankers have told me that many of their American clients own gold bullion. None of them has ever been harassed or prosecuted by the U.S. government.

In fact, to the best of my knowledge, no American has been fined or sent to jail for owning gold. If the gold is kept outside the country, it can't even be confiscated. The few cases of governmental action have been against large companies, where millions of dollars' worth of gold were involved.

Taxes can be evaded in many ways, too. Some of those ways are risky, but many of them involve very little chance of disclosure.

I imagine that many individuals make sure that they receive a good part of their income in cash, and then report only enough of that to justify their general living standards. The rest is salted away somewhere.

And I'm sure there must be thousands or millions of people who have never filed an income-tax return. They probably work in ways that eliminate the need to have taxes withheld or the need to have a Social Security number.

Many people use foreign banks to handle their financial affairs in ways that won't be reported in the U.S. Others simply cheat on their returns in ways that don't involve penalties.

These and other methods will continue to be profitable—so long as the people who use them don't try to get together and organize their activities. A little research can uncover a wide variety of avenues of tax evasion.

Then there are all the little irritants of governmental regulation—compulsory schooling laws, zoning laws, licenses, etc. If you gripe about them or campaign against them, you probably won't get anywhere. But use a little imagination and they don't have to control you.

For instance Karl Hess decided he didn't want to attend high school—despite the compulsory schooling laws. So he registered at two different schools, then filled out transfer slips from each of them. Authorities at each school assumed he was at the other and no one ever bothered him about it again.[2]

There are many, many private schools operating now, in many parts of the country, that aren't legitimatized by the various state compulsory schooling laws. I know of one in which all of its three hundred students are legal truants, and less than one half of its teachers have legal credentials; but its high academic results have made the school practically impervious to prosecution.

If you want to start a new business, don't go looking for all the licenses and regulations you're supposed to observe. Just operate. Try to arrange your business so that you can contact your prospects without public fanfare—and you may never come to the attention of the authorities. But if you do, the worst that could happen is that you'll have to do what you would have done at the outset anyway.

DEALING WITH GOVERNMENT

At some time you may need to decide whether or not it's in your self-interest to deal directly with the government—accept subsidies, sell to the government, buy from it, or work for it.

Such decisions are purely subjective, and you have to decide in a way that comfortably suits you.

In my own case, I've decided to avoid the government as much as possible. I use government roads and the post office because the government has declared monopolies in those fields, and that makes the alternatives many times costlier. But I've decided against accepting normal subsidies like "free" schooling, health care, mortgage guarantees, etc.

In general, government services are usually of very low quality. I often wonder, for example, if *no* education

[2] *National Observer,* March 1, 1971, p. 18.

might not be better than some of the "free" education I see.

Most people agree that you can't get something for nothing. And yet, I think they might also assume that what they get from the government doesn't cost them anything. There's always a price to pay, however. Even a thief who thinks he's obtained his haul costfree won't give *you* any of it without wanting something in return. And that goes for the government, too.

Government services involve obligations, red tape, and the need to put your name on a list as a "grateful" recipient of the government's favors. The gifts are always presented with plenty of strings attached; I don't want the strings, and I don't want to depend upon something that may be taken away from me tomorrow.

I don't think that most people recognize the strings and the prices, however. And part of the problem may come from thinking that money is the only cost to be considered.

For example, Abbie Hoffman's book *Steal This Book* lists hundreds of ways of getting free goodies from the government—along with ways of cheating companies. But in most of the examples cited, you have to exert devious, risky, and involved efforts to get the supposedly "free" benefits. For most people, it would be far less costly to pay the normal market prices of the stolen benefits.

My life is less cluttered as long as I simply avoid the government wherever possible. I find it easy to accept and pay normal prices as they occur—without wasting a great deal of time trying to circumvent the price by dealing through the government.

And, too, I see no reason to wage war against the government. Its employees are simply doing what each thinks best for himself—just as I'm doing for myself. Our methods may be different, but each of us is seeking his own happiness.

So I see no reason to be indignant over new or old

laws, no reason to campaign against injustice or inefficiency, no reason to waste my life fighting something that's always been here and probably always will be.

How you will deal with the government will be up to you. My observations have been mentioned only to illustrate the *kinds* of decisions one needs to consider in evaluating his relationship with the government.

YOUR COOPERATION

Governments invariably call upon their citizens to cooperate in efforts for the "public good." They want you to sacrifice to help solve economic crises, foreign-trade problems, and military conflicts; but these things were caused originally by government intervention. Even so, the calls can seem compelling, and social pressure can build on behalf of patriotic efforts.

I don't believe that you do anything for your country by fighting in a war (*any* war), giving up your money, or sacrificing in any way.

The national economy is a typical example of the government trying to solve a problem of its own making. During the past few years the American dollar has been sinking in international exchange, the economy has revealed critical problems, and inflation has proceeded unchecked. Politicians and economists would like you to believe that these problems are caused by gold speculators, greedy businessmen, powerful labor unions, or weak regulations.

They're not. They're the direct result of governmental interference in the economy. And any citizen who rallies to the government's solutions by rejecting his self-interest is making a futile sacrifice.

No matter how the problems are explained, it *is* important to deposit your money in a foreign bank while you still can; it *is* important to withhold as much as possible of your money from taxes. The economy will go its own inevitable way—regardless of what you do. But at least you can protect yourself.

There's no reason for you to go under if the government does.[3]

Whatever the issue, whatever the government's program, whatever the public acceptance, you can always accomplish more for your own life by withholding your support and using your resources on your own.

But do it quietly and anonymously. There's no reason to make a public issue of your views; that won't accomplish anything.

FREEDOM

It's not hard to be free of government—as long as you concentrate upon the direct alternatives available to you. It requires only a little initiative and imagination.

It may *seem* difficult, however, if you engage in political action to try to change what you don't like. You may feel quite helpless if you think you must convince everyone that things must be changed. But the objective of freedom is quite realistic; only the methods have been wrong.

Don't be awed by the government.

Don't confront it directly.

Don't organize.

If you act on your own, legally or illegally, there's a great deal you can do to be free of the government. And there's no reason to feel ashamed, unpatriotic, wicked, or guilty about it.

What you do to support the government contributes nothing to your own welfare nor to the welfare of society. What you do for yourself at least contributes to the happiness of one very important individual.

I like the way that Lysander Spooner put it:

[3] My reasons for these observations and my suggestions for protection are detailed in my book *You Can Profit from a Monetary Crisis*—which is listed in the Bibliography, along with other sources of protection.

. . . whoever desires liberty should understand these vital facts, viz.: 1. That every man who puts money in the hands of a "government" (so called), puts into its hands a sword which will be used against himself, to extort more money from him, and also to keep him in subjection to its arbitrary will. 2 That those who will take his money, without his consent, in the first place, will use it for his further robbery and enslavement, if he presumes to resist their demands in the future.[4]

When you withhold money from the government, you're acting as you would when you lock your home at night to protect it against thieves. In either case, you're acting to preserve what is yours from those who would like to take it without your consent.

And just as you can easily protect your home by using a watch dog, the right locks, or a burglar alarm, so can you protect your funds and your freedom from the government—if you'll direct your attention toward that goal.

The savings can be tremendous. If you need any incentive, determine how much you've paid in taxes for the past year (or five or ten years), then make a list of all the things you could have bought with that money.

The freedom is yours, the money is yours, the opportunity is yours—once you turn your attention toward yourself.

And your purpose will be as noble as any man could find—the advancement of your own happiness.

[4] *No Treason*, p. 20.

17

Freedom from
Social Restrictions

IT'S EASY TO FEEL that you have no chance to live your own life, that society imposes too many restrictions upon you. Employers, friends, lovers, family, and strangers seem to gang up on you to tell you how you must live.

Of course, "society" is a nonentity. It has no mind, no interests, no motivations. It is simply a collection of many *different* individuals who have different minds, interests, and motivations. So "society" can't restrain you.

The problems come from individuals—people who want you to act in certain ways and cause problems for you if you don't.

I think that the first step in freeing yourself from social restrictions is the realization that there is no such thing as a "safe" code of conduct—one that would earn everyone's approval. Your actions can always be condemned by *someone*—for being too bold or too apathetic, for being too conformist or too nonconformist, for being too liberal or too conservative.

So it's necessary to decide *whose* approval is important to you. If you just assume that you must have the approval of those nearest to you, social restrictions will be a very real problem.

But there are millions of people within your reach—

people of all different types. Included in those millions are undoubtedly many people who wouldn't demand the artificial attitudes you may think you have to display. They would want you as you really are.

I've often heard someone say that if such people exist, he's never seen them. But the problem is usually that he hasn't looked in the right places, or that he's given those people no chance to see *him*.

If you want to find someone who is much like yourself in attitude, tastes, and interests, you have to look where such a person is likely to be found. And you can't expect him to recognize you if you hide your identity behind a mask in order to get along with the people you're with.

Obviously, if you like rock music, you aren't likely to meet a kindred soul at the opera house. In the same way, if you're looking for someone who's honestly selfish and individualistic, you're not likely to find him at meetings of the local Improvement League or the Young Democrats Club.

Whatever your personal standards, the best place to find like-minded people is the same place where *you* would most like to be. If you crave companionship that's more intellectual, for example, you might try college or night-school courses in the subjects that have always interested you.

And since you could also run into potential friends almost anywhere, it's important to display your standards openly and honestly *wherever* you are. Only then can others recognize you as a kindred soul.

For if you wear a "socially acceptable" mask, those whom you seek will walk right by you. And those whom you *do* attract with the mask will only add to the pressure that you be something other than yourself.

If you make your own actions consistent with the standards you really admire, you'll know which people are compatible—just by their reactions to you. Those who disapprove will seek someone different to be with, and those who have standards similar to yours will react favorably toward you.

In effect, you let others tell you about themselves through their reactions to what you are.

So it's important to reveal yourself as you really are. If you're ambitious and show it, people who appreciate ambition are more likely to notice you. Or if you're careful to respect the property of others and clearly want the same treatment for your own property, you're less likely to wind up with thieving or freeloading friends.

When you act as *you* want to act, you stand a far greater chance of meeting the people who could be valuable to you. But when you let others determine your conduct, you acquire nothing but restrictions.

THE ALTERNATIVES

At this point, standing up for yourself might seem like a gamble with long odds against you, but I've never known anyone who's used this principle without achieving spectacular results. And this way offers hope and opportunity; hiding your identity offers nothing but more restrictions.

I think that many people hide their identity, tolerate restrictions, and remain in bad relationships because they're afraid of being lonely. But I wonder what they mean by "lonely." Aren't they *very* lonely when they deal with people who don't understand and appreciate them? I know *I'd* be lonely in such a situation.

I've also been lonely sometimes while looking for compatible people. But that loneliness was usually short-lived and more than rewarded by the discovery of people who wanted me for what I am. Around them, I *am* understood and appreciated in a way I never could have been among people with different standards.

There are many, many people in the world. You don't have to please any one person. There are other employers, other business prospects, other potential friends, lovers and spouses.

And when you find them, you'll have relationships that

impose no restrictions upon you. You'll be among people who will *want* you to be as you are.

YOUR VALUE

As you look for compatible people, it might be important to remind yourself that you have more value to offer than those around you may have led you to believe. They might have rejected much that is a part of your nature (or would have rejected it if you'd allowed it to be seen).

That can lead you to believe that you're out of touch with the world. And your lonely feelings can be worsened as you look at the popular trends, fashions, and interests—if those things aren't what you want.

You can believe that if you don't dance the new dances, no one will think you're much fun. Or if you don't join in the cries for "ecology," no one will think you're very knowledgeable. Of if you haven't been to an orgy, no one could think you're sexy.

But the popular trends are only a part of the General Market. In fact, they're usually not even representative of the majority of people; they are simply given a lot of publicity.

There are plenty of people who dance in the old way— or who don't dance at all. There are undoubtedly millions of Americans who don't join social causes and couldn't care less about your involvement in them. And I suspect that plenty of people still participate in sex on the old one-to-one basis.

I once met a young woman who had very long, lovely, wavy hair. I complimented her, but she replied that she was trying to straighten it. When I asked why, she said, "Wavy hair isn't fashionable these days; everyone likes straight hair."

Well, *I* much preferred her wavy hair, but then maybe I wasn't enough of a market to please her. So I pointed out that in the city of Vancouver (where we both live), there are perhaps 100,000 eligible men and about the same number of eligible women.

If straight hair is more popular, maybe as many as 90 percent of the men prefer it. If most all the women have straight hair, those 100,000 women will be competing for the attentions of 90,000 men.

So she could be one of 100,000 women competing for the attentions of 90,000 men. Or she could leave her hair the way it is and be uniquely attractive to 10,000 men. The odds are far greater in her favor when she's in a minority than when she tries to be part of the majority.

What she didn't realize was that her differences can often be her most powerful marketing assets. There's no reason to create artificial differences, but there's also no reason to suppress natural differences. By being willing to be in a minority, she could do away with most of the competition for the market that was hers.

FINDING OTHERS

What you are is the most valuable asset you possess for finding others.

And the best way to find those people is to *advertise* what you really are. Not by running an ad in the newspaper, but by being honest about who you are.

No matter where you go, you never know if someone you're seeking might see you. What a shame it would be if that person passed you by because you didn't reveal the qualities that both you and he admire most.

To reveal those qualities, you have to be willing to accept the disapproval of those you *aren't* seeking. It takes courage to overcome the embarrassment, self-consciousness, and even ridicule that might result from honest exposure of your nature—*at first*. But that shouldn't last long; soon, you'll form associations that are far more rewarding than what you've tolerated in the past.

If you've been hiding your collection of James Bond books for the sake of your cultural friends, get them out, go to "007" movies, and be free to enjoy yourself and find the people who won't pressure you. Chances are you won't miss the evenings of "culture" and you'll soon forget the people you weren't in tune with.

And why should you suppress your desires when you're having sexual intercourse? That way you'll *never* experience it in the way you dream of it. Do it the way you've always wanted to do it—cry or laugh or shout if you want to—ask for what you want. Sure, *someone* may laugh at you, deny you, or even condemn you. But is *that* the person who can fulfill your dreams? One of these times someone's going to respond enthusiastically and gratefully—and you'll know you've found someone wonderful.

The best method of advertising is simply to live the way *you* want to live.

Once you see the benefits of doing things *your* way, you may want to extend this practice to every area of your life. You might be encouraged to start handling your job the way you've always wanted to but for which you'd assumed there was no market.

And you might take seriously the thought that somewhere out there is someone with whom you could *happily* spend the rest of your life.

You are what you are. Your greatest pleasures will be those you experience when you can be yourself completely. Only then will you be free to enjoy every good thing the experience has to offer you. And you'll be more likely to find those experiences if you act sincerely at all times.

Being yourself is actually a skill. It takes time to become thoroughly acquainted with yourself, to throw off a lifetime of pressures, to relax and accept what you see in yourself (no matter how it may conflict with social standards), and to learn to act in ways consistent with your nature.

Advertising is a skill, too. It takes practice to learn how to advertise yourself. There are techniques to acquire and to practice until they become comfortable.

One of those techniques is to emphasize your differences. Try to reveal frequently the things about yourself that distinguish you from most others.

Your best prospects will respond when they see in you something they want that hasn't been available before. So advertise what makes you unique and what is most important to you—and those who respond favorably will most likely be the ones you're looking for. If others respond unfavorably, they're simply disqualifying themselves from your interest.

What is commonly thought of as good advertising is usually very ineffective advertising. Superlatives—words like "best," "quality," or "sensational"—have little impact. Most people know intuitively that it may not mean "best" for the prospect.

Good advertising isn't flashy or imposing. Simply learn to reveal your qualities as they are appropriate to the situation. Let your differences be brought out in conversations—without trying to demonstrate that you're different.

I can give you a good example. For years, whenever it was appropriate in conversations, lectures, and writing, I've casually mentioned one or more things such as: I'm single; I have no interest in governments, groups, crusades, or religions; I'm crazy about opera and other forms of classical music; I'm lazy and have learned to live with it and enjoy it; and I see nothing wrong with being selfish.[1]

I'm never evangelical about these things. I simply let them be known, one at a time, as appropriate.

Of course, I *could* join in the usual conversational attacks upon greed and selfishness, act as if I were a fervent believer in God and country, show my interest in the prevailing social issues. But where would that get me? My competition would be overwhelming and my rewards inappropriate to me.

Far better to be honest. By doing so, I've been approached by many individuals who were glad to find that they had a friend in what they had thought was an alien world.

---

[1] See how easy that was.

In fact, I've also made many friends whose ideas are considerably different from mine in some matters. They're quite willing to accept the things we have in common and leave the other matters alone. They don't pressure me to change my views—probably because I'm not self-conscious about them and therefore not a likley convert.

A NATURAL MONOPOLY

As I've indicated, far from cutting down your market, revealing yourself as you are *increases* your best market—whether you're concerned about personal or business relationships.

I was once asked by another writer if the uniqueness of my ideas didn't make me lonely. Wouldn't I feel more comfortable if more writers agreed with my views?

Obviously, no. My ideas may be the opposite of the popular views. But that doesn't mean there's no market for me. My market is bigger than it would be if I joined the crowd in an attempt to sell the more popular viewpoints.

My first book, published in 1970, suggested that the dollar would be devalued and that the economy was in bad shape—the opposite opinion from literally dozens of contemporary books on the subject. By looking only for a publisher who already shared my viewpoint, I spared myself the grief of being rejected by the more orthodox publishers. The second one I contacted bought the book eagerly.

When it was published, it far outsold any of the books that expressed the more popular opinions. The other authors may have felt comfortable in their conformity, but they didn't make as much money from their books.

Should I feel sad that I held the minority opinion? There were literally millions of Americans who felt as I did about the future and who wanted suggestions for dealing with a sagging dollar and a vulnerable economy. They were an eager market and I was the only one offering anything to it.

There's no one in the world exactly like you. And when you find the market that wants what you are, your position is as solid as you could ever hope for. You have a *natural monopoly* in that market—one that exists just because of what you are and requires no artificial devices to limit competition.

When you fight to compete with the crowd, competition is all around you and there's no way you can keep it out. But when you emphasize what *you* are, your market won't want anyone but you.

When you find the lover who's been looking for you, you won't need to restrict competition in any way—for no one else will be able to provide what that person needs most. Any exposure to others will only point up your unique value by comparison.

When you emphasize your unique professional talents, your customers won't be interested in the competition because it won't be offering what you offer.

In any area of life, you have a natural monopoly of the unique combination of traits that you possess. The only effective way to rule out competition is to find the market that wants your qualities above all others. And you'll find it and keep it by having the courage to stand up for what you are.

When you find that market, you'll wonder why you ever restricted yourself in order to get along with those who were incompatible with you.

DEALING WITH RESTRICTIONS

Most social restrictions are self-inflicted. Your life is yours to live as you choose. If you give up what you want because of someone's disapproval, you have only yourself to blame—because *you* made the choice; he didn't. He told you what he wanted, but he has no power to enforce it.

You can do with your life what you want. You don't have to work at a "normal" job. You can try your luck at anything. Do you want to be an artist? Tour guide? Gigolo? Do what you want to do—so long as you can make enough to survive while you're doing it.

You don't have to spend money on a new car and a respectable home to impress your neighbors, business associates, and friends. Why should you? Let them eat TV dinners in their new cars while you use your money to take the vacation you've always wanted.

Do you want to grow a beard or have longer hair? Do it. If your employer objects, look for a job where that's not a problem. Don't expect your employer to forsake his self-interest for you; but neither is there any reason for you to forsake yours for him.

If your social contacts object, so what? How important are they to you? If their approval is based upon matters of fashion, are you sure they have anything to offer you?

Is it necessary to go to parties and attend other social functions in order to be accepted? That depends upon whose acceptance you're seeking. Go where *you* want most to go; you're most likely to meet the people you seek there.

Do you want to smoke marijuana? Do it. Since it's legally prohibited, don't do it at the Policeman's Ball—but that might not be where you'd expect to find new friends anyway. Don't make a social movement out of your personal tastes and you won't get into trouble. Just smoke it quietly with those you value and trust.

Do some people get upset when you express your emotions—if you cry when you're moved, laugh when you see something ridiculous? Don't be bullied by those who say you shouldn't be so emotional. Find those who understand such things and appreciate your honesty.

Do those in your social circle make you feel pressured to live up to certain intellectual standards? If so, you may be in the wrong place. It might be that you haven't yet accurately identified your own beliefs and standards—and these people seemed to be the ones you wanted. One way to tell is by noticing if that kind of pressure exists. If it does, keep trying to recognize yourself more clearly, and then look for people who are more like you.

There isn't any society to disapprove, to disallow, to denounce or to ostracize you. It's a myth. I wonder how many millions of lives have been tossed on the junkpile to appease an entity that never existed.

Be honest with yourself and with others and act toward others as you'd like to be treated, and you'll have a far greater chance to attract people valuable to you. The others are unimportant to your future—if your future is to be free.

There's a beautiful world out there. Why clutter it up with relationships that don't belong in your life?

It's an easy life. Why complicate it by trying to be all things to all people?

Adopt the image that's most effective—your own.

Whoso would be a man must be a nonconformist.
                                        —RALPH WALDO EMERSON

18

Freedom from
Bad Relationships

WE'VE SEEN THAT IT'S FOOLISH to waste time trying to deal with incompatible people. There are plenty of people around who would want you to be as you are.

That doesn't mean, however, that you're likely to find individuals with whom you'll be 100 percent compatible—with the exact same tastes, values, attitudes, and ideas that you have. You're more likely to find individuals with whom you'll have one or more important things in common.

In the areas that you have in common, you'll please the other person most by doing what you want to do. That's the way it should be. No sacrifices are required by either person.

Such relationships can make your life far more exciting. They provide something to look forward to, something to enjoy, and the wonderful glow that comes from knowing that someone else is seeing and enjoying things in much the same way you do.

Unfortunately, such good relationships can deteriorate into bad ones. What was once a good friendship can deteriorate into a relationship of obligations, conflicts, and distrust. A love affair that started with an ecstatic glow can degenerate into a forum for arguments. A business relationship that began as a source of opportunity can decay into a bitter conflict of interests.

Why do such things happen? Is it because *no* relationship can be expected to last? Is it just impossible for people to get along indefinitely?

I don't think so. I think the problem has to do with the way relationships are handled. Once again, too many assumptions are taken for granted—and they create problems because the assumptions aren't realistic.

LABELS AGAIN

The biggest problem probably stems from the ease with which you can *label* a relationship and then, in effect, treat the individual as if he were the label. One is called a "friend" or "partner" or "lover" or "wife." And the labels imply subtle expectations concerning the role the person is expected to play in your life.

For example, a "friend" is someone who'll lend you money when you're in trouble; a "wife" is someone who'll cook, clean house, make love when you want to, and center her life around your family.

But what the label requires may not be in the self-interest of the person involved, so conflicts can result. "Loyalty" is demanded and the relationship becomes a source of aggravation for everyone concerned.

Suppose you meet someone, become friends with him, enjoy his company for several weeks, and then are confronted with a request to take care of his Great Dane while he's on vacation. That's the beginning of a new relationship. What had previously been completely beneficial to you now becomes a source of obligations and conflicts of interest. You'll never be able to relax completely and enjoy that person again.

If your wife makes friends with a neighbor and then expects the two families to take their vacations together, you may wind up taking your vacation in the Group Trap. The individuality of all the other members of the families will be eroded by the attempt to enlarge upon a simple enjoyable relationship between two women.

If you expect your secretary to wait on you hand and foot, do your Christmas shopping for you, and lie to your wife when you're out of the office, you're probably asking for more than she bargained for, and you may lose what you had hired—a good secretary.

Relationships can be fruitful only when they're in the self-interest of each person. Unfortunately, the normal labels and assumptions go far beyond that—and so problems develop.

In this chapter, we'll explore the general principles that can keep good relationships from falling apart. And in the next four chapters, we'll apply those principles to love affairs, family situations, and businesses.

PRINCIPLES

There are three principles that I find helpful to remember:

1. *Don't think in terms of groups.* As we saw in the Group-Trap chapter, groups don't think, act, or have motivations; only individuals do. It's misleading to think of a group as being of one mind and purpose. Each individual is different from every other individual.

2. *Limit the relationship to what you have in common.* Don't expect more from the relationship than what is in the self-interest of each person involved. When you extend the relationship beyond the areas of mutual self-interest, someone will have to sacrifice.

3. *Don't attempt to perpetuate a relationship by contract.* Change is inevitable. Alternatives, knowledge, and desires change. Any relationship should last only as long as it's beneficial to each party. If an individual is required to continue in a relationship past the time it's beneficial to him, he loses. And it won't be possible for him to satisfy

the needs of anyone else in the relationship if he's acting out of duty and not enthusiasm.

Don't make the relationship an end in itself that must be perpetuated at all costs. That will lead to demands for sacrifices in the name of "making our marriage work," "keeping our friendship," or "making the business succeed." Relationships are only means to the ends desired by each of the people involved; when the ends are no longer served, the relationship should end.

In commercial situations, contracts are sometimes required. This is usually because the supplier doesn't want to make a given investment unless he's assured of an appropriate return on his investment. This can be handled, however, by including in the contract a provision for early termination, accompanied by a cash payoff that provides the appropriate profit for the investment made.

The three principles are saying, in effect, don't make an institution of a relationship. Don't add inappropriate activities to it, don't try to fit it within a traditional context, don't add duties and obligations to it that are irrelevant to the desires of the people involved. Let the relationship evolve as it will—as mutual self-interest leads it.

BEER BUSTS

Let's apply these principles to an example. Suppose three men with the unimaginative names of A, B, and C find that they have something in common. They discover that they all like to drink beer, and they enjoy one another's company and conversation when they drink.

Suppose they find that they greatly enjoy getting together on Saturday nights to drink beer. All well and good.

Our first principle suggests that they are still individuals, not a group. Neither of them should allow his self-interest to be submerged into an artificial entity known as "the group."

For relationships with one another are a small part of

their lives. Each of them has many, many interests and concerns apart from beer and conversation about the football scores.

And since each of them is a different person, their relationships with one another will be different. A and B will probably have some things in common that B and C don't have. To think of the group as a single entity might prevent A and B from taking advantage of the common interests that concern only them.

They might both enjoy bowling, for example. If they feel they can bowl together only if it's agreeable to C (who prefers golf), they'll lose an opportunity to add to their enjoyment.

There are actually three separate relationships—A and B, B and C, A and C.

The second principle suggests that the relationships be limited to only what the participants have in common. To enlarge the relationships beyond the small areas in common is to open the door to many conflicts of interest.

For example, if A expects B and C to help him paint his garage ("What's a friend for?"), it will probably be a loss to all three. For one thing, B and C may be lousy garage painters; A might lose by not paying the necessary price to have it done right.

And for B and C, the relationship is no longer just good beer and good conversation. Now it includes duties and obligations. No one will be able to relax completely any longer, for he'll never know when he'll be called upon to set aside his own self-interest. Even if he refuses such requests, it will be a strain on the relationship.

The third principle says that you shouldn't try to perpetuate a relationship by contract. In a burst of exuberance and good fellowship, the three buddies might agree to meet together every Saturday night for the next ten years. But that would probably be a big mistake.

For all three of them are changing constantly. Each of them is discovering new alternatives, new motivations, and new interests. One of them may decide that he prefers wine. Another might even meet a girl someday and decide that she offers him more than his Saturday-night buddies.

To attempt to preserve the relationship by contract is only going to bend each of them out of shape. In fact, other common interests might be suppressed by the fixed structure of the relationship; as long as they're committed to one routine, they might ignore other things they could do together that would be more enjoyable.

Each relationship should be taken on its own merits. The relationship should evolve as it will—with no preconceived goals, structure, expectations, or rules.

Our friends A, B, and C don't have to share uncommon interests. They can limit their relationships to the enjoyment of the things they do have in common (including their dumb names).

The beer-bust example is rather obvious. So much the better that it is. For these same principles can be subverted subtly and easily in more complicated relationships. And when they're subverted, problems develop—and what was once a source of pleasure and opportunity can turn into a loss of freedom.

TAKE THINGS AS THEY ARE

You're bound to be disappointed when you apply labels to people and relationships and then expect them to live up to the labels.

Your definition of a "friend" may be considerably different from the one your friend has. What you expect from him may be far more than he's willing to give—regardless of what you may feel you've done for him.

Relationships don't have to be structured, perpetuated, tied down. They'll work out best if you let them evolve as they will—limiting your expectations to what is, and continues to be, *mutually* beneficial.

When you find a friend who's intellectually stimulating, enjoy him for the excellent discussions you can have. But don't expect him to help rearrange your furniture or lend you money. Those things are separate parts of *your* life, not a part of his.

If you need money and can't borrow it at a bank or finance company, don't jeopardize good friendships by appealing for money on the basis of loyalty. Offer terms that would make it worth more to a friend to lend the money than to use it himself. Make sure the terms are such that he'd be *eager* to be involved in the deal—even if his friend weren't to be the borrower. If that isn't possible, go without the money; it can't be as important as a good friendship. Choose between the money and friendships; you won't get both.

If you keep the three principles in mind, you can let each relationship grow naturally. You'll probably avoid most of the conflicts, arguments, and burdens that most people take for granted in their important relationships. The other person will be a positive benefit to your life.

If the relationship grows and seems to be broadening, approach each new area of mutual interest on its own merits. Don't lump activities together simply because you like someone. You'll continue to like him more if there are no dealings between you that aren't entered for their specific value to each of you.

If you find a friend who's closer to you than anyone you've known, don't get carried away and try to impose your separate, different tastes upon him. If you fall in love, don't expect that every interest, every decision, and every value will be exactly the same between you.

If you can accept the *differences* that exist between you and those you care for, you can make the most of what you have together. If you try to overcome the differences, you'll only make it harder to enjoy the things you *do* have together.

GRANTING FREEDOM

Recognize each person you associate with for what he is, what specifically he has to offer you, and what he might value in you. Don't confuse the issue by bringing in external matters that can only reduce the value of the relationship.

Relationships shouldn't be sources of restrictions. And they won't be if you take them as they are.

Perhaps the three principles can be summed up as one important principle: *Let others be free.*

Don't try to tie them down with obligations, loyalties, duties, commitments, or appeals of sympathy. Make it your policy that you don't expect anyone to do what isn't in his self-interest.

Don't try to restrict your lover's activities. Don't try to make your spouse give up his interests for you. Don't give your friends reason to feel that you expect anything from them but what is in their self-interest to give.

If you let others be free, you'll be a rare person—and a valuable one. You'll be in demand because you won't create the conflicts and arguments that so many people have had from others.

Your freedom is just as important, of course. You have to learn to say "no" in a way that doesn't create strain and conflict. When you learn that, others will usually respect *your* individuality.

Your freedom and the freedom of those you deal with are equally important to you. If people come to you because they *freely* want to, you'll receive more *genuine* love, friendship, understanding, and appreciation than you could possibly get by asking for it or demanding it.

Loneliness is never more cruel than when it is felt in close propinquity with someone who has ceased to communicate.　　　　　　　　　　—GERMAINE GREER

19

Freedom from Marriage Problems

THE GREATEST RESTRICTIONS upon many people are those imposed by marriage and family problems.

Some are dominated by parents. Others are trapped by duties and obligations to relatives. And others are entangled in the problems of raising children.

The most common restrictions come from marriages. Conflicts of interest develop between husband and wife; each feels that he's getting less than he wants out of life, perhaps because of restrictions imposed upon him by the other.

There are probably no subjects as emotionally charged as those of marriage and family. The "sanctity of marriage" and the pressures of parents and in-laws are only two of the many cultural expectations involved in these subjects.

And labels seem to be applied more readily and restrictively here than elsewhere. A "wife" is expected to give up her career and her own interests on behalf of her husband and children. A "husband" must be a good provider. And a "son" is someone who's supposed to make his parents proud of him—by his parents' standards, of course.

The problem, as usual, is a type of trap—the acceptance of labels and cultural dogmas without recognizing that there are better alternatives available by which an individual can satisfy his desires.

Love, closeness, affection, family opportunities—all these things can be enjoyed without having to build elaborate, restrictive structures that destroy the independence of everyone concerned.

WHY PEOPLE GET MARRIED

Let's begin by noting the reasons *why* people get married. The most common reason, I suppose, is because they're in love. Labels can be very compelling, so it's assumed that once you're "in love" with someone, you should confirm it by getting married.

That isn't the only reason people get married, however. I couldn't possibly think of every motive for marriage, but here are a few of the well-known reasons:

1. To enhance a love relationship.
2. To confirm that one has "won" his lover—once and for all.
3. To achieve social respectability (such as to prove one's desirability or to satisfy one's desire to be known as the "head of a family").
4. To make sexual intercourse easily accessible.
5. To be financially supported.
6. To avoid loneliness.
7. To guarantee that someone will be around in one's old age.
8. To have children.
9. To escape the need to do something more challenging with one's life.
10. To have a housekeeper.

There are alternative ways to satisfy these objectives, but it's frequently assumed that the traditional marriage is the only way. So a license is obtained, a church is hired, some words are spoken, and vows are made.

The lovers assume they've made a contract with each other, but they haven't. They have obtained the permission of the government to be married and signed a contract with it. And the government has decided many of the terms of the relationship—financial arrangements (property laws), sexual rules (adultery laws), legal responsibilities, inheritance matters, etc.

If they ever decide to terminate the marriage, they will need the permission of the government—which may or may not be granted. Not only that, the conditions for termination may be different from what they were when they signed the contract.

It isn't necessary to become involved in such legal problems to fulfill the objectives of the relationship. Neither is it necessary to assume the normal burdens that accompany legal marriages.

A BETTER WAY

There are better ways to handle things. Let's look at how the objectives of a marriage can be better achieved without a marriage. We'll use the desire to enhance the love affair as the example, and then look at the other possible objectives later.

Let's imagine that you find yourself in a luscious romantic situation. You're involved with someone who seems to be everything you want. Your attitudes toward life are generally the same, you like to do many of the same things, you find yourself thinking about him a great deal of the time, you see him as physically attractive, your body is alive in anticipation of sexual union, and you feel the wonderful glow that tells you you're in love.[1]

With all these things going for you, you probably feel that this person is the best friend you've ever had. He understands and appreciates what you are and what you

[1] Unfortunately, the English language doesn't include a separate word to refer to an individual who could be of either sex. Instead, I'll use the words *he* or *him* in referring to someone who could be either a man or woman. I trust you'll make any necessary translation.

want. Each of you accepts and understands the differences between you.

Such a relationship is unusual—probably because most people never try to find someone so appropriate to themselves. But as long as we're going to base this example on a love relationship, we might as well make the love as real and satisfying as possible.

With so much going for you, I think it's safe to assume that the most important objective would be to preserve that love. Once having felt such a wonderful glow, who'd want to take any chance of losing it?

MAKING IT LAST

To make love last, let's see how the three principles we covered in the last chapter apply to the situation.

1. Don't think in terms of groups.
2. Limit the relationship to what you have in common.
3. Don't attempt to perpetuate the relationship by contract.

As the first principle indicates, you aren't a couple, a twosome, or anything but two separate, individual human beings who have found a great deal to enjoy together. No real merger can take place—because it's literally impossible to merge human beings—in thought, motivation, or emotion.

What exists is an overlapping of interests, attitudes, and feelings. And the most should be made of that.

But—as the second principle indicates—it's important not to try to merge the *un*common interests. You can't destroy the nature and self-interest of an individual; if you try to submerge it by making the marriage an end in itself, or by making the uncommon interests common, you're bound to get reactions other than what you'd hoped for.

You'll have common interests that sometimes require that you consult with each other to make decisions, but it's a mistake to think that you have to agree on everything.

To expect that is to make the marriage a compromise—and that leads to situations where one is expected to sacrifice for the other.

Sacrifice is often regarded as one of the main factors in a successful relationship, but it leads to a loss of value for the participants. And if freedom is living your life as you want to live it, we should hope for a better kind of relationship than one in which the participants must give up that freedom.

In effect, the success of the relationship will depend most upon the way *differences* between the individuals are handled. Must they result in compromise—or is there a better way? We'll see.

The third principle warns against trying to perpetuate a relationship by contract. Too often, it's hoped that marriage will make permanent the love that one feels when he marries.

Unfortunately, it doesn't work that way. Love isn't a trophy you can win at a wedding and then place in a showcase to represent a permanent victory. Love is an emotion. Emotions are involuntary reactions that occur as a result of who you are and what happens to you.

You can't guarantee the durability of an emotion. If you know yourself well, you're in a better position to *predict* your future emotional responses, but it isn't something you can guarantee.

You can't promise to love forever—and neither can your lover. You'll continue to love and be loved if each of you continues to provide what the other's emotional nature reacts to. If you don't get married, you'll have to continue to be that very special person in order to retain the other's love. If you *do* get married, the situation is exactly the same.

A contract to love can make it more difficult to get out of the relationship—because of the recriminations, accusations, and guilt resulting from broken promises. But it won't perpetuate the love that prompted the contract; so of what value is it?

In fact, if you get married, it may be even more diffi-

cult to perpetuate the love—because the pressure upon
you to feel love may be greater by virtue of the promises
and expectations. And that pressure can make it more difficult to relax and enjoy everything you have together in
whatever way it unfolds.

It's important, then, to keep things in perspective. Don't
assume that your separate selves will no longer exist because you're in love; don't try to force interests that aren't
mutual into the relationship; and don't attempt to perpetuate it by contract.

It's *especially* important to keep things in perspective
when you're consumed by love. It's a wonderful, fascinating emotion—which means it can be harder to make decisions with a clear recognition of the consequences.

Enjoy the present to the maximum, but be careful
about committing your future. And a common example of
the Emotional Trap is to commit one's future in an unrealistic way because of the love one feels in the present.

If love is wonderful (as I think it is), then you should
be particularly careful to do what will *preserve* it, not destroy it.

And the key to achieving that will be to preserve the
relationship *as it is now. Don't change it from a love relationship to something else.* Don't assume that your lover
should automatically become your business partner, your
housekeeper, your fix-it-man, your bookkeeper, your
necessary companion in your separate interests, your social image-builder or anything else. Keep him as your
lover—just as he is now.

If you want to retain the love you feel now, don't introduce into the relationship anything that doesn't facilitate
that love. Limit that relationship to matters of love—not
finance, household affairs, compromised interests, or duties.

MAKING THE MOST OF IT

As the love grows, you will probably want to take advantage of the deeper feelings by finding ways to be closer than you were before. That's the critical point of the relationship. At that moment, you'll either find a way to satisfy the specific desire you have—or you'll take on a number of irrelevant obligations that have nothing to do with what you really want from each other. Which way you choose will be critical to the future of the relationship.

So decide first what it is you want. Do you want to live together? Have more time together? Sleep together? Enjoy sexual intercourse together?

All of those things can be accomplished without a legal marriage and without unrelated obligations that could inhibit the growth of the relationship and the individuals in it.

If you want to live together, the answer is to live together.

That doesn't require a license, a ceremony, engraved announcements, a written contract, a blessing from anyone. All you have to do is to live together.

In most states, there are no laws forbidding adults from living together (usually unless one of them is legally married to someone else).

However, you won't avoid the problems of marriage simply by avoiding the legalities. Many people who live together encounter all the same difficulties, conflicts, and loss of love that married people do.

Common-law marriage isn't the answer. The answer is to make it a *non-marriage*. And to do that means that you do nothing—nothing that would attempt to change the individuality you took for granted before the new situation developed.

Most love relationships probably falter because the individuals in them are unable to handle the *differences* between them. A non-marriage recognizes those differences, allows for them, and thereby permits the feelings of love to grow rather than be stifled.

Neither of you becomes a different person because of the relationship. You don't each become half of a "union." Each of you is still an individual human being—with his own nature, work, property, interests, and ways of doing things.

To attempt to change that will drive you straight into the Identity Trap. You can't be anything other than yourself; if you try to be, you'll most likely lose the good feelings you once felt for the person who is now responsible for your having to change. And to tell yourself that you'll love someone whose presence requires that you be something other than yourself is to drive yourself into the Intellectual Trap—the attempt to make your feelings conform to an unrealistic pattern.

There's no reason why you can't love each other and still remain two individuals. In fact, if you could change the nature of the person you love, you'd wind up with someone other than the person you fell in love with.

One way love diminishes is through the vulnerability one feels to the differences of the other person. If you're tidy and he's messy, the requirement that you live in chaos can eat away at your affection for the person who causes that chaos. If you're frugal, it can destroy your good feelings for him if you have to watch him throwing your money away.

But none of that has to happen. It didn't happen before you married—or non-married. And it doesn't have to happen now.

TWO INDIVIDUALS

All you have to do is to continue the relationship as it was before—even if you're living together.

Each person should continue each of his own interests that are separate from the other's. If you like country music and he likes jazz, keep your separate phonographs and play the music in separate rooms. If he likes golf and you like tennis, continue playing your own games with the people you played with before.

If the differences between you are too great, the relationship probably wouldn't have lasted without your living together—and it won't last now. But if the differences didn't get in the way before you lived together, they don't have to get in the way now. And they *won't*—provided you *accept* the differences and allow for them.

Each person should continue to have his time alone, his own friends, his own interests. *The time spent together should be preserved for those things you enjoy together—* so that every moment together is a joy rather than a burden.

It is vital that each person continue to know that his life is of his own making—that he can choose for himself without being vulnerable to the different decision-making methods of someone else. If one person must be dependent upon the decisions of the other, he's involved in an indirect alternative. He must "make the other understand" or compromise or sacrifice. His freedom is lost through the Group Trap.

The non-marriage recognizes the sovereignty of each person. In a non-marriage, no one expects anyone else to act in any way but in his own self-interest. The non-marriage recognizes that you can find lasting love and happiness only with someone with whom the differences aren't great enough to make a lasting relationship impossible. And the non-marriage allows for those differences that do exist to continue without sacrifice of self-interest.

In a non-marriage, you simply continue being the person you were before you started living together. You continue to work where you want to work, pursue the interests that concern you most, and at the same time enjoy the opportunity to be closer to the one you love.

PROPERTY

This means you retain your own property, your own income, and make your own decisions. There's no need for joint decisions, because each decision will primarily concern one person and only incidentally the other.

It's just as unrealistic to merge your property as it is to try to merge your minds. And property is very important. The control of your own property is the most tangible expression of your freedom.

It's as important as your time—because, in fact, it's the same thing as your time. When someone destroys your property or steals it or usurps your decision-making control over it, he has taken from your life the amount of time necessary to earn that property or to replace it. If an individual's time is important, his property is just as important.

Only when you can control your time and property with direct alternatives are you free. If you must compromise your control by gaining someone else's agreement to use it, you don't really own it. And to whatever extent your freedom is compromised, your lover doesn't represent a positive value in your life.

If each party to a relationship continues to be sovereign and control his own property—and to respect the same for the other person—most of the typical problems of marriage will never arise.

ARRANGEMENTS

The fact that you live together doesn't have to interfere with that in any way. Each of you can continue to own what he has had before and to acquire new things. You wouldn't expect to control your neighbor's property—and there's no reason to control that of your lover.

You simply continue to treat each other as you did be-

fore you started living together. You never expect the
other person to forfeit what is his for your sake.

As new situations develop, you can handle them as you
would with anyone else. As things arise that concern both
of you, you can make mutually beneficial arrangements
between you. And, needless to say, *no* arrangements
should be made that *aren't* mutually beneficial.

If you want to live in the same house, make an arrangement. Some people handle it by splitting the household
expenses down the middle. I'm not too fond of that arrangement because it involves joint decisions—such as
how much will be spent, to whom, and for what.

I think it's better for one person to supply the house or
apartment (either buying or renting), provide the utilities,
cleaning services, etc., and then be a sub-landlord who
rents to the other. The sub-landlord then has the responsibility to see that things are taken care of through his own
decisions. None of your precious time together is wasted
trying to decide how large a sofa you can afford.

If the sub-landlord's methods are unacceptable to the
other person, then you aren't going to get along very well,
no matter how you handle it. But this way less time is
wasted taking care of decisions that could more easily be
made by one person alone.

The sub-rent can be negotiated to determine a price
acceptable to both. Again, if you can't agree upon a price,
then you wouldn't have been able to agree how much
money to spend if you had pooled your assets.

In other words, if differences show up in this type of arrangement, they would have shown up anyway. And this
way, the differences can be handled much more openly,
with a greater chance to be resolved without lingering resentments.

Neither one should expect the other to give up his self-
interest. There's no reason to be upset if you can't negotiate a particular new arrangement easily. You can always
revert to your previous arrangement and continue to enjoy
each other as you did before.

If you respect the sovereignty of your lover, you'll approach each new arrangement in the way you would with an outsider—with full respect for the other's self-interest. If you want your lover to keep house for you, you'll offer him enough to make it worth his while; you won't expect him to do it because of a label attached to him, or because he should "give a little."

If both parties want to work outside the home, the sub-landlord can arrange for periodic cleaning, a cook, or a housekeeper—and the sub-rent can reflect that service.

I strongly suggest that the housekeeping be done by a third person. Too often it's assumed that "we can't afford outside help," and the enjoyment of the relationship is jeopardized to save the few dollars involved.

Anything that comes up can be handled. All you have to do is to remember the sovereignty of each person, and you'll usually see a simple, obvious, natural way of handling every question. Just ask yourselves what you would do if you *weren't* living together, and that will probably suggest a simple solution.

Differences can be handled very easily that way. For example, if one of you is messy and the other tidy, you can have separate rooms within your home. You can still sleep together whenever you want to, but you won't have to live in a room that doesn't conform to your life style. The cost of the extra room will be insignificant if it helps to preserve the best of your relationship.

If you were living separately, you'd have to pay for separate rooms. If you're living together only to save money, then the preservation of your love is secondary. But if you're living together to enhance your love, that should always have the highest priority.

RULES

You can build your relationships with each other in any way you choose. There is only one rule in a non-marriage: *Don't ask either person to sacrifice his sovereignty.* Don't create situations that require joint control of property, time, or interests. Allow each person to live and grow and develop as his own self-interest leads him.

Other than that, there's no guidebook. What others choose to do might be best for them; but you'll have to determine what's best for you. Your relationship will be totally unique, because each of you is totally unique.

Always keep in mind that you're together because you love each other—and only for that reason. Keep all other relationships separate. If your lover is your sub-landlord, keep that relationship with him separate from your love relationship.

If you want your lover to stay home and keep house for you, don't appeal to his love for you. Appeal to his pocketbook and offer him what he needs to make it worth his while.

If your lover doesn't enjoy the same forms of entertainment you do, let each enjoy his own—and reserve your time together for the things you *do* enjoy together.

If you keep other things out of the love relationship, it will have a far, far better chance to succeed. Simply approach the matter as if you were single individuals (which you are), without accepting any of the normal assumptions concerning marriage. With that in mind, you can always work out arrangements that will suit each of you.

SEPARATION

If you should ever decide to part, you can part friends. You won't be involved in any of the financial haggling, accusations, bad feelings, desires for revenge, and recriminations that accompany most marital breakups. Each is still his own person with his own life and property; there's nothing to be untangled.

But by retaining the individuality of each person, it's more likely that the love between you will grow and deepen, rather than wither—as is normally expected. If you can't make it this way, it's extremely unlikely that the love would have survived in a normal marriage.

Just imagine the kind of relationship you'll have. *You'll be living with someone who's there because he'd rather be there than anywhere else in the world.*

You'll be free of the nagging conflicts that many married people take for granted. You won't be subject to the bad consequences that Group-Trap relationships create. You'll be responsible for yourself; you won't be a 50 percent partner in a collective you can't completely control.

The time you spend together will be devoted to enjoying each other—instead of haggling over details.

I think you'll find, too, that you'll have far fewer financial problems than most married couples have. The respect for sovereignty tends to eliminate most of the exuberant overspending that can characterize a marriage. You won't be relying upon the other person to bail you out of your financial problems. You'll be less likely to involve yourself in long-term mortgages and contracts—something married couples do easily because of the alleged "permanence" of the relationship.

Instead, you'll be more likely to enjoy each day as it comes—making the most of it without committing your future to satisfy emotional whims of the present.

You'll be living with your best friend—who'll continue to be your best friend instead of becoming your adversary. If there's a problem in the relationship, your best friend will want to know about it, to work with you to correct it if possible.

Neither party will feel that his burdensome marriage is his lot in life, so that he must suppress his resentment and put up with it, thus letting it get worse. Since he doesn't feel trapped, he won't feel that he has to try to take advantage of the other person—in order to make the best of a bad deal.

When you don't have to depend upon the other person's agreement to live as you want to, you can be far more benevolent toward him, far more understanding of him and his problems, far more anxious to do what's possible to help him make things right. In such circumstances, the initial feeling is more likley to grow and reach new levels of affection and excitement.

And none of this involves sacrifice or compromise. Why so many people think a happy marriage is based upon sacrifice, I'll never know. Life is to be lived, not sacrificed. You love someone because of the way he makes *you* feel, because of the way he enhances *your* life. If what you are doesn't do the same for him, no amount of sacrifice is going to make things right.

I've seen several non-marriages that are based upon this respect for self-interest and sovereignty. Invariably, they are simpler, more loving, more enjoyable relationships than the traditional kinds in which the participants must spend so much time working out decisions with each other.

You've probably heard the old saying that, in a marriage, you should expect to give 60% and get 40%. In a non-marriage, you should expect to give 40% and get at least 60%—and so should your lover. Why should either of you enter a relationship unless both of you profit from it?

EXISTING MARRIAGES

If you're already married, the same principle can be used to enhance your relationship.

If you honestly believe you already have the perfect relationship, skip over to the next chapter, for I have nothing to offer that might improve upon perfection.

But if you see ways in which the arrangement I've described could improve your relationship, it's not too difficult to convert to such a system. Only three things are required:

1. Terminate the legal contract—so that you have a two-way relationship instead of a three-way contract with the government. That means getting a divorce—which is only a legal formality.

2. Divide the property so that each thing is owned by one person or the other, thus recognizing individual sovereignty and removing the need for most joint decisions. Several ways to do this are described in Chapter 31.

3. Do everything possible to make it easy for each of you to be totally honest with the other. That will be the hardest part but also the most rewarding. Self-interests

can't be served if they can't be expressed. Once you're free to discuss everything openly and unashamedly, problems should be much more easily resolved.

Recognize that you don't have to do everything together. Each can pursue interests that are of no concern to the other. Think of yourselves as independent individuals who gain from being together in ways that are mutually satisfying.

LOVE CAN TRIUMPH

We've based this example of a non-marriage on a relationship that has love as its premise. At the beginning of this chapter I mentioned nine other common reasons why people get married. If you look over those reasons again, I think you can easily see how they would be affected by this type of system.

If the individual's freedom is important, he can achieve his objective through a non-marriage better than through a marriage. If his freedom isn't important, a normal marriage might be more advantageous—but such matters are outside the scope of this book.

The romantic legends of those who "live happily ever after" are always treated skeptically because it isn't normal for romance to last indefinitely. It's assumed that the initial glow and excitement will fade away with time and a more "mature" relationship will replace it—which is just a polite way of describing an uneasy compromise.

Such things *are* the rule because individuals are usually squarely in the Emotional Trap at the time important long-term decisions are made. Their "romantic" notions discourage them from wanting to think of what the relationship might be like a few years hence if handled in the normal ways.

Consequently, the romantic notions don't last very long. The romance fades and further confirms the opinion that love is at best a temporary thing.

But love, romance, excitement, and respect *are* possible.

They can grow rather than shrink. When you remove the cliché structures and attitudes, you're free to love each other, free to allow the seeds of your love to bloom and prosper—instead of trampling them under in the name of duty or marriage or sacrifice or social responsibility.

It's not difficult to use and enjoy both of your mental capabilities—your *emotions* that can bask in the pleasure of the present and your *intellect* that can protect your future. If you're infatuated with someone, enjoy it to the hilt—it's a wonderful feeling. But don't commit your future; there's no reason to.

If you know yourself well, you can eventually find the person whose self-interest most nearly matches yours. And when you find him, you'll have a future. But you never have to make the decision. You don't have to make a commitment, a plunge, an irrevocable decision of any kind.

Just let the relationship grow and develop on its own merits. Let things evolve as they will. If you reach a point where it seems you have more to gain by living together, do it. But you don't have to sign your life away for that; it just isn't necessary. To do so is to create a pressure for success that can be a significant way of destroying the natural affection you feel for each other.

Let things evolve. If you're with the wrong person, marriage won't make it right. But if you're with the right person, you may wake up one day to realize that you *do* have a lifetime relationship. Even then, there will be no decision to be made—all you'll have to do is to enjoy what you have.

You'll get to that point only if you recognize each of your sovereignties. That means recognizing the importance of *his* freedom as well as your own. Not a freedom that's grudgingly granted or negotiated by trading restrictions or privileges but a freedom that's encouraged and taken for granted.

The more free, the more independent, the more an individual your lover is, the more he'll be capable of loving—loving *you*.

And the more he'll value you, because you'll be one of the rare individuals who's able to let him be free.

To be genuine and profound, love depends upon freedom. For one example, only free people can afford to love without reservation, to unleash all their emotions in the supreme act of enjoyment—sexual intercourse.

Other people enjoy sex, or don't enjoy it, as just another part of life. They have to remain on guard always, on the lookout to be sure this brief escape doesn't lead to further bad consequences.

The free individual knows who he is and why he's where he is. He doesn't have to hold back anything. He can be loving, affectionate, and understanding because he isn't threatened or vulnerable. Isn't that the kind of person you'd like to have love you?

Love is too valuable to allow it to be killed by marriage, social pressures, or any other restriction.

To me, love is the most exciting thing in the world. The joy of having one's thoughts and emotions filled with another person is the most wonderful experience that life has to offer. It's the culmination of everything else. All other enjoyment values seem to lead inexorably to the moment of sexual intercourse with the person who represents everything one wants in life.

Nothing should be allowed to stand in the way of that.

O you and I, what is it to us, what the rest do or think?
What is all else to us, who have voided all but freedom
and all but our own joy?
                                    —WALT WHITMAN AND FREDERICK DELIUS

20

Freedom from
Jealousy Problems

JEALOUSY IS perhaps the most difficult problem in a romantic relationship. It's hard to let someone be free if he uses that freedom in ways that hurt you.

There's no easy cure for jealousy; you won't eliminate it by saying you shouldn't feel jealous. But some of the *problems* caused by jealousy can be eliminated—and this, in turn, can alleviate some of the bad feelings.

Jealousy is the negative emotion caused by the fear of losing someone (or something) to someone else. *Envy* is of a different character; it's the desire for something possessed by someone else. Envy is simply an intellectual recognition of what you'd like to have. It doesn't necessarily cause problems because it doesn't usually affect the emotions.

Jealousy, on the other hand, permeates the emotions— thus distorting your ability to make decisions and creating the urge to do things that might be self-defeating. In a jealous state, one can feel compelled to do or say things he doesn't really mean; he can become moralistic, hateful of someone he loves, accusing, possessive, vengeful.

When you're jealous, it's ultimately the attention your lover gives to someone else that hurts. The attention may be represented by physical attraction, romantic interest, intellectual stimulation, time spent with the other person, or sexual activity—but I think these are all symbols of the attention that's being diverted from you to someone else.

If some of those things cause jealousy while others don't, it's because some of them represent to you a higher degree of attention and involvement with the competitor.

RECOGNIZING JEALOUSY

There are ways to reduce the bad feelings that come from jealousy, and we'll look at several different factors that have a bearing upon it. We'll confine our attention to jealousy as it affects romantic relationships; the same principles should apply to any other type of jealousy.

First, it's important to emphasize that jealousy is an emotion—an involuntary response to something that happens. There's no reason to be ashamed of it, to try to suppress it, or to deny it. When you try to act as if it doesn't exist, you're in the Intellectual Trap—and you'll probably feel worse if you don't get the jealousy out into the open where you can deal with it.

If you feel jealous, accept it. That in itself should take some of the sting out of it.

It also helps to be able to tell your lover of your jealousy. If you're afraid to do so, it probably means that you don't have the best kind of friendship with your lover. If you have to hide your emotions, you're not free to fully enjoy the relationship.

The deepest, most satisfying, most durable relationships are bound to be those in which both parties can be totally honest with each other. Without that freedom, you'll always be at least partially in the Identity Trap—unable to express yourself as you really are, unable to let yourself relax and enjoy what you have.

It's also important to your lover that you be honest. He can't be your friend and help you if he doesn't know what you're feeling; he can't be as valuable to you as he might want to be.

So honesty is very important. But that means the *real* truth, not the emotional whim you feel at the moment. If the truth is, "I'm jealous when you're with him," you're not speaking the truth when you say, "You have no right to be with him," or "I hate you," or "*I* haven't done that; therefore *you* shouldn't."

As always, it's in your self-interest to let others be free. There are very few people strong enough to do that—so if you're one of them, you automatically have a head-start on the competition. And the greatest benefits come from a lover who's with you because he *wants* to be with you— because he'd rather be with you than with anyone else in the world at that moment.

Jealousy and restrictions are two different things. One doesn't necessarily follow the other. You can be jealous— openly and honestly—without imposing restrictions upon your lover.

And if you're free to voice your jealousy openly, without condemnation or demands, you may find that the mere act of saying what you feel will alleviate some of the pain of it. Too often, jealousy smolders and grows because it's suppressed or denied and the discomfort is attributed to something else.

NO SURPRISES

Jealousy is often caused by surprises. If each of you expects a certain type of conduct from the other, but you never discuss and define that standard, surprises can result. If you abide by what you think is the standard and then find that your lover hasn't, you can be hurt and can feel that you've been taken advantage of.

But it's possible that the problem isn't one of misconduct—but rather that no attempt was made to identify what each of you expected from the other.

If you're closely involved with someone, define the rules

of the relationship clearly so there can be no misunderstanding. If there are no rules, then *that* should be openly expressed and understood also—so that neither party expects from the other what he doesn't intend to give.

FIDELITY

This, of course, brings us to the question of fidelity. You have to decide how free each person is to associate with others—especially others who might be romantic rivals. Is it understood that each person may associate with anyone he chooses? Have other romantic involvements? Have sexual intercourse with others? If not, what are the limits regarding associations with others?

These things must be clearly understood between you. Otherwise, there may be surprises that could pile additional hurt feelings upon already jealous feelings.

Be realistic when you decide such things. Don't try to be something you're not; recognize your own emotional nature and self-interest. If you pick a standard determined by someone else, you'll probably have problems. You could easily be tempted to suppress your emotions when they seem to contradict the standard you've chosen.

The rules must be of your own choosing—in keeping with your own natures. I'll offer my observations on the subject, only because they might be helpful to you in defining your own.

I think that *any* restriction is harmful to a good relationship. I want to be free and I want those closest to me to be free, also. I don't want to be anyone's jailer; I don't want anyone to feel that his life is restricted because of his association with me.

That doesn't mean I'm never jealous. But I'd rather suffer occasional jealousy than to face the problems that restrictions create in a relationship.

I realize that life often involves giving up a short-term pleasure for a long-term gain—and restrictions are often justified on that basis. But I want my lover to feel that she's getting the most possible from me while giving up the least possible.

NATURAL MONOPOLY

The answer to the problem of restrictions is to find the relationship in which they're unnecessary. When you find someone who is not only attractive and interesting, but very appropriate to you in most every way, you won't need restrictions. Competition will be irrelevant or absent if you find someone who wants and needs exactly what you are.

The urge to restrict stems from a feeling of vulnerability—the fear that someone else might offer more of what your lover wants and take attention away from you. If there isn't an overwhelming mutual self-interest between you and your lover, you'll continue to have that fear—no matter what restrictions are imposed.

But if your relationship is the result of mutual understanding, mutual interests, mutual views of the world—in short, if your lover is also your best friend—you won't need restrictions because you'll have very little to fear. You'll have a natural monopoly upon the attentions of your lover.

And one of the ways of creating that is by letting him be free. If he can be free with you—free to say what he means, free to express his desires and secret feelings (even when they involve attraction to others), free to see whomever he chooses, free to do as he wants to do—then he'll have less need to seek out others. He'll be getting from you most everything he needs. You'll be the most important person in his world.

The paradox, in a sense, is that he'll probably stay closer to home if you don't *demand* that he stay home.

If you have a natural monopoly, access to others will be valuable to the relationship. For the more your lover associates with others, the more he'll be aware that he gets much more from you than he can get from them. Only by being with others can he see that clearly.

But if you restrict his relationships, the opposite can happen. At a distance, many people can appear to be attractive, appropriate—even perfect. All their virtues will beckon, but none of their drawbacks will be apparent. That's an undesirable position for *you* to be in; you're being unrealistically compared with an ideal image. Let him go and find that out for himself.

DOUBLE STANDARDS

Restrictions often result in a double standard—in which one person is free to do things that are denied to the other—even if the restrictions weren't intended that way.

It's possible, for example, that the man's work may involve regular contact with women, while his lover's routine might not include contact with other men. If that's the case, restrictions upon dates with others will deprive *her* more than they will him. He'll have the opportunity to meet and associate with other women, possibly even meet one more appropriate to him, while she'll be confined to her relationship with him.

In other ways, one person is usually affected more than the other by a restriction. Whenever the restriction is lifted, or when the relationship ends, the one most affected by the restriction will have suffered for his obedience to it. In effect, he'll have deprived himself until it became in the self-interest of the other person to have the restriction lifted.

In addition, some exceptions are often made to restrictions. Certain outsiders may be considered acceptable companions while others are off limits. When that happens, it's easy for one person to feel that the exceptions have favored the other person. In fact, both parties can feel simultaneously that they're being discriminated against.

I'm convinced that any relationship will be more open,

more honest, and more benevolent when there are no restrictions. You'll have to decide your rules for yourself, however, and they should be defined in terms of what you believe and what you're capable of handling.

MINIMIZING JEALOUSY

Even if it's in your self-interest to have your lover associate with others, your emotions might not accept the situation so easily.

One's imagination is often his worst enemy when he's jealous; but if used properly, your imagination can minimize your emotional discomfort. The trick is to face up to your secret fears so that they no longer terrify you.

If your lover is going to spend an evening with someone else, imagine the situation you're afraid will happen. Imagine the worst. Picture them talking, laughing, kissing, making love—whatever it is you fear will happen. Keep doing it over and over again until it no longer affects you emotionally.

This technique has helped me several times. It neutralizes my fears, but never seems to eliminate the good emotions I feel toward someone.

I remember using it once when I was involved with a woman with whom I didn't have too much in common. The inappropriateness of the relationship made me feel quite vulnerable.

One night I had to give a lecture and she announced that she was going out with someone else. I was sure they'd wind up in bed—and it infuriated me. I didn't want to stop her but I still felt terribly jealous.

On the way to the lecture, I stopped for dinner. For the past three hours, I'd been unable to think of anything but the terrible thing I was sure was going to happen. I finally decided that I wouldn't be able to give the lecture unless I calmed down.

After ordering my dinner, I started to use the technique. I had never seen the other man involved—which always seems to make such a person more formidable. So I pictured him as the exact opposite of me, the kind of man I wouldn't like, the kind of man who could sweet-talk women away from their lovers. I imagined them doing together every obscene thing I could think of.[1]

I was determined to keep thinking about the scene over and over again until it no longer bothered me emotionally. However, I suddenly realized that I was thinking about the lecture I was going to give; I hadn't made it all the way through the imaginary sex scene even once. So I turned my mind back to the horrible scene and concentrated on it again.

But it quickly became apparent that my mind had wandered once again. And then it dawned on me that the scene no longer held any terror for me—not even any interest, in fact.

So I spent the rest of my dinner time planning my lecture and never gave the jealousy problem another thought. In all, it had taken only about five minutes of attention to eliminate all the pain and fear.

Of course, it doesn't always work out so easily. But if you'll give the technique a try, I think you'll find it can minimize jealous pangs when your lover is going to be with someone else.

THE RIGHT SITUATION

Find the person who's most appropriate for you and you'll probably discover that jealousy is much less of a problem.

Examine yourself, find out what you have to offer, determine what kind of person could make you most happy. And then find that person. If you're honest with yourself and then find the person most appropriate to you, chances are that person will feel the same way about you. You'll have a natural monopoly.

[1] In this context, *obscene* means all the sexual things I like to do—when done by someone else.

In that situation, you'll know that just being what you are is earning for you what you want—and you'll know that it will be highly unlikely that a third party can come between you.

That doesn't mean you should never become involved with someone who's less than perfect for you. It's easy to become infatuated with someone for purely superficial reasons. There's no reason to ignore that or to attempt to deny your feelings in such a situation.

Accept your infatuation and enjoy it. You might even find that the situation will lead to more than you'd expected. But don't count on your feelings (or his) remaining as they are indefinitely. Be prepared for the possibility that one of you may soon meet someone else more appropriate—or even that the infatuation will just fade away.

Enjoy such relationships but don't let them keep you from watching for the person with whom you could have a better relationship. Go to the places where you'd be most likely to meet such a person; display yourself as you are at all times. That will increase your chances of meeting the person who can mean the most to you.

That person will want you just as you are. He'll understand and appreciate what you are. He'll understand your thoughts and feelings and respect you for being honest about them.

You'll have found the person who can be both your lover and your best friend. And every benefit that comes from having a friend or a lover will be magnified many times over because they're combined in one person.

With him, you'll have far less reason to feel jealous. You'll have the natural security that comes from knowing you've earned honestly what you have and that it's unlikely anyone could replace you.

That doesn't mean you'll *never* be jealous. But you'll be able to deal with it openly and honestly with your lover—because he'll also be your best friend.

He won't sacrifice for you; it's not in your self-interest that he do so. But he'll understand how you feel and make it much easier for you. Together, you'll be able to work out problems because you'll have a common viewpoint toward such situations. You'll be able to discuss problems rather than argue about them.

And you should feel a great sense of self-esteem when you know that your lover wants you more than anyone else in the world. He genuinely *wants* you—not because you've limited his alternatives, but because he's seen the competition and he prefers you.

Love sought is good, but giv'n unsought is better.
—SHAKESPEARE

21

Freedom from Family Problems

MANY PEOPLE might respond to the idea of a non-marriage as something excellent—"but of course impossible if you have children, in-laws, or relatives."

Having children doesn't have to interfere with the love relationship. In fact, there are many reasons why the non-marriage framework provides a better setting than marriage for raising children. There are fewer complications, and the relationships between everyone involved can be more easily understood.

Once again, it's necessary to try to set aside the normal ways of thinking about these questions. The normal ways aren't working—and usually because the sovereignty of each individual isn't respected.

The raising of children is a far-reaching subject, and I wouldn't presume to answer all the questions involved within a few pages. But I think there are basic guidelines that can provide a harmonious framework within which children can grow to be clear-thinking individuals.

One of the values of the non-marriage arrangement is that it keeps all things on an individualized basis and precludes the need for group decisions. All property and decisions are controlled by one person or another—not by both.

Though a child is not a "thing" to be owned, some of the same principles apply to decision making and custody that apply to property. Someone must make decisions concerning the child; and if there's a separation, the question of custody will arise.

One of the most difficult problems a child can face is in being subject to conflicting authorities when the parents disagree. He's put in an unfortunate position when two people whom he loves are claiming authority and telling him to act in two different ways. He knows he has to disappoint one of them when there are disagreements.

How much simpler for everyone concerned if one person has the major responsibility and sets the main plans for the child's upbringing.

If the parents' differences of opinion are so great that one couldn't stand to live with a child raised by the other, they probably shouldn't have a child—no matter what the arrangement. But if they're compatible enough to live together harmoniously, the chances are good that one will not object to the methods used by the person who has the main responsibility.

CUSTODY

I think it's important, then, that it be clearly established before the child is born which parent is the ultimate custodian of the child. That parent will have the final say in decisions concerning the child and will automatically have custody of the child if the parents should separate.

If you think ahead to such a decision, you can see that the woman will ultimately control such a question of custody. She has to deliver the child, and she doesn't have to get pregnant if she doesn't want to. Also, she can leave any time during the pregnancy and take the unborn child with her. So she will be the ultimate custodian unless she agrees otherwise.

Any agreement made before the birth can be altered later if both parties agree. In fact, if after the child is old enough to have some conception of the consequences of his choice he chooses the non-custodial parent (and that parent agrees), it's probably best for all concerned that his choice be honored in the event of a separation of the parents.

Before the child is conceived, the ultimate custodian should consider whether he's prepared to support and raise the child *with or without* the other parent. It's foolish to ignore the possibility that you may be on your own again someday.

If you're to be the custodian, ask yourself if you'll be able to raise and support that child by yourself. If you're not sure, you ought to be doubly cautious about having a child.

If you're a woman, you might assume that the law will make your husband responsible to support the child after a separation—but such assumptions are dangerous. The world is full of divorced women with children who are trying desperately to get their ex-husbands to fulfill their obligations.

And if you expect that you might have to depend upon the law to enforce your relationship with your husband, then your entire relationship is probably misconceived. Why would you want to live with, and raise a family with, a man who must be forced to do what you think is right?

I favor the idea that it should be agreed from the beginning that the custodian will be totally responsible for the child in the event of a separation. That merely recognizes what may be the case anyway. And if it develops that both parties want custody, it won't turn out that one will get custody and the other the bills.

If a woman agrees to assume custody of a child, that encourages her to maintain her income-producing ability throughout the relationship—instead of becoming financially dependent upon her husband and thus less free.

If the woman doesn't think she could handle such financial responsibility, but both parties want to have a child, the man can establish a monetary fund before the birth of the child. The fund can provide the financial means for the woman to be solely responsible for the child if it ever becomes necessary. That will eliminate the sense of dependence that might otherwise cause her to remain in an unrewarding relationship.

All these matters are subjective decisions to be made by you and your lover. But it's important that the decisions be made—in advance of the time that they might be necessary.

RAISING THE CHILD

As early as possible, it's valuable to establish relationships with your child that are similar to the relationship you have with your lover.

The child should have his own world where he is clearly the sovereign. That means a room of his own that is subject to his control alone. If he doesn't take care of it, he'll learn the consequences of that sooner or later. But if he's *forced* to keep it as his parents wish, he'll never discover for himself the consequences of alternative courses of action.

He should also have other property to use in whatever way he chooses. Property isn't owned if it can be used only in "approved" ways.

You'll have to decide how he'll obtain his property. He can earn it, receive an allowance, get outright gifts, or he can receive property in any combination of these ways.

But once he receives something, it's important that he learn to understand what it means to own something and be responsible for its preservation. He shouldn't be taught to expect automatic replacement of any of his property that he might destroy.

The importance of his sense of ownership can be seen by observing the difficulties many adults have in dealing with the world. For close to two decades, most people are led to believe that they aren't sovereign.

Then, suddenly, they're thrust out into the world and expected to make far-reaching decisions concerning their lives. It's no wonder that they have difficulty foreseeing the consequences of their actions and fall back on any authority that appears to be competent to make decisions for them.

I believe the child will be far better equipped to face the world if he understands how the world operates right from the beginning. He can easily learn what it means to make decisions and to experience the consequences of his decisions.

This means, too, that he should be helped to understand that you have your property, also. Show him which areas are off limits to him or require permission before he can use them. Even the dining table he eats on will belong to someone; part of his arrangement with the owner can include table privileges.

Obviously, a two-year-old child won't have an explicit understanding of these matters. But there are two ways that he *can* understand them at the earliest possible age. One is that he can learn by example if the entire family operates in this way.

The second way is by never being taught otherwise. For some reason, many parents seem to think it important to change systems at some point in a child's age. They first teach him he has no authority over his life, and then try later to instill a sense of responsibility in him. In the same way, they first want him to believe that Santa Claus loves and rewards him and then later want him to understand that it's the parents who love him. I think it would make a considerable difference if the child were never taught anything that you intend to reverse later.

It's important that each of the three of you be a separate human being with his own life, his own interests, and his own property. None of you is living for the benefit of the others; rather, each should be there because he wants to be. And each will want to be there if it's a setting where he can live a meaningful life of his own choosing.

It obviously isn't necessary that each member of the family own his own washing machine, stove, and living-room furniture; nor is it necessary for permission to be requested every time a non-owner wants to use something. Various things can be made available to other members of the household on a "till further notice" basis. But the ultimate ownership should never be in doubt.

If these principles don't seem attractive to you, it may be because you've never been married. You may never have seen the hundreds of insignificant joint decisions that preoccupy most married people.

I've never known a family who used these principles who didn't find them a great relief and advantage over the normal ways of handling such matters.

A SOVEREIGN CHILD

If you want your child to understand that he lives in a world in which his future will be of his own making, encourage that by letting him deal directly with the world as much as possible. Let him experience the consequences of his own actions.

Naturally, you don't intend to let him discover first hand a very dangerous consequence of something he wants to do. But it's important to decide in advance where you *will* draw the line. How far will you let him go in making his own decisions? Don't leave it to decide each time the matter arises. Have a clearly defined policy in advance; that will prevent inconsistencies.

Be available to let him know your opinions—without implying that your opinions are binding on him. Let him think of you as a wiser, more experienced person—but not as a moral authority who stands in the way of his living his own life.

Be a source of information and opinion concerning the consequences of acts. Let him learn that the nature of the world he lives in (not the attitudes of people bigger and smarter than he is) sets the limits on what he can and cannot do in the world.

If you recognize him as an individual who is allowed to learn for himself, a genuine friendship can develop between you. He'll be willing to talk to you about his ideas, plans, and problems—because he won't have to fear the moral retribution that most parents inflict when they disagree with their children's ideas and actions.

Parents who fear letting their children make decisions fail to realize that their children *do* make decisions on their own. You can't possibly control all your child's actions. So the best security you can have comes from two conditions: (1) allowing the child to learn as early as possible that his actions have consequences to him; and (2) developing a friendship that will make it possible for him to come to you when he needs help.

If either of those conditions is missing, you shouldn't be surprised if you find out about crises only *after* they've happened. A child who knows that acts have consequences and who knows that he has a wise friend will be more likely to consult his friend *before* risking something dangerous.

Love and understanding are important to a child. And you'll show your love more by respecting his individuality and appreciating him for what he is, not for what you force him to be.

THINK IT OVER FIRST

It's unfortunate that it's almost impossible to learn second hand what it means to have children. As a result, parents learn only *after the fact* the responsibilities they have assumed by bringing a child into the world. If it were somehow possible to learn beforehand, there might be fewer unhappy parents and disturbed children.

I've observed many situations in which people conceived children without any real notion of the responsibilities they were taking on. Often, it's an example of the Emotional Trap, in which the desire for a child is taken out of the context of the consequences involved.

It's true that you can put a child out for adoption if you can't get along with him, but few parents are willing to do that, no matter what the problem. So you're usually assuming eighteen or more years of responsibility. And no matter how much you may cherish the child, it will place restrictions on your own actions.

It's usually assumed by parents that if they do all the right things, the child will cause very few problems for them. And I'm convinced that a recognition of the principles covered already in this chapter will eliminate many of the normal difficulties.

But the fact is that it's a human being you're bringing into the world, not a robot that needs only to be programmed correctly. The influences that come from school and neighborhood, as well as from yourself, are not totally within your control.

You can't realistically approach child-raising unless you're willing to accept that the child will have his own nature, no matter how you might raise him.

So, in effect, you're inviting a stranger to live in your home for eighteen years or more. There are *risks* involved—plenty of them. You're committing a large part of your future to satisfy a desire that may be only a part of the present.

In other words, I'm suggesting that you be very careful in making a decision concerning the conception of a child. If you have a truly loving relationship with your spouse, there will probably be less desire (and less feeling of need) to amend the relationship by adding a child. And if you don't have an excellent relationship with your spouse, bringing a child into it will probably worsen the situation, not better it.

I think that the worst time to have a child is when the parents are in their twenties. They've hardly had time to understand themselves and decide in any durable way what they want from their lives. Their plans and ideas may change many times before the child would be even ten years old.

There's nothing disastrous about having a child when the parents are in their thirties. A child born to such parents is more likely to be treated with greater consistency,

with more love, and with more perspective than one born
to younger parents.

My parents were both around forty when I was born
and I can see many advantages that I gained from that.
They were much more ready to devote themselves to children; their basic plans and life styles had been clearly established and never changed while I was growing up.
When they ran into financial difficulties later, they treated
such matters with a realistic perspective, and I never had
any reason to feel that I was somehow responsible for
their difficulties.

If you like children, there are ways to enjoy them without becoming a parent. You can be a YMCA counselor,
den mother, school helper, or Boy Scout leader—limiting
your exposure to children to the ways you desire.

When you become a parent, however, you're bringing a
stranger into the world with the requirement that you get
along with him—no matter who he is.

EXISTING CHILDREN

If you already have children and the suggestions made
earlier make sense to you, they can be implemented, no
matter how old your child is already.

Naturally, the earlier you start, the easier and more effective the methods should be. But there's no reason to refrain from taking a course of action you deem right, no
matter how long you may have been doing things another
way.

It's important to realize, however, that your child may
not understand the value of the change as well as you do.
For instance, the prospect of making his own decisions
could be frightening if he's used to being given orders.

I suggest that the changeover be gradual, with the speed
dictated by how well the child understands what is happening and can recognize the benefits to himself.

If you have a teen-age child with whom you *haven't*
cultivated a friendship, don't expect to make friends

quickly. And don't *tell* him you're now going to be his friend—just do it.

Take it slow, be patient, and prove your friendship by actions, not by declarations of intent. Take any opportunity that arises to try to understand his thinking—without exercising your moral judgment. His thoughts and actions are his—whether or not you approve—so you won't accomplish anything by condemning what he does.

When he decides that you are capable of understanding his thoughts and motives, he may begin asking your opinions. Even then, take it slowly. Point out what you believe to be the likely consequences of various actions, but let him know that it's *your* opinion and acknowledge that he may not see it the same way.

The establishment of independent property can be handled in the same gradual way, no matter what the age of the child. Let his understanding and acceptance dictate the speed of the changeover.

NON-INTERFERENCE

The principles of individuality discussed in this chapter can help considerably to create a rewarding relationship with your children, replacing the series of conflicts and crises that so many parents take for granted.

Your own individuality and your relationship with your lover can be preserved more easily this way, too. For a child who recognizes his own sovereignty and the sovereignty of others will understand the importance of your having your own life and your own relationships with others.

Jealousy among members of the family will be less likely if each person understands that there are separate relationships between each of the people involved—and that each relationship is of a different kind.

You and your lover will be free to develop your own interests and to do the things that will add to your love.

And as the years pass, you'll spend less of your time worrying that your children might be getting into trouble.

Treat your child as a human being—not as a household pet to be taught tricks. If you do, it's unlikely that he'll prevent you from having a life of your own and a satisfying relationship with your lover.

THOSE RELATIVES

Another family area that creates restrictions upon one's life is the existence of relatives.

There appears to be an unwritten law that blood is thicker than self-interest. One supposedly has a duty to value his blood relatives—simply *because* they're relatives.

This means, for openers, that you owe something to your parents. And then you have a multitude of responsibilities to anyone else who happens to be in the family tree by accident of birth.

If your cousin has a heart attack, you might be expected to chip in for the hospital bill. Or if your uncle lives in the same city as you do, you might be expected to curtail some of your own activities so as not to embarrass "the family."

Or if your child chooses to have ten children of his own, you're expected to buy ten birthday presents and ten Christmas gifts every year for the grandchildren. And you might even be called upon to take care of some of the grandchildren if the load becomes too great.

Since my family has never imposed these kinds of burdens upon me, it was only a few years ago that I became aware that this sort of thing was so widespread. At first, I was amazed to discover how much of an individual's life could be monopolized by his relatives.

To be responsible for someone who happens to have been born into the same family doesn't make sense. Any relationship that isn't based upon mutual self-interest is bound to have poor consequences.

YOUR PARENTS

The most serious problems usually develop with one's parents.

My friend Marian Hall Landers once pointed out that, too often, a parent-child relationship is a unilateral contract, initiated and ruled by the parents. They decide not only what they will give to the child but also what the child owes them in return.

The parents seldom even state precisely what this is. They can simply invoke a claim at any time for anything, justified by "all we've done for you."

The parents might claim money, attention, time, love, or favors; or they might demand that the child live his life in a way approved by them.

As a result, the child can carry a vague, indefinite and—for all practical purposes—infinite debt. He's never wholly free to plan his own future without potential interference from his parents.

This, of course, takes us back to the Identity Trap, the Morality Trap, and the Unselfishness Trap. All kinds of pressures are used to enforce the parents' claims; but more than anything else, the weapon used is *guilt*. The child is made to feel guilty for disappointing the parents.

It may be redundant to point out once again that no one is qualified to run your life for you, but the point can't be made too often.

Whatever your parents expended "for you" was actually what they did for themselves. They took a calculated risk that the time, effort, and money they expended would produce a child they would enjoy, and they hoped it would lead you to a life they would consider favorable to them. If you choose not to live that kind of life, they lose on that part of their investment.

Your parents decided for themselves how they would live their own lives. They may have chosen to do what *their* parents wanted, or they may have chosen to go their own ways. They may have accepted the authority of the church or the government or someone else.

Whatever they did, they *chose* to do it. They may have chosen wisely or they may have chosen foolishly—but they chose.

Now you have to choose, too. And you have to choose in a way that fits *your* nature. That's the only way you have of achieving a satisfying life for yourself. If your parents prefer that you be an obedient but unhappy child, then they can hardly be considered necessary or valuable friends.

They may never understand that you have to choose for yourself. If you base your hopes upon getting their agreement before you act in ways of your choosing, you're relying on an indirect alternative—and you may wait the rest of your life without ever acquiring the opportunity to be free.

If you choose for yourself, you'll undoubtedly make mistakes along the way. But you'd have made mistakes, too, if you'd followed your parents' advice. And the mistakes you make on your own will teach you far more than the mistakes made following another's rules.

HANDLING GUILT

Whether your restrictions are imposed by your parents or other relatives, their principal weapon is most likely guilt. They can make you suffer emotional discomfort for going your own way—even if you're convinced you're right.

Because guilt is an emotion, there's no easy way to eliminate it. But it helps to realize that once the guilt is inflicted upon you, there's usually never enough you can do for your relatives to get rid of the guilt. You're going to feel guilty even if you do most of what's asked of you.

If that's the case, you might as well go ahead and enjoy your life as you want to. If you're going to feel guilty anyway, you might as well have a good time while you're doing it.

And you might be amazed at how quickly the negative feelings can be alleviated by the rewards of your independence—and even just by the *feeling* of independence.

If you're going to do something that your family will disapprove of, and you expect to feel guilty about it, try using the technique suggested in the Box-Trap chapter.

Take a few minutes to be by yourself. Relax and imagine the experience that you're going to go through. Picture what you will do, and imagine the reactions you'll receive from those you're concerned about.

It may be a painful experience. If so, go through it again—and again—until it's no longer painful for you. In effect, you're desensitizing your emotions in advance, so that you'll be less likely to get the guilty emotional reaction when you actually go through the experience.

Picture the very worst that you can imagine might happen as a result of your planned action. Be prepared for very bad reactions from others. You'll be less likely then to be thrown off balance by surprises.

In this way, you might be able to reduce the emotional pressure.

In addition, the emotional difficulties will probably lessen if you have less contact with those who are imposing the guilt upon you. There's no point in exposing yourself to someone with whom you have a primarily negative relationship.

If you rely upon your parents for financial support, you have to decide which is more important to you—the money or your independence and emotional relaxation. Whichever way you decide, it will help to recognize that you *have* made a choice; whatever difficulties ensue can then be understood as the price you're paying for what you want.

GETTING FREE

If you feel imprisoned by your parents or relatives, it is you who must make the move to be free. No one else is going to bestow your freedom upon you.

In any kind of disengagement, you don't have to be brutal, indignant, resentful, or unfeeling. You have only to decide carefully what you believe the limits of your involvement should be, and then set about to make that a reality. Recognize that everyone involved is doing what he thinks best, that it is a conflict of interest that creates the problem.

Don't overreact to a difficult relationship by destroying the good parts while trying to weed out the bad. Emphasize the good parts in discussions with the others. But make it clear that you won't participate any longer in the bad parts.

If you continue to show respect and affection while living your own life, the decision will then be up to them. If they're hostile, that's their decision, not yours. The break will have come from them, not from you. Naturally, you should prepare yourself emotionally for such a possibility.

IT'S YOUR CHOICE

A discussion of the possible problems one can face with relatives could go on endlessly. But whatever the problem, the principles discussed in this book apply, and especially those concerning relationships.

You are an individual, not part of a group. Your relationship with anyone should be confined to those areas that are mutually beneficial. And no relationship should have a lifetime contract implied in it.

You will decide for yourself what you'll do with your life. You can choose the indirect alternative of trying to please others by your actions. Or you can choose the direct alternatives and live your life as you want to live it.

No one is holding you back. Those who want to restrict you have no power over you; they rely upon your willingness to stay in the traps. All you have to do is to reject the traps and climb out of the boxes. It's entirely your decision to make.

Because of common backgrounds, and often common interests, families can be a great source of pleasure. If you remove the boxes, debts, and obligations from the relationships, you may find that a new and valuable framework is available in which you can deal with your relatives on a mutually rewarding basis.

If that happens, they may come to see the benefit to themselves in what you've done. They may appreciate the fact that you care for them because they happen to be relatives.

That consequence isn't guaranteed. But no matter what happens, it can't be worse than giving up your life to try to pay an unending debt.

Relations are simply a tedious pack of people, who haven't got the remotest knowledge of how to live, nor the smallest instinct about when to die.

—OSCAR WILDE

22

Freedom from Business Problems

RELATIONSHIPS WITH BUSINESS ASSOCIATES frequently become boxes. The traditional ways of structuring business enterprises lead easily to restrictions, bad feelings, and conflicts of interest between employers, employees, and partners.

Suppose, for example, that you and a friend discover that you have certain complementary talents and see a market for those talents. You might decide to go into business by setting up a partnership or corporation in which you'll share 50/50. You'd probably agree that you'll both work hard and split whatever profits come from the business.

You've already made your first mistakes.

As we saw in Chapter 6, partnerships are a form of the Group Trap. They discourage incentive and create problems by ignoring the principles of good relationships we covered in Chapter 18.

The "partnership" isn't a living entity with a single purpose and a single mind. Each of you will remain individuals—with individual motives, talents, goals, and attitudes. So your ideas about the business will differ in some ways.

For instance, you may each agree to work hard, but the word "hard" defies precise definition. What you each mean by your intentions probably won't be mutually understood until you have a disagreement and one of you thinks the other isn't working hard enough.

Even if you work equally hard, you won't produce the exact same value. So the one who's more valuable will be subsidizing the other to some extent. In fact, each of you could come to think that he's the stronger partner and that the other is thereby getting a better deal.

Often, a partnership is established to combine two different talents—one may be the producer and the other the seller. Both functions are essential to the business, but they won't necessarily be equal in value. So to share 50/50 (or by any other ratio) can open the door to resentments.

As we saw in the Group-Trap chapter, if your reward is dependent upon more than your own output, you won't have a 100 percent incentive to produce more. For anything you do, you'll receive only half the reward—the other half going to your partner. As a result, there will be a natural incentive to produce less and to encourage your partner to produce more.

Dozens of other problems are inherent in partnerships, but we don't need to detail them here. If you've ever been in one, you probably know them all. You may feel that you made a bad choice of partners, but it's more likely that you made a bad choice of structures.

Action involves thinking, deciding, valuing, and doing—by *one* human being. If two people are going to act together, each will think, decide, evaluate, and do in his own way—in accordance with his own nature.

As in any other type of relationship, it's important that neither be dependent upon another person's way of doing things. Each person should control and evaluate his own action in terms of the personal consequences to himself.

And he should have the opportunity to achieve his objectives by dealing at any time with anyone who offers him a way to fulfill those objectives, without having to deal with anyone whose objectives or methods are in conflict with his.

Unfortunately, the normal ways of operating a business

overlook these principles. They amalgamate individuals into groups and hope for collective action. They broaden business relationships beyond the common interests that are required to fulfill one's objectives. And they attempt to achieve success and longevity through contracts that transcend the individual's self-interest.

Since most businesses violate the basic principles of good relationships, most businessmen are entangled in many restrictions that aren't necessary. The normal ways require a great deal of supervision that shouldn't be necessary. And the employees of the business have greater restrictions upon *their* time than is necessary.

If a relationship is structured so that each person has his own area of responsibility over which he has complete control, most of the typical headaches of business can be eliminated.

A BETTER WAY

This should be clearer as we apply these principles to a business enterprise.

Suppose you have an idea for a product or service you think would succeed in the market. You won't have the talents or time necessary to do everything in the business, but that doesn't mean you have to take on a partner, nor even that you need employees.

For instance, you're not going to construct your own typewriter, mill your own stationery, nor operate your own telephone company. Other people will do those things; but you wouldn't think of taking them into your business as partners—nor would you hire them as employees to be paid on an hourly or weekly basis. You'll *contract* with them—but *only for what you need from them.*

Why can't you contract for *any* service you need?

You may not even know how to produce the product you want to market. If that's the case, find someone who can produce it—but don't make him your partner. Find out how much he'll charge you to manufacture the product for you.

Then check with other potential manufacturers to determine your alternatives. Pick the one that offers you the most of what you want.

You can check the marketplace at any time to see if you're getting the best possible deal from your supplier—but you can't do that with a partner.

You can acquire any service you need in the same way. Perhaps you don't even know how to operate a business. Find someone who does. Then find someone else who does, and perhaps even someone else. See what each has to offer and at what price.

Select the best one to run the business for you and pay him on a basis that makes his income an incentive to provide exactly what you want. Define what it is you want from him—and pay him as he provides that.

In the same way, you can contract for every service necessary to make the business work. You don't have to acquire partners or employees. You simply contract with people to provide whatever you need.

If you need a salesman for your product, find one and pay him on the basis of how much he sells. Don't pay him for the time he spends in the office; compensate him on the basis of sales.

If you need a bookkeeper, what you want from him is usable information regarding your financial status. Determine what information you need and pay him *for the information, not for his time*—which might include coffee breaks, trips to the restroom, and flirting with the receptionist. Pay him for what you want to receive and let *him* determine how much time he needs to do the job.

When you pay for results, not for time, you get three important benefits: (1) you have an accurate understanding of what each thing costs you (and can easily compare alternatives); (2) you no longer have to supervise the individual's time—all you have to do is check his results; and (3) each supplier has the same incentive *you* do with regard to his service—he'll profit most by doing what is most valuable to you.

It's important, too, that you don't try to create group incentives. Don't offer to pay someone on the basis of the net profits of the business. He doesn't control the amount of net profit by his one service, so he has little incentive to try to increase it.

The only exception might be a manager hired to run the business. He would be in a position to affect the profits—and so you might decide to pay him on that basis.

Sometimes adjustments are necessary as you go along. You might make a contract with someone to have him provide a specific result for you. But the compensation might not be directed in such a way that his greatest incentive is to provide the result you want. If so, you may have to make adjustments until his incentive is exactly the same as yours.

At that point, he'll apply his creative talents to discover ways of doing the job more efficiently. Very few people are stupid; it's just that most employees have no real incentive to use their intelligence in their jobs. So they reserve their mental energy for their hobbies, personal relationships, and other things outside the office. In fact, with normal compensation systems, an employee often uses most of his initiative figuring out how to work less without losing his job.

With the right system, that mental energy can be unleashed on your behalf.

Another benefit of this system is that it allows you to begin with much less capital—and thus, with less risk. You pay for things only as you need them; there's no weekly payroll that must be met regardless of the need for it; as a result, you need fewer permanent facilities.

Even if you don't have enough money to begin, you can pay interest on borrowed money; you don't have to take in a partner. Arrangements whereby an investor is made a partner are risky; if the business is a success, you'll be sharing your profits long after you need the initial capital. While that's a decision you might willingly make, you may regret it five years later. And taking in a partner always opens the door to joint decisions and disagreements.

Whatever you need—services, money, advice—you can usually pay for on a single-exchange basis.

YOUR OWN SYSTEM

Obviously, this system could raise enough questions to fill a book by itself. There's a whole world of its own involved in business compensation systems. But you can probably work out a very effective one yourself if you keep the three basic principles in mind:

1. Deal with each individual on an individual basis. Make sure his compensation is dependent only upon his own value to you.

2. Contract only for what you want. Determine what results you want from someone and pay for those results only. If he delivers, you needn't worry about how he uses his time—that's not your concern.

3. Don't attempt to perpetuate a relationship by contract. If any contracts are necessary, make them for the shortest practical period of time, with ways of terminating with relatively short notice. Try to avoid any situation in which you or anyone else is obligated to perform services beyond the time in which it's in his self-interest to do so. You won't get good value when the individual no longer wants to be involved.

I've seen a number of businesses operated profitably in this way. The owners of those businesses avoid the normal problems that most businessmen take for granted. "Employees" (suppliers) are more devoted to their work, very little supervision is required, costs are always clearly discernible and the lowest available commensurate with quality.

I mentioned in Chapter 16 that I had avoided payroll taxes by transforming employees into independent contractors. That was only one of the benefits. The business had been losing money so fast it was about to go under.

After eliminating all employees (including myself) and contracting for services needed, the business was in the black. Those who continued to work with me made more money per hour worked, and I was able to cut *my* working time about half. Nothing else changed but the system of compensation—and that one change provided many benefits.

Even if you don't operate a business, you're in a better position if you act as a supplier of a service rather than as an employee. You can contract with companies to perform specific services for them at specific prices. In addition to the tax benefits, you can choose your own working hours, usually make more money, and have more free time.

If you avoid the assumptions that most employers and employees take for granted, you can earn the money you want without sacrificing your freedom to get it.

Work expands so as to fill the time available for its completion.   —C. NORTHCOTE PARKINSON

The strongest man in the world is he who stands most alone.   —HENRIK IBSEN

23

Freedom from Insecurity

IN A WORLD OF CONSTANT CHANGE and unfamiliar elements, it's natural to look for security—something reliable and protective.

The three forms of security most often sought are *financial security* (the assurance that one will never be poor), *intellectual security* (the assurance that one is right in his beliefs), and *emotional security* (the assurance that one will always be loved).

It's natural to want these things, and it's realistic to think that they're possible. Unfortunately, though, most people look for security where it can't be found—and in the process they become even more insecure. They hope that someone outside themselves can guarantee security and end their need to be concerned about it. But all they do is make themselves more vulnerable, and hence more insecure, by becoming dependent upon someone else.

Security comes from your ability to deal with the world, not from a guarantee by someone else. When you know that you're capable of dealing with whatever comes, you have the only security the world has to offer.

And your ability to deal with the world depends upon three assets: *self-reliance, vigilance,* and *honesty with yourself.*

To be self-reliant is to recognize that no one else is as concerned about your future as you are and that no one knows as much about you as you do. You can delegate decisions to others, but a secure individual recognizes that he's taking a risk when he does so. He knows that the responsibility for anything concerning his life remains with himself—and he accepts that responsibility.

To be vigilant is to recognize that there will be constant change in the world. There are always unknown factors that can affect your plans. So the secure individual is always mentally prepared for changes and surprises. He doesn't necessarily have a plan in mind to handle those changes and surprises, but he's aware that they can happen and is prepared to deal with them as they arise.

To be honest with yourself means to acknowledge mistakes as they become known. If you can accept your mistakes, you can correct them, pay for them, learn from them, and see that they don't interfere with your security. The individual who *can't* acknowledge his mistakes will remain vulnerable and be doomed to repeat them.

If you have these assets, you have no reason to be afraid; you'll know you can have love and financial security, and you won't need anyone to tell you that you're right.

Let's look at each of the three forms of security to see how these principles work.

FINANCIAL SECURITY

All financial dealings depend upon the reaction of the General Market. Whether your assets are in cash, investments, skills, or property, the worth of them will depend upon market acceptance.

As tastes and values change, the General Market changes. Stocks go up and down, currencies rise and fall, property changes in value.

Many people thought they'd found security in the 1920s by putting their money in the stock market, or by having it handled by a bank. They felt that their interests were being protected by people more capable than themselves.

They were proven wrong in 1929, and they paid for their willingness to rely upon others.

Naturally, it's helpful to utilize the information provided by people who specialize in various fields and to use the services they offer. But it's a mistake to think that those people know everything necessary, or that they will always act in your best interests.

In the same way, it's foolish to believe the government can protect or guarantee your future. Governments are subject to the same laws of economics as anyone else. The only "security" they offer is the promise to take care of you with other people's money. But what if those other people don't produce enough to take care of everyone who is relying upon the government?

Many people have faith that the government can somehow overrule the laws of economics, or that the government can use more resources than actually exist. So they trust the claims that their bank deposits are insured, that medical care will always be available to them, that "Social Security" will eliminate the need to provide for their futures. But the government has no power to transform stones into bread; and if there's another great depression (as I think there will be), this will become all too evident.

This doesn't mean you have to spend all your time watching your money. It only means that you must allow for many different possibilities. Diversification, periodic monitoring, and the willingness to acknowledge mistakes are the necessary ingredients of a secure future.

For example, Swiss banks *in general* are more realistic and more conservative, and so are safer depositories for savings than American banks. But the alert individual will increase the odds for safety by using two or more Swiss banks so as not to be vulnerable to any one of them.

Security doesn't require absolute knowledge of the future. It's simply the recognition that changes will take place and the knowledge that you're willing to deal with whatever happens.

You'll have that attitude if you're willing to rely upon yourself, recognize the state of constant change, and be willing to acknowledge any mistakes you make along the way.

Financial insecurity is inherent in any situation where you're relying upon someone outside your control. Then you're vulnerable—he *has* to be right—and you'll naturally worry that things may not work out as you want them to.

INCOME

The same principles apply to your ability to acquire income in the future. No one can take the gamble out of life for you, no matter how much he may promise to do so. But when you recognize that *you* have the power to deal with anything that lies ahead, an uncertain future can be a source of adventure rather than a fearful liability.

I haven't the faintest idea what I'll be doing five years from now. I may be writing books; I may be doing something else that I can't even conceive of now. I don't know where I'll be living; I don't know whom I'll be with. I know only one thing—that life will continue to be as exciting and as full of happy surprises as it is now.

My life is an adventure because I'm not vulnerable to someone else's mistakes. I'm not depending upon someone to guarantee my income—someone who could fail. If *I* fail, it will be a simple matter to pay for my mistakes and move right on to better things. If I were to stake my future on someone else's ability, I'd be constantly afraid that he might not do the right things—afraid that *he* might make a bad mistake but wouldn't have the honesty to acknowledge and correct it.

If a factory closes, most of the people who worked there will sulk over their misfortune. They had depended upon the continuation of that one source of income. They were vulnerable because they couldn't conceive of any other possibilities.

Meanwhile, a free man will move on to something better. He may have no new alternatives in mind at the time of the closing, but he knows that other alternatives exist—and that he can always find a way of being valuable to someone in exchange for money.

He's prepared for such a possibility, because he never believes that any situation *has* to be permanent. He's ready for change whenever it might happen.

No one can guarantee a steady pay check for you. Anyone who promises to do so is simply being unrealistic.

Your income will always depend upon the changing values of the General Market. You can't expect to receive money unless you're providing a service to someone who's willing to pay for it. That applies whether you perform services or make investments.

If you realize that there will always be people willing to pay to have things done, and if you're willing to find out what they're willing to pay for, you have nothing to be afraid of. You'll know that you can always strike a bargain with someone to do something—even if you're flat on your back.

You may decide to have the managers of a company provide a market for your services, but don't assume it must be permanent. For if you do, you'll be insecure. They can be wrong; they can fail; they can lose interest in their work. But you'll never lose interest in yourself or your own future—so why not depend upon you?

INTELLECTUAL SECURITY

For the past twenty-two chapters I've been saying that you are sovereign. You're the absolute final judge of the worth of information you receive; you're the one who decides every one of your actions; you're the person who determines what is right and wrong for you.

That's the simple reality of it. But many people don't want that responsibility—even though they can't possibly discard it. And so they hope to be handed a ready-made philosophy of life. Such a person wants someone else to guarantee that he's right—no matter what happens.

You *are* responsible, because you will experience the consequences of your own acts, and those consequences are the final judge of whether you've been right or wrong. They provide a verdict from which there is no appeal.

The insecure individual hopes somehow to bypass that verdict. He looks for a way to believe he's right, no matter what consequences he experiences.

He looks for a source of "truth" that he can believe in. When he finds it, he accepts it totally. He feels that this gives him the security to know that he's right, and he prefers that kind of security to the need to rely upon his own ability.

The philosophy he finds usually contains three basic ingredients. They are *moral rightness,* a *leader,* and an *enemy.* These ingredients arm him with an assurance that allows him to disregard the test of consequences.

The sense of moral rightness permits him to believe that *he's right no matter what the consequences he receives in life.* He settles for whatever happiness he gains from knowing he's adhered strictly to the code. He "knows" he was right in what he did—righter than his successful, wealthy, peaceful, joyous neighbor.

Such a philosophy will usually have a leader to give the individual the confidence that he doesn't have in himself. If questions or doubts arise, the leader can set them to rest. The insecure individual may feel, "I can't tell what is right, but *he* says it's right—and he must know."

It always seems necessary, too, for the philosophy to have an enemy. That provides a ready-made explanation for any bad consequences that may occur.

Since the philosophy is usually expressed in terms of "moral truths," the battle with the enemy becomes a moral one. "We" (the good guys) are moral and "they" (the enemy) are immoral.

The moralistic overtones create an evangelical fervor. The enemy isn't pictured as a group of misguided individuals who don't understand things as well as "we" do. Instead, "they" *know* what they're doing and *know* that it's wrong. They're acting deliberately; they're "evil."

This eliminates the need for the moralist to be tolerant or understanding of anyone whose interests conflict with his. Instead, he can be aggressive, violent, nasty, vitriolic, outraged—because he's dealing with someone who is immoral and thus not deserving of benevolence. It's an ideal way to relieve the pent-up frustrations that come from having to bear the bad consequences that might come from living by the philosophy.

So the insecure individual looks outside himself for intellectual security. He hopes to find a philosophy that will guarantee him moral rightness, a leader to compensate for his lack of confidence, and an enemy to justify whatever goes wrong. Unfortunately, he lives in a fool's paradise. He still has to deal with the world and with the consequences of his own actions.

Meanwhile, the individual who recognizes his own sovereignty considers the consequences of his actions to be the only standard of right and wrong. He knows that he's capable of seeing those consequences and reacting to them as necessary. He can change any course of action that doesn't work; he can handle change and surprises as they occur. He can deal with whatever comes.

He would feel insecure only if he had to act in accordance with someone else's judgment. He would be genuinely afraid if someone else's decisions were determining his future.

He knows that the future is uncertain. But he's willing to be vigilant—to check the results of his actions. And he's willing to be honest—to acknowledge any mistakes and correct them immediately.

He's found the only kind of intellectual security that makes sense—reliance upon his own sovereignty.

EMOTIONAL SECURITY

The desire to be loved, to be understood and appreciated, is universal. Unfortunately, many people don't feel they're worthy of such benefits, and so they hope to have them guaranteed without having to earn them. They seek perpetual love and understanding by getting married, by joining groups, or by having children.

If you rely upon yourself, you know that you can find the kind of people who will appreciate you. If you rely upon marriage, family, or groups, you know intuitively that you're vulnerable; you can be deserted despite the guarantees. And you know that the appreciation isn't for what *you* are but instead for your role in the family or the group.

You may find someone to marry, but that doesn't mean he'll always love you or that he'll understand and appreciate you. You can join groups, but don't be surprised if you find a lot of other lonely people acting as if they're having a good time.

Only if you know that you have something to offer can you be sure you'll be appreciated or loved. Only then can you hope to find someone who'll appreciate what you are.

You have to earn anything you want in life—and emotional security is no exception. You earn it by living up to the standards that have meaning to you, finding other people who value those standards, and *continuing* to live up to those standards.

There's no final resting place—short of death—where you can stop having to earn what you want. If you're loved now, you'll continue to be loved only if you continue to satisfy the values of the person who loves you.

That fact only bothers the person who doesn't feel that he *is* genuinely worthy. Chances are that he's tried to live with an identity that isn't his own, and he's constantly afraid that he won't live up to it—afraid that he'll be found out and deserted.

Meanwhile, the individual who accepts his own identity knows that he is something real, something honest, something worthy. He doesn't expect everyone to appreciate that—but he knows *someone* will. He's willing to expend the effort to find that someone (and others who are similar), because he knows the rewards are worth it.

He recognizes that values constantly change. When a

friendship is no longer in the best interests of both parties, he accepts the ending of it. When a love affair ends, he doesn't try to perpetuate it by appeals to loyalty, dependence, or the preservation of a marriage.

Because he's self-reliant and honest with himself, he's constantly growing. And so every relationship he has is more fruitful than the ones that preceded it. He has no fear of the future because he knows the future can only mean better things for him.

Emotional security is entirely within your power to achieve. When you recognize and depend upon your own sovereignty, you'll know that you're capable of finding and enjoying valuable relationships—no matter how those you know now may change.

The insecure person hangs on desperately to whatever exists in the present. The secure person accepts and enjoys whatever he has in the present, but as change occurs he feels no fear of the future. He knows that changes are only preludes to better things.

SECURITY

Insecurity comes from vulnerability. The insecure person relies upon protectors—institutions and people who will guarantee results for him. Because he knows intuitively that his interests can't possibly be the paramount interest in someone else's life, he's vulnerable and he knows it.

He depends upon his "rights" to protect him, he hopes for safety and durability from his ability to make others understand him, he clings to situations that are no longer right for him, and the constant frustrations of these situations only heighten his insecurity. He has good reason to be afraid of the world.

But security is always possible—financial, intellectual, and emotional security. However, it can come only from the willingness to handle whatever comes and the knowledge that you can do so.

The knowledge and willingness aren't hard to come by when you form the habit of thinking in terms of the areas that *you* control. When you realize how much you can do that doesn't depend upon the agreement of others, you know there's nothing you can't handle.

When situations are wrong for you, you can find better situations. You don't have to be frustrated by trying to make those around you treat you better.

If you're willing to depend upon the direct alternatives available to you, if you're willing to be alert to changes as they develop, if you're willing to be honest with yourself and with others, you have nothing to be insecure about— because there's nothing important that you can't handle.

If you earn whatever you want, you know that it's yours. Then life is an adventure. The uncertainty of the future is a challenge, not a source of dread.

Why, then the world's mine oyster,
Which I with sword will open.
—SHAKESPEARE

In battle or business, whatever the game,
In law or in love, it is ever the same;
In the struggle for power, or the scramble for pelf,
Let this be your motto—rely on yourself!
—JOHN GODFREY SAXE

24

Freedom from Exploitation

MANY PEOPLE EXPLAIN THEIR PROBLEMS by describing themselves as "exploited."

Some feel they can never be free so long as the economic system exploits them. Others blame their poverty on businesses that sell them goods at "exorbitant" prices.

On a personal level, some people attribute their job problems to exploitation by their employers or associates. Others complain about the continual mistreatment they receive from their friends, families, or lovers.

Freedom from exploitation comes not from changing other people or the economic system; it comes from a recognition of the direct alternatives available to you. If you feel you're exploited, it's probably because you feel trapped in a situation to which there are no alternatives. But there are always alternatives.

WHAT IS IT?

By definition, exploitation is usually considered to be the utilization of someone or something for purely selfish ends. But as we've seen again and again, all persons' motivations are "purely selfish." You can't expect to deal with anyone who won't be acting in his own selfish interest—

whatever it may be. So you'll never be free from exploitation if you hope to arrange things so that others won't act in ways they think will bring them mental well-being.

Each person will act upon the best alternative he thinks is available to him. So when you think someone is exploiting, it's simply that he's doing what he thinks best. He may seem to be taking advantage of someone, but we also know that the other person (the "exploited") is doing what *he* thinks best.

And so we come to the key question: If someone is being exploited, *why does he permit it*? Why does someone willingly put himself in a position where it appears to us that he's being taken advantage of?

Let's look at some examples of exploitation in different kinds of relationships to see if we can get an answer.

PERSONAL RELATIONSHIPS

I've often been bored by someone telling me over and over again how his spouse mistreats him, how his friends take advantage of him, how his boss abuses him, how his lover "uses" him. *Why does he permit it?* Why doesn't he terminate the realtionship rather than allow the same person to "exploit" him over and over again?[1]

Obviously, the individual permits it because he believes it's the best alternative available to him. He might wish he had a better alternative, but he doesn't know of any—and so he stays where he is.

It's surprising, then, that he usually aims his bitterness at the person he's dealing with, when he really wishes that *someone else* would offer something better.

I think it's a general rule that if you feel you're being exploited, the person you're dealing with is usually the last person you should blame.

In a sense, an individual can be made to suffer for his

---

[1] And why do I permit myself to be bored by such complaints over and over again?

good qualities. For it's his good qualities (those that *you* value) that make him attractive to you. Otherwise, you'd simply ignore him. But because he seems to offer you something, you want to be involved with him. And if there's something about him you don't like, you can be tempted to try to change him.

But it won't work. Each person is what he is. To try to change him is to frustrate yourself with an indirect alternative. The resentment that many people call "being exploited" is usually the result of such frustration. Your only direct alternatives are to look for someone better, or to change the nature of the relationship so that his differences don't have to get in the way (as we saw in Chapter 18).

If there are better alternatives available to you and you don't take advantage of them, then it's *you* who is abusing you.

You don't have to be involved with cheaters, frauds, cheapskates, liars, demanding people, or anyone else you don't like. It's up to you to choose the people you'll deal with.

Friendships don't have to be excuses for continual demands. And love affairs don't have to include constant arguments or sacrifices. If *your* situation does, it's because you've chosen to permit it.

You'll free yourself from such exploitation only by enlarging your range of alternatives. What other way is there?

ECONOMIC EXPLOITATION

I've often heard it said that the profit system allows businessmen to exploit workers. The working conditions during the Industrial Revolution are frequently cited as evidence; men, women, and children were supposedly forced to work in terrible conditions for little pay.

Again, the question to be asked is: *Why* did they permit it? *Why* did they work in such miserable conditions?

The only conceivable answer is that they wanted to. Individuals left their farms and other occupations and migrated to the factories because it was an *improvement* over what was available to them before.

You probably wouldn't work twelve to fourteen hours a day in a hot, stifling factory for a dollar. That is, you wouldn't do it in the 1970s. But millions of people did so willingly in the nineteenth century—because that was better than other opportunities.

Should the businessmen be blamed for improving the lot of the workers?

The introduction of machinery made it possible to produce more in the same number of man–hours. Consequently, profits went up, wages went up, and prices dropped. People bought more because they could afford more at lower prices. And many competed for the factory jobs because the work offered an opportunity to improve their living standards.

There isn't any other logical explanation. To think otherwise is to assume somehow that millions of people gave up good pay and good working conditions to debase themselves in factory work.

Without the Industrial Revolution, most of us today would be working on farms, barely producing enough to feed ourselves, making our own clothes, living without things we now consider necessities, working twelve or more hours every day of the week.

And without the profit system, the Industrial Revolution probably never would have happened. Men were inspired to create improvements in production because of the rewards they could get from them.

The men who made millions of dollars from the innovations provided far *more* wealth to other people. Otherwise, those other people wouldn't have paid them for what they did. No one pays money if he thinks he has a better alternative.

It's ironic that the men who are pictured as symbols of greed and exploitation are the ones who have done the most for other people. It would seem that most people aren't happy with the things they take for granted.

For example, if Henry Ford had been prevented from making his billion dollars, we might have been deprived of the availability of low-cost mass-produced automobiles. If you don't think automobiles are a blessing, you don't have to buy one, of course.

I fail to see how we've been expoited by people who have advanced our standards of living and become wealthy in the process. The General Market determined how much their services were worth to people. And for every man who became wealthy, there were hundreds who tried but didn't offer what people wanted.

If the people who gave money to the men who became wealthy had felt they were being exploited, they could have stopped it by not buying their products.

COMMERCIALISM

A frequent complaint is that someone is charging too much for his services. But he can be charging "too much" only if someone else is willing to offer the same service for less. If no one else will offer the service for less, how can we say the price is too high?

We hear of businessmen who exploit Negroes and others in the "ghetto" areas. It's said that they charge higher prices than are charged in other areas of the cities. If that's true, and there's no real need for the higher prices, it should be a marvelous opportunity for someone to go into those areas and outsell the exploiters by charging lower prices.

Why don't those who are concerned about exploitation do that? They could offer a humanitarian service and make a good profit while doing it. There must be a reason why they don't; and when you find that reason, you'll know that no one is "exploiting" anyone.

There's no way anyone can get into a position where he can charge any price he wants to charge. For competition always exists—even if the competition isn't selling the same thing. A man who sells ballpoint pens has to compete with people who sell other ballpoint pens, pencils, fountain pens, typewriters, crayons, etc. If he charges more for his pens than they're worth to people, they'll find other ways of satisfying their needs.

If a water company decided to charge $25 for the amount of water necessary to water your lawn, would you buy it? Probably not. You'd water your lawn less often. And if car prices are too high, you might buy a new car every four or five years instead of every three.

Individuals can always get by for short periods of time with minor inconveniences. But a lack of sales is a *major* inconvenience to a company. It has an investment to recoup, a payroll to meet. Most companies can't last very long on their reserves; they *have* to make sales.

As a result, they charge the prices they think will bring them the greatest profit—which means a price that's low enough to keep competition away and low enough to make it profitable for people to buy their products.

You don't have to buy from anyone. If you *do* buy, it's because you value the product or service more than you value the money you're spending.

To resent a price is to wish that the seller would be "kinder" and charge less or give more in return. That's wishing that the other person were less selfish than you are. And while that would be nice if it were possible, it isn't possible. So why even think about it?

No one has to produce for others; he'll do so only when he believes it's to his advantage. And no one has to buy from anyone; he'll do so only when it's to *his* advantage. The desire for the service, together with available alternatives, will determine the price.

Since no one *has* to produce what I want, I'm relieved and grateful when I find that the things I want are available. I feel fortunate that others have chosen to produce the things I'd like to have.

I feel lucky that there are operas to see (I certainly couldn't produce one all by myself), that there are so many different cars to choose from, that there are people who produce phonograph records, books, movies, and the other things I like. Sometimes I might wish they had done things differently, but how can I object to the fact that they *have* produced the things I want?

ALTERNATIVES

In the same way, the people I associate with on a personal level offer me more than the other alternatives I'm aware of. How can I complain? If I continue dealing with someone, I'd better accept him as he is.

I'm grateful for every relationship I've had. Because I seek happiness, I'm on the lookout for better relationships and better ways to handle relationships. But if I find them, that doesn't detract from the value of what I've had in the past.

You don't have to buy from anyone.

You don't have to work at any particular job.

You don't have to participate in any given relationship.

You can choose.

If you feel exploited, you have four alternatives available: (1) you can stay and complain that you're being "used"; (2) you can try to change the other person; (3) you can change the relationship so that the other person's drawbacks don't affect you; or (4) you can withdraw from the relationship and look for better alternatives. Only the last two alternatives offer any hope for a better life.

You only sap your strength when you become preoccupied with the drawbacks of the person you deal with. He'll continue to be what he is. Let him be that; it doesn't have to affect you.

You can have so much more if you recognize your own sovereignty. In the final analysis, the only person who can exploit you is you—because you make all the final decisions for your life.

Freedom from exploitation is perhaps the easiest freedom to get. All you have to do is to stop participating in any relationship—of any kind—that doesn't suit you.

It is as impossible for a man to be cheated by anyone but himself, as for a thing to be, and not to be, at the same time.   —RALPH WALDO EMERSON

25

Freedom
from the Treadmill

FREEDOM IS living your life as you want to live it.

Many people feel that freedom is impossible because of the many hours required for work, because of their debts, and because they can't afford to live the way they'd like to.

The treadmill enslaves many people who can't conceive that life could be any different. They stay where they are, leaving things as they are, making changes only when someone else initiates them.

But why should it be that way? You're a sovereign human being with numerous talents and a great many alternatives available to you. Whether you want to increase your income, reduce your working hours, get out of debt, or work in a less monotonous job, there's always a way. More than anything, the need is to use your imagination to look for alternatives.

Several years ago I faced a large debt that had to be paid off almost immediately. At the time I was doing miscellaneous sales jobs for several different companies. I went to the manager of one of the companies and asked what his worst problem was. What he told me was something I couldn't do anything about, so I asked him what his second worst problem was.

In reply, he explained the difficulty he was having because various administrative personnel weren't supporting the company's sales programs. I offered to give them a series of sales lectures, and he accepted the offer. I created a lecture series, together with an incentive system that would reward the administrative personnel for their sales help.

That one extra job led to others. After our initial discussion, the manager mentioned many other problems to me and I had opportunities to solve some of them. Each problem meant extra money for me if I could solve it. The debt that had bothered me was paid off very quickly.

I remember the incident well, because the day before I saw the manager, I was sulking in my living room, saying to myself, "There's nothing I can do."

There's *always* something you can do. And usually the way to find out *what* you can do is to ask. Ask your employer or your customer what he needs right now more than anything else. He can probably name a dozen things—and one or more of them may be things you can do.

SOLVING PROBLEMS

Every problem you can solve means more money for you. A problem is a market for a solution. Be sensitive to the problems of everyone you do business with.

If you don't see problems, ask about them. Almost everyone has irritating concerns that he'd like to have out of the way. Treat each of these opportunities as a separate matter, with a separate fee for the solution of the problem—to be paid *if* you can solve it.

To make the most of the opportunity, always handle the problem for a fee—never for an hourly wage. Find out what it would be worth to have the problem eliminated, and then decide if that price would be worth your time to do it. If you contract in terms of objectives, rather than hours, you'll probably find that your hourly income can be two or three times as much as it would have been otherwise.

There are always plenty of opportunities of this kind around—more than enough to keep you busy without having to work for a salary or an hourly wage. Even during times of high unemployment, the person who looks for unsatisfied needs will always find numerous profitable alternatives.

Always try to determine the self-interest of anyone you deal with. And the best way to discover that is to ask him. What does he need?

Above all, remember that the person who's paying for the service decides what it's worth to him. Don't ever expect someone to pay for something unless *he* sees it as valuable to him. If you're sure he's being shortsighted, look for someone who appreciates your value.

You're not a slave to anyone; you don't *have* to work for anyone. But neither is anyone a slave to you.

You may feel your talents or skills are limited. But you'd probably be surprised to find how many things you're capable of doing that other people would gladly pay for. Once you start asking what people would pay to have done, that may become apparent.

It doesn't hurt to make a list of your talents, just to remind yourself. Include all the things you've ever worked at, along with your hobbies and the subjects you excelled in at school. When you look at your list, you might notice many things you could do for others that would be more rewarding than what you're doing now.

Don't worry about college degrees and other credentials. When you offer to solve problems and be paid on the basis of results, customers are usually unconcerned about diplomas and other normal job qualifications.

I know a number of executives who never went to college, salesmen and entrepreneurs who didn't finish high school, and professional men who never bothered to get licenses. They simply look for people who want value for their money and offer it to them.

NEW JOBS

Why should you spend the only life you have in a job that doesn't excite you? There are undoubtedly many other things you could do—if you're willing to look into them.

Daydream. What did you always dream of doing while you were growing up? Is that still attractive to you now? If not, what do you dream of today? Whatever it may be, take your dreams seriously. Why shouldn't you at least try to make your life what you want it to be?

Did you always want to paint? Why not try it now? Maybe you wouldn't be a Rembrandt—but you might still be a good enough painter to make a decent living while doing what *you* want to do. You could even test it on the side without having to forsake your present job until you know what you can earn from your painting.

Did you want to be a lion tamer? Maybe you could still be one. If not, you might be able to find another interesting job dealing with animals.

Did you want to be a movie star? Even if you decide there's no hope for that, why couldn't you join a neighborhood theater group to see if you like acting and to determine if you have any talent? If you do, you could then look for something more professional.

Why should you have to resign yourself to a life you don't care for?

FREE TIME

Would you like to work fewer hours? There's always a way to cut down on your working time without reducing your income.

I mentioned earlier the contracting arrangement I made with my employees. I contracted with each of them for a specific result and no longer considered them as employees. Each former employee was then free to use his time in any way he chose; the only requirement was that he deliver the work on time.

Every one of them performed his work in less time than he had before. Some of them used the new free time to make extra money elsewhere; others enjoyed the luxury of working fewer hours.

You can use this principle in any kind of work. If you deal with customers or employers on the basis of results, you don't have to go on the payroll—nor do you have to punch a time clock or show up at the office. All your customer will demand is results. Your time will be free to plan as you choose.

I know a number of people—engineers, accountants, salesmen, secretaries, executives, and others—who would never dream of being on a company's payroll. They simply contact companies and offer to perform needed services for a given fee. They manage their own time and methods and never take on jobs they don't think will be interesting.

They often perform jobs that are similar to what the company's employees are doing. But because they offer more than the employees do, they get better arrangements.

When you solve problems and satisy needs, you put yourself in a unique position. You're doing something for the customer that he isn't used to getting from others. The others are simply going along, taking orders, doing only what they're asked to do. They aren't looking for ways to be of greater value, so they don't enjoy greater income and opportunities.

If *you* do, you'll be a rare person. You'll have a natural monopoly in your area. You'll be irreplaceable in the eyes of someone, because there will be no one as valuable at what you do.

When you're in that position, you may be amazed at how easy it is to write your own ticket.

I know a woman who works for a company in a big city. Since it's a large corporation, it has bureaucratic rules and traditions that normally defy individual arrangements.

She has a second home outside the city where she likes to spend her weekends. But the traffic problem makes it a struggle to get in and out of the city on weekends.

Because she's unusually valuable to the company, she was able to arrange to be in the office only Tuesdays, Wednesdays, and Thursdays, so she can commute during times of little traffic. She does her work at her country home on Mondays and Fridays and accomplishes more in that quiet setting than she could at the office.

If she had asked her employer to grant her this request as a favor, he'd have found plenty of reasons regretfully to turn her down. But because she's demonstrated many times over that she's unusually valuable, she has a natural monopoly in her job. Her work is far more important to the company than her presence in the office on Mondays and Fridays.

There are always ways to arrange more free time if you're geared to thinking in terms of results—results for the person paying you and results for you.

For example, you might be in a position to hire someone else to do the least important parts of your work. You'd probably pay him less than you receive for that work. You can then use the extra hours to make more money or to enjoy yourself more.

The keys to a non-treadmill life are to find out what other people will pay for and to recognize what you're capable of doing. Get in the habit of asking your employer and your customers what they need and they aren't getting. Get in the habit of thinking of things you'd like to do but aren't doing now. Get in the habit of making changes that give you time to enjoy life more.

DEBTS

Too often, an individual remains on the treadmill because he has too many debts to allow him to reduce his working hours. A great deal of freedom is lost when you have to spend the present paying off the past.

I've never liked debt. I've had plenty of it and I dislike the way it immobilizes. To me, freedom includes the opportunity to spend money as I choose, to spend it at the time I receive it.

I was once so deep in debt that I thought it was foolish to even think I'd ever be out of it. I don't believe in bankruptcy, so I thought I was stuck for life.

One day I totaled all my obligations and found that I owed $13,000. The amount seemed so enormous that I thought it was pointless to pay $50 or $100 against it.

But I also began to feel that there wasn't anything more important to me than getting rid of it. I resolved to try to reduce it by some amount during the next couple of months. If the effort were to make my life too miserable, I could always go back to my old spending habits; but for two months I'd concentrate on the task.

I kept a running total of my debts and reduced the total everytime I made a payment against it. At the end of the first month, I'd lowered it by only $400. That meant it would take over two years to liquidate the whole amount.

But it was fun to see the total go down. Before long, no purchase was as exciting as buying a position of less debt. I was inspired to take on extra jobs—because every fee I earned meant a reduction of the total.

If it became necessary to replace a household item, I did it in the cheapest possible way—knowing I could always improve upon it later. For now, cutting the debt was my most compelling motivation.

Once a momentum was created, the debt shrank faster and faster. Finally, I was totally out of debt—seven months after I'd believed it would be impossible to *ever* get out of debt.

I happily gave up the austerity budget and went out and splurged on new clothes, dinners, and dates (paying cash, of course). I never want to have to go back to such a task, so the experience has kept me from being tempted to jump back into debt.

What I did isn't necessarily what you will do—possibly it would be more difficult for you. But I cite the experience as an example of how wrong it can be to think there is no way out. There's always a way out—once you make up your mind what is most important to you.

If it's important to you to be debtfree, then work extra hours, cut out nonessential spending for a while, or sell items you don't need. Find a way to put yourself in the position you'd like to be in. If you know why you're doing it, and it's important to you to do it, you don't mind the temporary austerity.

SMALL PRICES

I've also found that I'm better off—during good times or bad—by never worrying about small sums of money.

John Kamen, publisher of the *Forecaster*, once told me that he never worried about any price under $10. He'd pay for anything under $10 without considering his budget or the possibility that it might be a waste. If someone created a dispute about $10, he'd pay it without arguing.

When he told me this, I realized that I'd been doing the same thing. I've always disregarded small sums because it seemed a waste of time to argue over them or worry about them. After hearing John's rule, I set for myself a conscious limit of $100. If I ever find that the limit costs me more than it saves me, I can adjust it. Until then, I refuse to ponder restaurant prices, repair bills, or any other small expenditures.

Meanwhile, I see people who will spend hours (if not weeks) pondering a $15 expenditure. They feel they have to, because of their limited means. They never consider that their means are limited partly because of the time they waste over pennies.

Such choices are subjective, of course. Some people love to shop; but many people think they're bargain-hunting out of necessity. They may be costing themselves more than they're saving.

Freedom from such concerns is important to me. I'd much rather spend my time listening to a Puccini opera or making love than trying to choose between a $6 item and an $8 item.

YOUR DECISIONS

Your life is yours to spend as you choose. You don't *have* to be wealthy; you don't *have* to be involved in a family; you don't *have* to be successful. If any of those things are a part of your life, it should be only because you choose them. There are no rules for what your life should be.

When you decide what you want, it's important to recognize that there are probably *many* things you want. You can envision many more desirable alternatives than you could satisfy in a lifetime. Desires always exceed resources. That's why you choose—to satisfy the desires most important to you.

It's essential to realize that you can't have everything, you can't do everything. There's always a price—and the price can be expressed in the alternatives that must be given up for something.

There are many things you *could* do with your life. But which ones do you want *most*? What would you be willing to give up in order to advance your career, to become famous, to be wealthy? Are you willing to set aside the next twenty years of your life for the *possibility* that you may become wealthy? Are you willing to forego the leisure, the entertainment, the family life, and other things most people take for granted?

Always view your desires within the context of your whole life. There is an unlimited number of things you can do to make money. But that's the point: Since there *is* an unlimited number, you have to draw the line somewhere. It's unrealistic to say you'll "do anything you have to" to make money.

To say that is to give up everything else in life that you

might enjoy. So it's best to draw limits at the beginning—limits that are appropriate to your own nature. If you do that, you'll be less likely to be burdened by thoughts of what you *could* have done to make more money. You'll know what you received in place of the extra earning hours.

I've always wanted to be rich, but I've always been very lazy, too. One day I had it out with myself and decided that, given a choice, I would prefer a lower financial status to working long hours at something I didn't enjoy.

I still wanted money for the things it could buy. But I established limits beyond which I wouldn't go to acquire wealth. I defined them clearly and they were compatible with what I knew about myself. So I never had to feel guilty when I wasn't working.

For the past few years I've worked only at things I've generally enjoyed. I knew that it was better to do that (no matter what the monetary return) than to commit myself to a lifetime of intense effort and joyless drudgery.

Perhaps it isn't surprising that I've made far more money during these past few years than I ever made before. For I'm much more valuable doing what I enjoy than I am doing what is distasteful to me.

If it hadn't turned out that way, I wouldn't be sorry. I made a choice that was appropriate to my nature and I was quite willing to live by it—no matter what the monetary result. I knew I would never be happy living any other way.

If you're not willing to give up the things that you enjoy, accept that and don't waste your time and attention pining over what you should have done to be more successful. Establish a set of priorities; place limits upon the effort you'll make to be professionally successful; and then remind yourself of those limits whenever you're tempted to be regretful.

On the other hand, if wealth and achievement are what you *do* want—more than parties, friendships, love affairs, family activities, more than anything—then recognize *that* and accept it. Do what is necessary to succeed and don't

let anyone browbeat you with accusations that you're
"self-centered" or "greedy."

Do what *you* want to do. But recognize that there are
many things you want to do and you can't have them all.
So establish priorities in your values and stick to the ones
at the top. When you have to give up the lesser values,
don't waste your time bemoaning the loss of what could
have been obtained only by giving up something more
valuable.

THE FUTURE

Another way many people keep themselves on the
treadmill is by being preoccupied with the future. It's easy
to justify a rigorous schedule in the present as an investment in the future. Many people work long hours, put up
with disagreeable effects of their work, and forego enjoyments—all because it promises a brighter future.

But what if the future never comes? Who knows what
will happen to the economy, to your ability to enjoy yourself, to the things you'd planned to spend your money for?

I don't believe in committing my future to pay for in-
dulgences of the present. But neither will I sacrifice today
for a vague, indefinite tomorrow. I could die next week.
What then would be the worth of my well-laid plans for
twenty years from now?

It makes sense to enjoy yourself at the time when
you're best able to do so—mentally and physically. At
sixty-five, the luscious dreams of today may not be so attractive. So leave sixty-five to be handled at sixty-five. Do
what you can to be sure you can provide for yourself
then—but don't put off your dreams until then.

The time to be free, to start living, to enjoy yourself, is
right now. Now is the time when you can best appreciate
the unplanned hours that can be enjoyed as you choose at
each moment.

If you don't have any free time or money, do something
about that. If you don't know where your time and money

are going, stop everything and check your expenditures and activities carefully. Find out how you're spending your life.

Get rid of all the nonessentials—especially those that are vague investments in the future. Don't feel that you have to give sixty hours a week to your work—unless that's what you enjoy most.

Be free—free to act upon opportunities as they arise, free to take advantage of the things you've wanted to do. Find ways to satisfy your dreams. After all, what is life for? If it's really just a vale of tears, what's the point in being alive?

I believe that life is to be enjoyed, to be tasted—or there isn't any point to it. I've found ways to live freely and joyously—because I was convinced there was no other reason for living.

I didn't become free by working sixty hours a week— except during very brief periods when there were immediate and important rewards for doing so. I didn't become free by accepting the routine that others expected of me.

There will be plenty of people to tell you that you must go along with things as they are, that you have no right to expect a happier, easier life, that there are other people who have less than you do. But so what?

There's so much to be had from life. There's pleasure and satisfaction and love and entertainment and excitement. And there are enjoyable ways of earning a living, and there are adventures, uncommitted hours, challenges, and happy surprises.

Use your imagination. Look for alternatives. Don't settle for less than the kind of life you need to make it worth having lived.

Riches are for spending.   —FRANCIS BACON

Why do you have to postpone moving to a warmer climate where you can swim all year until you are so old that you're afraid of the water?   —DAVID S. VISCOTT

26

Freedom from Pretense

WE'VE SEEN HOW HIDING YOURSELF can cause all kinds of social restrictions to be imposed upon you. In the same way, little acts of dishonesty can be a surprisingly easy way to throw away your freedom.

It's such a small thing to shade the truth a little—but the long-run consequences can create tremendous restrictions on your life.

For example, suppose there's something you want to do, but if a given person knew about it there might be problems. So you tell a simple lie to him to cover your tracks.

Then one day you're with him and another person, and the matter comes up in discussion. It becomes necessary to repeat or confirm the lie you told before. But the other person doesn't understand the inconsistency between what you're saying now and something you've said to him before. So you have to invent an explanation that will satisfy both of them.

Now whenever you're with either of these people, you have to remember the separate fictions involved—to keep the original lie from being exposed. And it can become even more complicated as other people become involved.

So to avoid revealing your actions to someone, you can eventually pay a very complicated and expensive price. If you admit to the second person that you lied to the first, your honesty would be suspect in the future. No matter how you handle it, you pay for dishonesty.

In fact, it's a very easy way to jump into a box. When you've lied about something, your actions are restricted by the need to maintain the fiction you've created. You can no longer react freely and spontaneously to new developments; you always have to keep your guard up to avoid doing anything that might reveal your previous acts.

Ironically, I think dishonesty usually comes about as an attempt to *avoid* prices. A friend, Lynda Raff, once pointed out that lying is an attempt to get something for nothing. It's the hope of being able to do something without the consequences that would naturally follow—the reactions of certain people.

And yet, you usually wind up paying a higher price dealing with the problems required to continue the deception.

The value of honesty is greatest to the person being honest. It may be helpful to someone else if you're honest with him, but you're helping *yourself* far more by your honesty.

PROBLEMS OF DISHONESTY

Here are a few of the problems you can bring upon yourself by being dishonest:

1. You have to remain on guard, using precious resources to cover up past acts.

2. You miss opportunities to be accepted for yourself, because you're hiding that self. The people who would like you as you really are will never see you if you keep your real self hidden.

3. Dishonesty toward others can lead easily to dishonesty toward yourself. Lying can become automatic. If you're very concerned with maintaining an image, you can remember past lies more clearly than what really happened. After a while, it may become impossible to remember what was true and what wasn't.

4. This can lead to an anxious feeling that what you've obtained by lying can't be preserved. You can feel that you don't really deserve what you have—and so you can't relax and fully enjoy it.

5. Sooner or later someone is going to become aware of your dishonesty—possibly because he has participated in it. Because he knows you've been dishonest in the past, he can't be sure you're being honest in the present. You'll have fewer alternatives available when your word can't be accepted without question.

BENEFITS OF HONESTY

You can avoid those problems by being honest and gain other advantages, too. Here's a brief summary of the various benefits I find that honesty brings:

1. When you prove that you're willing to be honest—no matter what the short-term consequences—others will accept your word more easily. This can open up many opportunities that wouldn't exist if your listeners had to wonder about each thing you say.

For example, when I was promoting my last book through radio and television appearances, I was often asked, "Why did you write this book?" I always answered, "To make money."

A public-relations man suggested to me that I be less honest. "Don't admit you're selfish," he said. "People don't want to hear that. You should tell them you wrote the book to help people."

I asked him how many times he'd heard an author or politician say that he was "only interested in helping people." He acknowledged that he'd heard it many times—and he also acknowledged that he never believed it when he heard it. And finally he admitted that he doubted that other people believed it either.

He hadn't understood that I was helping myself, not hurting myself, by my statement. If I were willing to admit my selfish intentions (usually the first thing someone would lie about), people could more readily accept other things I said when they knew I wasn't covering up anything.

Honesty allows other people to relax around you. They don't have to be alert to evaluate the truthfulness of each statement. Consequently, there's more chance for your words to make an impact.

2. Honesty allows *you* to relax, too. You can say what you think and mean and would like to say—without having to check first to be sure your statements won't contradict a previous remark.

3. As you reveal yourself honestly, you often find that you didn't really know what others wanted to hear; you only assumed you knew. When you tell the truth, you may be surprised to discover that it projects a more attractive image of yourself than one you might have fabricated.

I've often found that others would reveal their feelings only after I'd revealed mine frankly. When they saw that someone was willing to admit the truth about himself, they felt free to follow suit.

4. When you've been honest with everyone you're involved with, you'll know you've earned whatever you have—and you'll feel much freer to relax and enjoy it. You won't have to fear that the truth might someday be revealed and destroy what you've achieved.

5. You'll be free to share your innermost secrets with others. When you decide that you don't have to fear the judgments of others, you won't be afraid to confide in them. When you can verbalize your emotions and desires honestly, you'll probably understand them better and you'll be able to satisfy them more easily.

PLENTY OF ENCOURAGEMENT

Honesty has many advantages, but somehow dishonesty continues to get a good press and plenty of encouragement. Both fiction and real life are filled with examples of "smart" and even "noble" people telling lies.

I imagine you've seen in movies, books, and newspapers how people lie to get what they want, how they lie to avoid hurting someone's feelings, how they disguise their own desires in a show of self-sacrifice, how politicians and diplomats lie in the service of their countries, how lovers lie to arrange secret meetings, and how "little people" lie to get even with big business.

Perhaps the most common encouragement to lying is the idea that you're doing someone a favor when you lie to him.

But I think that idea is dishonest in itself. When a person lies to protect someone's feelings, he's most likely doing it to keep the person from disliking him. A phony compliment usually isn't meant to make an individual feel better about *himself*; it's meant to make him feel better about the person doing the complimenting.

It doesn't work, though. He probably knows the truth already. If you lie to a person about what he already knows, he'll probably respect you less, not more.

And you also hurt your credibility with anyone else who knows about it. Suppose, for example, that you and I are having lunch with Charley, who's known for his large nose. When Charley asks me, "Do you think my nose is large?" I could answer, "Of course not, Charley."

Later, you might ask me if I really meant my remark. Suppose I answer, "No, but I didn't want to hurt his feelings." That may seem noble, but the next time I say something "nice" to you, you'll have no way of knowing whether I meant it or was just trying to make you feel good. My so-called kindness has hurt my relationship with you.

What's the alternative to lying? Do I have to be brutal and hurt Charley in order to be truthful? No. Too often, the "brutal truth" is only a partial truth. When it seems that honesty has caused problems, the trouble is often *too little* truth rather than too much.

For example, when Charley asks me if his nose is too large, I could say, "It sure is!" Would *that* be the truth? Only part of it. It would be more completely honest to say, "You have a large nose—but it doesn't make any difference to me."

Another example of too little truth is the person who angrily says, "I hate you," and then excuses his venom by saying, "Well, you want me to be honest, don't you?" But *is* he being honest? Usually, such an individual doesn't really hate the person—or he wouldn't be in contact with him to begin with.

It might be more accurate to say, "There are many things I like about you, but I dislike very much what you've just done." Or just "I am very angry right now."

That recognizes the broader context in which the issue at hand is only one small part. It makes quite a difference; honesty makes it much easier to deal with whatever has caused the problem.

So if you sometimes fear saying the truth, check first to see if perhaps the problem is one of too little truth rather than too much.

And recognize that you're sacrificing your own reputation and reducing your alternatives when you lie as a supposed favor to someone else. Any problem he has in facing the truth is *his* problem. It isn't your duty to protect him from himself.

100 PERCENT

An important principle underlies the examples we've seen in this chapter: An individual can be sure of your honesty only if you're honest with *everyone*.

How can he be sure you're not lying to protect his feelings if you've lied to protect someone else's feelings?

If you've said you'd lie only if it's "absolutely necessary," how can he be sure you don't consider *this* situation an "absolute necessity"?

If you say you'd never lie to your close friends, how can he be sure he hasn't done something to be demoted from your close friendship?

If you want to prove your honesty to someone, you can

do it only by being honest with everyone. He can relax and accept what you say only if you've demonstrated that you'll be honest even when it's uncomfortable for you to do so.

I once had a lady friend who played the typical games with the phone company—placing collect or person-to-person calls that were never completed, just to get a prearranged message through.

Obviously, the phone company didn't create its facilities to enable people to send free messages. To use those facilities fraudulently is just as dishonest as lying to someone's face.

My friend justified her tactic by saying, "But that doesn't mean I'd lie to *you*! And I resent the inference that I would. You're far more important to me than the phone company."

But that's the point. If she'd lie to the phone company to save 85¢, why wouldn't she lie to me if she thought it would save our relationship—especially since she says I'm more important to her than the phone company?

You can prove your honesty to any one person only by being honest to everyone.

There's a greater difference between being 99 percent honest and 100 percent honest than there is between 70 percent and 90 percent. The first exception to your honesty destroys one of its most important benefits—the absolute trust of others.

TESTING YOURSELF

Most people probably think of themselves as being basically honest, even though they tell a few white lies here and there. In fact, it can be so habitual that it doesn't even register with the person as being dishonest.

The Identity Trap can be compelling. One can be so anxious to put his "best foot forward" that he doesn't even notice that it isn't his own foot.

I find it valuable to test my honesty periodically. To do

so, I pick a period of thirty minutes or so when I'm talking on the telephone or in person with others. I observe closely everything I say. Did I speak the absolute truth as I know it—or did I say what I felt I "ought" to say in the circumstances?

Through this test, I sometimes realize that I've lied without being aware of it.

It *is* possible to change that, however. And I've found a little exercise for that purpose. In fact, it follows from the test I just described.

Take an hour when you'll be talking with someone. Instead of checking your statements *after* you say them, think twice about them *before* speaking. Stop your first impulse to speak, and check what you were about to say. Is it the truth? If it isn't, determine what is and say that.

After an hour, you may be exhausted from the concentration. So don't overdo it at first. An hour each day might be enough to start with.

After a few days of this, it becomes more automatic and requires less effort to keep up. So you can increase the amount of time you'll devote to the exercise.

Eventually, you should discover that your first impulses to speak *are* truthful. At that point, the monitoring can be dropped; honesty will have become natural.

The way I've described the exercise might make it seem as routine as doing an hour of calisthenics each day. But there's a lot more to it.

During the exercise time, you might face some decisive moments. Suppose you've been exaggerating your affection for your wife, and on the first day you try this she asks if you love her? On the third day, you might be divorced.

You might need to answer a question in a way that contradicts an important lie you've been protecting for a long time. If you're not prepared to accept the consequences of that, there's no point in undertaking the attempt.

As I mentioned in the Box-Trap chapter, it's foolish to start using a new technique before you're fully prepared to handle the consequences. You have to be convinced the benefits are worth the discomfort that will accompany the adjustment period.

As with anything else, you can approach absolute honesty on a gradual basis. But it would help to begin thinking of ways to handle the major adjustments that might be required when you acknowledge major dishonesties of the past. I don't think it's worth doing unless you're prepared to go all the way with it eventually.

If you do decide that honesty will be your policy, the rewards should far outweigh the problems. In fact, you'll probably discover benefits far beyond anything I might suggest.

You might develop valuable new relationships—even out of old ones. You may find that more people will respond favorably to you because your honesty is a refreshing difference. As you deal with others, you'll probably feel a great sense of freedom when all need for pretense evaporates. You'll be able to forget about the contradictions and complications you had to keep track of before.

Let me warn you, however, that the only way to demonstrate your honesty is by simply responding honestly to everything. The most ineffective way of demonstrating your honesty is by saying, "I'm being honest with you."

WHAT YOU ARE

When you start reaping the benefits of honesty, all temptation to be dishonest may fade away. You'll want to reveal yourself to others as you are—because you'll know that's the way to attract the kind of people who have the most to offer you.

The real you has a lot more to offer the world than the lost-in-the-crowd façade that so many people try to assume. Who wants one more person whose identity is just like everyone else is trying to be?

I've found that my most useful assets are many of the things I used to try to hide—my selfishness, my laziness, the ease with which I cry when I hear good music or see good drama. Those things have helped me find likeminded people who appreciate the same things. And those are the people I've always wanted to be with—not the ones for whom I'd have to suppress myself.

I've found that suppressing embarrassing things about myself costs me far too much freedom to be worth it. So, if I feared that a given person might discover something I had been trying to hide, I went to him and told it to him myself. The experience never failed to give me a wonderful sense of freedom. I no longer had to worry about it; the price had been paid once and for all, and I didn't have to think about it again.

In the same way, if there is something about myself that makes me self-conscious, I examine it closely. I invariably discover that it's either nothing to be self-conscious about or something that can be easily changed.

INTEGRITY

Honesty is displaying yourself to others as you really are. But, of course, you can't be truthful about something you don't know.

And that's why it's so important to examine yourself, understand yourself, and accept yourself. Only when you know who you are can you honestly represent yourself to others.

The individual who doesn't know himself can't speak with authority about himself. He can't make promises, because he doesn't know himself well enough to foresee his future emotions and actions. He can't express authoritative opinions, because he doesn't really know what he believes.

He uses the word "I" dishonestly. He begins statements with "I think . . ." but he's only repeating what he's heard. He says, "I will . . ." but he doesn't really know what he's going to do.

The word "I" is one of the most important words in the English language. It refers to a unique, individual entity, different from all others in the world. When you use the word, you should be sure you're really expressing the unique, individual entity that is *you*—not simply repeating something that sounded good to you.

To be honest, you must know yourself well. And that involves integrity—which is honesty's twin asset. *Integrity is knowing yourself well enough to be able to mean what you say.*

The person with integrity can use the word "I" with authority. He *knows* what he thinks—for he's thought it out for himself.

AN UNCLUTTERED LIFE

The effort to prevent discovery of facts about yourself can be costly and draining. But it's perhaps the easiest self-destructive habit one can practice.

I've had to work with it—and work with it again. It's so important to me that I don't like to go for very long without rechecking myself to be sure I haven't unthinkingly relapsed into dishonesty. And, unfortunately, sometimes my rechecking reveals that I *have* fallen back.

But my efforts to correct it have been worth the trouble many times over. Discovering myself and displaying that self has brought me countless benefits, valuable friends, a clean, uncluttered life, and a wide expanse of freedom that I didn't even know existed until I tried being totally honest.

As I've said before, there may be more things depriving you of freedom than the particular restriction that prompted you to pick up this book. Freedom can be lost through many traps, boxes, and temptations. And what seems to be harmless dishonesty can turn out to be one of the greatest restrictions of all.

Dishonesty is a form of the Identity Trap. When you lie to someone, you're falling for the temptation to think that you'll be more attractive (and get more of what you want) if you appear to be something different from what you are.

Learn to trust your own nature, your own identity. Accept it, live it, reveal it. Don't suppress it; don't attempt to shade it with little lies and half-truths. When you do, you miss so much of life and the happiness that can be yours.

By being only what *you* are, you can awaken each morning to a new day that's an opportunity to seek whatever you want—with no previous deceptions to get in your way.

To be honest, as this world goes, is to be one man picked out of ten thousand.   —SHAKESPEARE

How could you get what you want if the other person really doesn't see you as you?   —DAVID S. VISCOTT

PART III A New Life

27

Who Are You?

PERHAPS THE MOST IMPORTANT PART of the quest for freedom is discovering yourself, and that can be the hardest part. When you try to live up to an image dictated by others, it can be very difficult to know exactly who you are and what you want.

You're a unique individual—different from anyone else in the world. And what you are is revealed mostly by how you react to things around you—what pleases you and what causes you discomfort. These are the signals that let you know what kind of life you crave, what will bring you happiness.

Unfortunately, the signals become distorted if you've lived most of your life in involved relationships. If you've grown up living with your parents, then lived with a roommate, and then married, your apparent tastes and values may be more the result of the people around you than a reflection of your own nature.

Even if the people around you haven't been demanding or tyrannical, you've still had to consider them when making decisions. As a result, what you now consider to be your tastes might be more a reflection of your past routine than of your natural emotional needs. If so, your experiences might be much less than they could be—perhaps pleasant, but not joyful and exciting.

You need time alone to act completely on your own desires—to discover the kinds of entertainment that please

you, to realize such things as what color you'd most like
your living room to be, to daydream and discover what
you're now missing. Your desires will be best learned
when there's no one around to influence and inhibit you.

SOURCES OF INFORMATION

There are three basic sources of information to tell you
what you want most—past experiences, daydreams, and
new experiences. If you examine each of them more
closely, you'll discover a great deal about yourself that will
tell you what kind of life you need in order to be happy.
Each of them requires time to yourself—time when you
can do what you want to do and discover how much it
pleases you.

Start by looking back over your life. Take some time
alone and think about things you've done before. Try to
recapture those moments of full-bodied happiness—times
when you were almost dizzy with joy.

Try to remember all such experiences, no matter how
long past. Remember the joy you felt—the feeling that for
once you were totally satisfied. And then examine the experience to try to determine what it was that made it so
ecstatic.

You might want to disregard such experiences if you
think they can't be repeated. Maybe they can't. But why
not create new experiences that are similar? Perhaps people who were important to that happiness are lost to you
now. But if you can understand what made those people
so important, you can find others like them.

Reminisce. Indulge yourself in your past joys. And then
start to figure out how you can make such things happen
again.

Your fantasies or daydreams are another important
source of information. Most people don't take their daydreams seriously. They consider them nothing more than
an escape from the rigors of the real world. They're unfree, and they don't believe that their dreams could be sat-

isfied. But if taken seriously, dreams can provide the motivation necessary to break out of boxes.

The next time you daydream, imagine that you're free to actually live the experiences you're fantasizing—totally free of all commitments, obligations, and boxes. Don't try to figure out how you'll remove the restrictions; just imagine that they're already gone. In a later chapter, we'll look at ways to use your dreams to get rid of boxes and leave you free to make the dreams a reality. But it begins by taking your fantasies seriously, by using them to learn what you need to be happy.

And the third source of information is to try new things. Be willing to test new experiences—to discover your own responses, uninhibited by others' reactions.

These last two sources are the most dynamic ways to bring new interest and pleasure to your life. If you never feel intense enjoyment, the way to find some is to experiment with new activities and new environments—paying attention to your reactions.

DO SOMETHING

Do novel things. You may react in novel ways. Pay very serious attention to those reactions—they're telling you who you are.

Experiment in imagination—daydream. Experiment in fact—taste new experiences.

Your imagination will have to be cultivated. It isn't a machine that can be turned on like a television set. You have to develop the art of imagining what you could enjoy that isn't in your life now.

Play, bit by bit, with little memories of delightful moments, days, years, places, people, ideas, wishes, dreams, stories, plans. Play with your imagination. See how good you can become at fantasizing. Imagine the people involved, how you deal with them, what you get from them.

Notice, as you do, when you get the greatest joy from a situation you're imagining. Take that reaction seriously and make a note to see how you can turn that particular dream into a reality.

Use your imagination to find better alternatives. If you later decide to stay where you are now, do so only because you've imagined many alternatives and none of them is better than what you already have.

If possible, don't leave it all to your imagination. Sample. Actually play with the world, open doors to fresh situations that are entirely new. Some of what's beyond those doors will be dull—but a lot of it may be far more delightful than what you have now.

Even the experiments that don't pay off can help you to know what *would* pay off. If something doesn't please you, ask yourself what it was you craved but didn't get in that experience. Then look for a way to get it.

Naturally, be cautious about the consequences of these explorations. There are limits to the ways you can experiment without becoming vulnerable to bad long-term consequences. But within those limits is a world of new and surprising adventures. You'll make mistakes and even be hurt occasionally, but don't let that stop you from trying new things.

Some new possibilities may seem foreign to you, but perhaps only because of a routine you've settled into. As you change your circumstances and remove restrictions from your responses, your emotional reactions to various things can be stronger and different from what they were before. I've found this to be very true in my own experience.

For example, I once thought sex was overrated and often nothing more than a burden. Now that I've learned what I like and I'm free to seek and find it, sex is a totally new, excitingly wonderful means of expression and satisfaction. If I had relied only on my previous experiences, I'd never have known what I was missing.

In the same way, I've discovered new entertainments, new foods, new intellectual adventures, new challenges— since I removed the boxes from my life. As a result, I'm far more willing to try new things and to try again activities I'd previously rejected.

Life has so much to offer that can provide profound and durable happiness. There's so much to discover that can enable you to spend more of your time genuinely enjoying life, rather than just passing the time. You'll find those new joys if you take advantage of past experiences that have been fruitful for you, if you take your daydreams seriously, and if you're willing to try new things.

ACCEPT YOURSELF

I realize that the search for yourself can be a bit frightening sometimes. We've all lived with external standards that can conflict with our natures. And when you discover something about yourself that doesn't suit the accepted standards, you may not be willing to accept your discovery.

The critical points in your self-exploration are the moments when you dislike what you find. If you ignore the discoveries, you're rejecting the opportunity to find a way of life that will bring you happiness. You're resigning yourself to a life in the Identity Trap.

You are what you are. If what you are seems "wrong," it might be because you've accepted standards that are wrong for you.

Or it might be that you haven't probed deeply enough—or that you haven't yet learned how to gratify your desires without bad consequences.

Suppose, for example, that you discover that you have an urge to steal. Your immediate reaction might be a desire to ignore the discovery; it may seem that even to acknowledge the discovery will get you into trouble.

Not necessarily. If you probe more deeply, you might find your urge to steal is only a superficial symptom of a more basic desire—perhaps the desire to have money, or the desire to get away with something, or the desire to rebel against standards that you've seen advocated in a smug, self-righteous way.

If you fight your initial discovery, you'll never come to understand the more basic motivations within you—motivations that might be gratified without the bad consequences that can come from stealing.

Don't feel that to find some desire in yourself is to be compelled to a given course of action. Once you know what you are, you can find ways to make the most of that without getting into trouble. But you'll never find those ways if you don't first accept what you see in yourself.

It may take time to acquire that sense of self-acceptance, but it will come if you let it—and it will bring with it a greater happiness than you could find living in the Identity Trap.

AN EXAMPLE

I've mentioned my laziness before. *How* I discovered it is an excellent example of the difficulty of self-acceptance.

For years I assumed that I was a productive, achieving individual. I wanted to demonstrate my ability to make money and accomplish more than other people could. I associated with people who seemed to reflect those values; often they were successful, self-made industrialists and professional people.

I was always a little uncomfortable around them, partly because I was never as successful as I thought I should be. And when I was alone, it was always more appealing to relax and listen to good music or curl up with a novel, rather than to spend my time in intellectual pursuits, or to lay out grand plans, or to make extra efforts to achieve more.

Naturally, I felt very guilty about my private preferences and activities. In addition, I was in debt and, although I was making a fair living, it seemed that I would always be in debt if I didn't work harder. I wasn't very happy.

Whenever the thought struck me that I was really very lazy, I rejected it. *I didn't want to be lazy.* What would my friends think of me? What about the standards I espoused? How would I ever get out of debt? The apparent consequences were too horrible for me to accept my own laziness.

I can't tell you exactly when I made the breakthrough, for it happened over a period of time. But eventually I became willing to accept my laziness as a part of me.

As I learned to accept that facet of my nature, I made changes in my life. I no longer tried to carry out plans that required more effort than I was capable of giving. I looked for ways to make money that capitalized on the things I could do best (and thus required fewer working hours) and which I enjoyed doing. I stopped worrying what my friends would think and looked for friends who were more relaxed, less compulsively active and productive, and more willing to accept pure enjoyment as a respectable activity.

Dramatic improvements appeared in every area of my life. Friendships and romances became genuine pleasures instead of situations in which a false image had to be maintained. I spent more time with good music and novels. I found new ways to enjoy myself—ways I could enjoy freely, for the burden of guilt was gone.

I constructed a realistic scale of values for myself. I realized that monetary success might cost me too much in discomfort to be worth the effort, so I willingly settled for a life with less strain—even if that also meant less money.

As it turned out, my new way of life brought me *more* money. When I concentrated on the work I enjoyed, my work became more valuable to others and I was paid more for it. My income increased and my working hours decreased. Now I've made more money than I'd even *hoped* to make before.

The acceptance of my laziness was so rewarding that it inspired me to take other revelations about myself more seriously. And I was able to use those discoveries to advantage, too.

I became more honest with others; I no longer said what seemed "proper"—I said what I believed to be true. I was able to speak freely, without embarrassment, of what I wanted and needed. When I did, those who weren't valuable to me drifted away and those who had something to offer made themselves known to me.

My example may be far removed from any problem you have in your life now. I cite it only to demonstrate the importance of self-discovery. It's easy to be afraid of a trait you discover in yourself, but don't jump to conclusions; don't think that the more obvious consequences of that trait are the only ones.

First take yourself seriously—and then find out how you can act upon what you find without bad consequences.

CHANGING YOURSELF

After recognizing and accepting what you find in yourself, you might still be dissatisfied with something about yourself that's in conflict with other, more important parts of your nature. If so, you can work to improve any part of yourself that displeases you.

Understand, however, that the change will probably be a long-term project. Don't let it interfere with what *does* make you happy in the interim. As hopeful as you may be, the change may never be successfully completed—so it would be foolish to throw away the happiness you can have in favor of something that might never be.

People often get into trouble by thinking that they can change themselves just by deciding to. They decide they're going to be different from what they've been, and then make plans based upon their new images—plans that never work out because they're unrealistic.

Always act with a recognition and acceptance of what you are at that moment. Don't expect to accomplish feats that require talents you don't have; don't ignore your weaknesses; don't act as if you were someone other than who you are. Work to improve yourself in any way that seems right to you; but in the interim, act in ways that are consistent with what you are at that moment.

You are what you are. That doesn't mean you'll always be the same—but what you do right now will succeed or fail in terms of what you are this minute.

YOUR DESIRES

As you look for ways to be happier, there are two types of desires to be considered.

One is the *long-term* way of life you want for yourself. That can include such things as the kind of work you want to do, the long-term love relationship you might be seeking, where you'd like to live, the improvements you'd like to make in yourself. It can also include a long-term plan to create a new free life for yourself that includes fewer commitments, obligations, debts, and responsibilities.

The other type of desire is the *short-term* pleasure you seek. That can include minor romances, various entertainments, traveling, projects, or hobbies you've wanted to try—anything that doesn't involve long-term plans.

Your personal morality can be of value in both areas. It can remind you to keep your eyes on the long-term goals you've set for yourself. And it can act as a monitor to assure that short-term pleasures don't interfere with your long-term plans.

Don't feel that you have to know all your long-term goals right now. In fact, you should *never* set a long-term goal until you're fairly sure that its attainment will truly make you happy. Even then, be prepared to alter it as you and your circumstances change. Don't ever be ashamed to change your programs as new information reveals better ways for you to be happy; just don't make important changes too suddenly or when your emotions are in control.

Until you're sure what you want for the long term, you can continue to live day by day, enjoying what you experience, experimenting with new things. You don't have to decide upon a career by any given age; nor do you have to know right now what you want most in a long-term love relationship. And there's no reason to commit your future before you know those things.

In fact, short-term pleasures can evolve into long-term matters without your ever having to make a formal decision. For example, as you work at various jobs, you might find one that suits you well enough to stay in it a longer time—without deciding that it will be your ultimate career. As your talents and opportunities in that field grow, you might one day realize that you *have* made a career of it. Even so, you might still wish to change it someday.

In the same way, if you accept each romantic relationship for what it offers you, you don't have to make a formal decision that one of them will be permanent. But it may turn out that one of them *will* be—without any conscious attempt to make it so.

When things develop in this way, you never have to make a long-term commitment or final decision about anything. You just do what you enjoy doing the most—and over a period of time, your pleasures can grow into lifelong enjoyments.

ADVENTURES

As you seek to discover yourself and look for ways to make your life joyful, you may often be told that you shouldn't be so preoccupied with yourself, or that you should accept the life you already have, or that it's too "idealistic" to expect to find genuine, durable happiness in this world. You may see others spending their lives working miserably to stay in their boxes.

Realize that what *they* do is up to them. What *you* do is up to you.

Your life can be an adventure—a continuing stream of new pleasures, excitement, and satisfactions. You can have meaningful, problem-free friendships; you can have love that's intense and exciting without burdens and compromises; you can produce income in ways that are fun; you can have thrilling experiences that don't lead to bad consequences.

There are plenty of people who live that way. And some of them may have once been locked in more boxes than those that restrict you now.

My freedom and happiness weren't achieved by compromising my standards to conform to the people around me. Neither did they come from a superhuman effort to change people.

I'm free and happy because I accepted myself as I am and found a life that suits me—and it wasn't nearly as difficult as I had thought it might be.

As I lie on my couch by the fireplace, looking out from my hillside home at the snow leading down to the ocean, with the right woman in my arms, a glass of Bordeaux beside me and a Puccini opera on the stereo system, knowing that I've earned the pleasure I feel, I'm so glad I didn't let someone else decide what's best for me.

28

Your Own Morality

A PERSONAL MORALITY is a systematic attempt to recognize all the relevant consequences of your acts. Its purpose is to prevent you from doing something hastily that might interfere with your long-term goals.

Many people might think that the idea of creating your own morality is outrageous—that you should accept what's been handed to you by others (in the interest of "society").

But a personal morality is simply the making of rules for yourself that will guide your conduct toward what you want and away from what you don't want. And the rules are made by examining alternative sets of consequences in important matters.

Your knowledge will tell you what consequences you believe will ensue from any given action; and only your values can tell you whether those consequences are good or bad. So your rules will be consistent with your nature and your goals only if you've created the morality for yourself.

The temptation to act "immorally" is usually the result of trying to be moral in a way that isn't really suitable to you. But if you've thought things out for yourself, you'll develop principles you can live with comfortably—principles that match your understanding of reality, principles that can help keep you pointed in the direction you want to go, principles you can act upon without mixed emotions.

A clear-cut morality is like a boundary line. Beyond the boundaries set by your morality, you know you can run into trouble. Within the boundaries, you can act freely and spontaneously because you believe no problems will be caused by your short-term enjoyment.

CRISES

If you construct your morality carefully, it should serve you especially well in a crisis. The worst time to reconsider long-range principles is during a crisis. When emotions are intense, it's very difficult to see realistically all the consequences that might ensue from your choices.

At such a time, your principles should already be clearly in mind. Your only concern should be with the specific facts of the situation—to which you'll apply the principles you already hold.

You might make important changes in your morality at other times; that's a matter of being humble enough to realize that you can grow. But it's unrealistic to believe you can make useful changes in your principles during a crisis.

So anticipate the various kinds of circumstances in which you might someday find yourself. Now is the time to determine the principles by which you'll act if such conditions should ever arise.

For example, are there circumstances that would make it right for you to coerce your child? If so, what are they? To stop him from taking drugs? And would you coerce someone who was trying to induce your child to take them? At what point would you intervene?

It doesn't help to say, "My child would never do that." Someday your child will want to do *something* that goes against your wishes. Where will you draw the line between letting him do as he chooses and coercively intervening to stop him?

As you think about it, ask yourself what the consequences of your intervention might be—and also what the consequences of non-intervention might be. Then decide at what point the consequences of one outweigh the consequences of the other. The result is your moral rule for that issue.

These things must be decided in advance. You might alter your judgment in the future, as you gain new insights. But a crisis could occur at any time—and you need to have firm, realistic, believable principles available to you when it does. Otherwise, you could throw away a large part of your future by making a rash decision.

RECOGNIZE EXCEPTIONS

As you decide upon such principles, the rules should be formed in a way that eliminates any need to break them. Exceptions should be recognized as you create the rules, and then incorporated into the rules.

For example, one of *my* rules is, "Never lie or appear to be something other than what you are." I see mostly bad consequences from lying. At the same time, I recognize that no consequences will matter to me if I'm dead. And there are also certain people in the world who are very valuable to me; if they were to die, I'd lose a great deal.

So it becomes a question of which of these values is more important to me. I've decided that my survival and the survival of those most valuable to me are more important than avoiding the bad consequences of dishonesty. My moral rule must take that into consideration.

As a result, it would be more complete and more realistic to phrase it "Never lie or appear to be something other than what you are—unless you're sure your life or the life of someone very important to you is literally at stake."

In a life-or-death emergency, I'll lie if I must. I know why I'll lie and I've already made that decision.

If I lie, I'll suffer the bad consequences that I know come from lying. But I'll do so because a superior value will be preserved—my life. I won't "justify" the lie by pointing to the circumstances; that won't change the consequences of dishonesty. When I suffer those consequences, I'll know that I'm paying a necessary price for remaining alive.

Because my rule already includes exceptional circumstances, there'll be no need to wonder during a crisis if I should change it. I'll know which way to act—and I'll be prepared for whatever comes.

And because I recognize these things now, I can do more to avoid getting myself into a situation where I must choose between my honesty and my life. That would be a negative decision—one in which either choice would cause problems—and it's important to avoid negative decisions.

MORAL QUESTIONS

To help you construct your own morality, here is a list of moral questions that I think require answers. Your answers should be your own, but I think it's important that you *do* have answers for them.

1. In what circumstances would you steal, if ever?

2. How honest should you be? Do different relationships deserve different degrees of honesty? If so, on what basis can you decide the degree of honesty appropriate to the relationship? (If you know in advance the circumstances that warrant lying, you'll be less likely to feel guilty when you do so in accordance with your rules.)

3. When would you use physical force to protect yourself? In what circumstances would you use it to get something you want? To what extent would you use it to repel an intruder from your property?

4. In what circumstances would you go to the aid of a stranger? When would it be unrealistic to do so?

5. Would you interfere to stop a fight between a friend and someone else? Between two strangers?

6. In what circumstances would you accept a government subsidy? (If such a question is important to you, rec-

ognize that there are many kinds of subsidies—"public" schools, government contracts, Medicare, for example.)

7. What is the limit to which you'll go to satisfy your parents' wishes? Your friends' wishes? The wishes of your lover or spouse?

8. How much sympathy, attention, or help are you willing to give your friends? Is there a limit? If so, what is it?

9. In what circumstances should you not act sexually as you want to at that moment?

10. Are there any circumstances in which you would allow your own desires to be overruled by a group decision? If so, what circumstances?

11. How involved should you be with someone whose answers to the above questions are quite different from yours? Which of the issues involved are the most critical to you?

In each case, ask yourself what consequences you could expect from various different answers to these questions. Picture yourself in such circumstances and act them out mentally. Follow each situation through until you see the consequences taking place. See if your actions will in any way affect future relationships with others.

When you have a good answer to a question, check to see if it includes all possible exceptions within the rule.

It would be helpful to write out your answers. You may be surprised by how much more precise you can make an answer once you've seen it on paper. If you don't feel inspired to write them out, try saying them aloud—or better yet, into a tape recorder.

If your first efforts seem rough or unsure, keep at it. That way you're more likely to get answers you can live with—and live well. When you verbalize your answers— on paper or aloud—they'll be more real and more precise.

Make a note of anything covered in this book that you believe is significant to your life. It doesn't matter whether you agree with my views; the important thing is to call attention to issues you feel you should think about in more detail. When you've finished the book, go back and review those issues; think about them until you have answers you're satisfied with.

There are undoubtedly many important issues other than those questions I've listed. As you think of them, make notes so you can consider them later in detail.

The range of issues might seem to be limitless. But as you develop a set of principles for yourself, you'll probably find that many apparently new issues are already covered by principles you've formed.

The process of forming a personal morality isn't something that's completed in an hour or two. You'll undoubtedly adopt some conclusions that are rather tentative, to be superseded later by mere thoughtful and confident answers. If you continue to grow in your knowledge and insight, you'll want to amend conclusions accordingly.

Don't rush; the job may take years—but it's worth it. And what could be more stimulating than thinking about your own life?

MY RULES

To stimulate your thinking further, here's a list of some of my most important moral principles. As you look at them, ask yourself what you think about them—and why. Ask yourself what you'd expect to be the consequences of acting by these rules and of not acting by them.

As you'll see, most of these rules are framed as negatives—prohibitions upon actions that might get in the way of my long-term goals. The more positive rules will depend more upon *your* personal values and goals; they'll be rules that attempt to keep you aimed in the direction most attractive to you.

1. Never expect anyone to act from your knowledge, perspective, or objectives. Assume that his viewpoints will differ in some ways from yours.

2. Never make an important decision when your emotions are dominating your mind.

3. Never lie or appear to be something other than what

you are—unless you're sure that your life or the life of someone very important to you is literally at stake.

4. Never invest any resource (time, money, emotional involvement) that you're not prepared to lose.

5. Never take on a new responsibility, time commitment, or liability without recognizing what must be given up to accommodate it.

6. Always leave some free time in your schedule to take advantage of new opportunities as they arise. If there are no new opportunities during the period, the free time can always be used for pure pleasure.

7. Never use someone's property in any way that he doesn't approve of—unless your life or the life of someone very important to you is literally at stake.

8. Never focus your attention on anyone's weaknesses—his temper, sloppiness, poor logic, dishonesty, whatever. Recognize these shortcomings, take them into consideration, but don't waste your time complaining about them. Instead, pay attention to what *your* actions should be in order to deal with him.

9. Never quibble over a price you didn't expect to pay. Pay it and move on to better things.

10. Never form a partnership (an agreement in which responsibilities or rewards will be shared) for any purpose.

11. Never become directly involved in violence unless it appears to be the only alternative to prevent more serious injury to yourself or to someone very important to you.

12. Never forsake your rules because of someone's actions or opinions.[1]

The last rule is especially important. Many philosophies encourage the idea that it's moral to respond in kind to something someone does—whether that be lying, cheating, stealing, or violence.

I believe that the consequences of an act will be pretty

---

[1] These are only a few of the rules I live by, of course. Others are mentioned throughout the book. And there are others that I take so much for granted that it wouldn't occur to me to mention them.

much the same, no matter what provokes it. It would be to *my* disadvantage to lie—even if I were lying to a liar.

If I lied to someone and then justified my action by saying that the person I lied to had already been dishonest toward me, my relationship with friends might not be the same in the future. For they could never be sure that a misunderstanding hadn't caused me to believe I was justified in lying to them.[2]

The same principle applies to stealing, violence or any other action that's normally prohibited by your morality. If others choose to lie, steal, make emotional decisions, or engage in violence, that doesn't change the consequences to you of your own actions. Don't allow others to run your life indirectly by letting their actions dictate yours. Make your own decisions based upon the consequences to you.

YOUR LIFE

It's also important to decide for yourself how much you believe you can get from life. Obviously, you shouldn't adhere to a code that's based upon goals you don't believe can be achieved. And you need to decide how much effort each of your goals is worth.

Don't allow the standards of others to influence you. Different people, with different views of life, have different ideas about what is possible. Let them choose for themselves—and you choose for you.

If you determine for yourself who you are, what will make you happy, and what code of conduct is consistent with that, you'll be able to act more freely and with more conviction. You won't be hindered by prohibitions that aren't appropriate to you—and you won't jump into po-

---

[2] An interesting question concerns whether one should lie to the government, and how that might create consequences in other areas of one's life—a question I haven't fully settled to my own satisfaction.

tentially dangerous situations just because others are doing so.

You're not acting irresponsibly by choosing for yourself. Your actions will produce consequences that you'll have to live with; you're accepting that fact when you create a morality for yourself. What could be a greater example of responsibility than an individual who chooses for himself and is prepared to accept the consequences of his own choices?

The irresponsible person will refuse to take the credit or blame for his own actions. He'll say that he did what he did because he was obeying a "moral law," or because he didn't want to hurt someone's feelings, or because society wouldn't let him do otherwise. He's disclaiming the responsibility for his own acts.

A free man has no one to blame. He has no boxes, no restrictions, no enemies to take the responsibility for his actions.

But because he's free, he can choose for himself to create a personal morality that fits his view of reality and will help him live in the way he wants to live.

If a man does not keep pace with his companions, perhaps it is because he hears a different drummer. Let him step to the music which he hears, however measured or far away.   —HENRY DAVID THOREAU

29

Is Your Life
What You Want It to Be?

WHEN YOU FIND an attractive long-term goal, it's easy to be induced to take on obligations that seem necessary to attain it. Unfortunately, however, years later the obligations may have turned into burdens—and the burdens can remain long after the goals have been reached or even discarded.

For example, an individual gets married because he's in love and wants to enjoy love, affection, appreciation, and understanding for the rest of his life. A year or two later, the love has evaporated—but the structure that was erected to achieve the goals still stands. The negative side of marriage remains long after the positive goals have been discarded.

In smaller ways, routines in your life can continue long after they've ceased to be valuable. It's easy to maintain pointless activities without reappraising their relevance to your current goals.

So it's important to periodically recheck your assumptions, reappraise your activities, and reexamine your goals to see how much relevance they still have to your happiness.

The simplest way I know to do that is to make a list of the things you do with each of the 168 hours in a typical week. Include every one of your routine activities, including eating and sleeping. Then apply labels to each of the activities to help you determine how much you're getting out of those hours.

There are four different sets of labels you can use—each of which will help you appraise your life from a different perspective.

1. GOOD-BAD LABELS

This set of labels will identify how much of your precious time is being used in ways that add to your happiness, and how much is being wasted.

Use the three labels *good, bad,* and *indifferent.* Put the *good* label on anything that makes you feel good. Put the *bad* label on the things that cause you discomfort, the things you dread, the activities that seem to be prices to be paid. And apply the *indifferent* label to those things that seem to be neutral—whatever provides neither pleasure nor discomfort (brushing your teeth perhaps).

Don't apply a label in accordance with what an activity *ought* to be. For example, don't automatically label an activity *good* just because it's supposed to be "entertainment." Maybe you play poker with the boys because it's a habit. Or perhaps you go out to dinner every Sunday only because you've done that for years. Or maybe you play bridge with the Culbertsons on Wednesdays because you've never thought of anything better to do.

Don't consider something enjoyable just because you don't know what you'd do instead. You won't find anything better until you first establish that you're not satisfied with what you're doing now.

On the other hand, the fact that you work forty hours every week doesn't necessarily mean that it's unpleasant and must be labeled *bad*. There may be parts of it that you enjoy and parts you don't. If so, separate the general category "work" into specific hours to be individually labeled.

The *indifferent* label is mostly a catch-all for those things that seem to defy either a *good* or *bad* label. There are many activities that you wouldn't consider unpleasant, but which add no enjoyment to your life—going to the mailbox, eating breakfast, walking the dog, reading the newspaper, etc.

As you look at items labeled *bad*, ask yourself, "Why am I continuing these activities?" If you answer, "Because they're necessary," get tough with yourself and demand to know why they can't be eliminated. If it's a box that you're maintaining, find a price and pay your way out.

And be impatient with the items labeled *indifferent*, too. Some of them may indeed be necessary to stay alive, but a lot of them may be just ways of passing time while waiting for something to happen. Start daydreaming and exploring to find new activities that can make more exciting use of your time.

It isn't necessary that your life be full of *bad* and *indifferent* activities. Take a close look at your present routine and rearrange things so that a great deal of your time is spent more enjoyably.

2. POSITIVE-NEGATIVE LABELS

Now analyze the list of your weekly activities from a different perspective, using a different pair of labels.

Label each activity either *positive* (those things you choose to do to increase your happiness) or *negative* (those things you do in order to avoid unhappiness).

A *positive* label would be attached to a Sunday afternoon in which you have no commitments, and can choose among several ways to enjoy yourself. A *negative* label should be applied to a Sunday afternoon you must spend with your relatives—if your motive is only to avoid recriminations and family turmoil.

After you've applied labels to your entire week, you should have a pretty good idea how much of your life is yours to enjoy as you desire. If it isn't much, start dismantling the boxes that tie up so much of your time.

3. ACTIVE-PASSIVE LABELS

This approach is similar to the last one. It will help you to see if you're making things happen in your life—or if you're just going along with what others want.

Label each activity *active* or *passive*. The *active* label applies to anything *you* have initiated, the things you do because *you* have decided they should be done. The *passive* label should be attached to those activities you do because someone else wants you to do them.

Do you simply react as other people initiate things? Do you find yourself hoping that others will suggest the things you'd like to see happen? If so, why don't *you* act? Why don't *you* initiate new, more enjoyable, more sensible activities? After all, others may *never* initiate the things you want to happen.

No one knows better than you what will make you happy. If you don't ask for what you want, you'll probably never get it. And if the asking or initiating is certain to meet with rejection or problems among your current relationships, then ask elsewhere.

As you apply these labels to your weekly activities, designate *passive* those things you do only to preserve a relationship (even if it's a relationship you value)—such things as conversations that bore you, favors, etc. As you look at the labels, you can see how much of your time is necessary to preserve the relationship—and that should tell you if the situation is as compatible as you'd thought it was.

Look for relationships that don't require that you tolerate unpleasant things in order to maintain them. With the right people, you should be spending most (if not all) of your time doing things that please you, that make sense to you—the things you want to do. Compromises seem necessary only because of inappropriate situations. If you're involved with the right people, the word "sacrifice" shouldn't even be in your vocabulary.

4. PRODUCTION-ENJOYMENT LABELS

Now analyze the list from one more perspective—to determine *why* you've taken on these activities and to see if they still serve any valid functions.

As you look at each activity, choose from five labels. The first is *enjoyment*—that which brings you happiness right now (golf, sex, reading, TV, travel, etc.).

The second label is *past mistakes*—anything you must do to pay for some costly thing you did in the past (alimony payments, child support, installment payments on something no longer useful, effort expended to undo a bad deed, etc.).

The last three labels designate activities that are supposed to provide happiness at some time in the future. They're assumed to be *productive*. The pay-off may be expected soon—or it may be a long-term project—or it may be something you now realize will never come to fruition.

The first of these three labels is *productive—short-term*, which applies to anything you expect will produce happiness in the near future. It can include any part of your working time that yields money you can spend enjoyably right away. It can also apply to the time spent planning and preparing for a forthcoming activity that will give you pleasure—such as arranging a party, building a boat, or planting a garden.

Productive-long-term labels should be attached to projects that you hope will produce happiness in the distant future. For example, you might be going to school to acquire a skill that will increase your income two or three years from now. It can also apply to the hours spent earning the mortgage payment that will give you a paid-for home many years from now (if having a paid-for home is important to you).

And as you appraise your weekly routine, you may dis-

cover activities that offer no hope or gain. They are the
things you might have once undertaken with a definite
goal in mind that has since become irrelevant. Label those
productive—never, and smile as you realize that you've
just found a few hours each week that will soon be free to
be used for something new and more rewarding.

That can include a language you've been studying because of a job you've since changed—or a business that's
been losing money and will continue to do so—or time expended for a community cause whose failure is obvious—
or a marriage you'd hoped would someday bring you love,
but hasn't.

Some activities can bear more than one label. Your job
might be productive of income to be spent, but it might
also include the enjoyment of various projects and discoveries—not to mention the more obvious things like enter-
taining clients at expensive restaurants, coffee breaks with
a cute secretary, or Rotary Club meetings if you enjoy
them. So break your work week into individual hours—
and apply the labels to each activity in your work.

The five labels identify those parts of your life that deal
with the past *(past mistakes)*, the present *(enjoyment)*,
and the future (the three *productive* labels).

You can't evade paying off the mistakes of the past, but
you can look for ways to reduce the costs. And you can
find ways to accelerate the payment so that you'll be free
of them sooner.

Neither can you disregard the future. It's important that
you don't do things today that must be paid for with regret tomorrow. But at the same time, it's very easy to get
into the habit of doing things that add nothing to your future but which are vaguely justified as being necessary for
the future.

When I review my activities with this technique, I immediately eliminate the *productive—never* items from my
life. I spend the most time appraising the *productive—
short-term* and *long-term* activities.

I'm very skeptical about long-term projects. In an uncertain, changing world, it's too easy for them to become

irrelevant by the time they're completed. I try to keep goals telescoped into the short term where they can be appraised realistically and discarded when they don't add to my happiness.

I've found that the most fruitful long-term projects have evolved out of short-term projects. The short-term projects have definite pay-offs at various points along the way; I never have to wonder for very long if I'm doing the right thing. If they then lead naturally into larger long-term pay-offs, so much the better. But I never have to undergo a long period of stoic self-denial based upon the hope of a brighter future many years away.

I also take a second look at each activity I've labeled enjoyment—to be sure I really enjoy those things. If I'm not very sure, I start looking for better things with which to replace them.

This technique should raise important questions for you as you appraise the motivations behind each of your activities. The goal is happiness—but it's easy to be sidetracked into worthless activities by vague promises of better days to come. Every day should include genuine enjoyment.

The many stories of single-minded success-seekers who patiently climbed to the top make good reading, but they can overlook a lot of relevant details. Often, the prize is attained when the winner is too old to enjoy it fully. In reality, I think that success is more often achieved by individuals who found ways of enjoying themselves while in the process of getting where they wanted to go.

LABELS

If you use these four techniques, you might wind up with a page full of labels. It may seem very mechanical, but it will help to demonstrate how much of your life can be wasted in purposeless activity. If you wonder why you aren't free, a few hours spent with these techniques may provide the answer.

Each of the four techniques can be utilized within sub-divisions of your life, such as your work. By reviewing each hour of your typical work week, you can determine how much of your time is spent in ways of your choosing, how much is actually contributing to your income, how much you enjoy your work, and how much you're controlling your own career future.

If you manage your own working time, the labels can inspire you to make changes that will increase the productivity and enjoyment in your work. If you don't manage your working time, the labels can only tell you whether or not your work is valuable to you. If your job is one in which you're just there for forty hours each week to do whatever you're told, don't waste too much time with these techniques—use the time to look for another job.

I've never been much for taking notes and writing things down. So I can understand if you think that making a list of your activities is too much work. If that's the case, you can still use the technique by mentally labeling each thing as you do it. After a day or two, it might become habitual to identify each activity and evaluate it.

I'd still like to urge you to write out the list, however. Only in that way can you see at a glance your total situation and make a realistic appraisal of your activities.

The use of these techniques can dramatically increase your self-control, self-confidence, and happiness. They will provide an answer to the important question: *How many hours a week are you happy?*

It's very easy to pay more attention to the lives of others, to complain about the state of the world and the mistakes of others, and to ignore one's own self-defeating habits. Without realizing it, you can spend most of your time doing things that contribute nothing to your happiness—and which actually perpetuate the conditions that make you unfree and unhappy.

Don't be too anxious to justify your activities as being necessary to long-term goals. The future has an annoying habit of forgetting its appointments—or arriving too late for them.

I've always found it hard to understand why so many people live so much for the future—especially when the present is such a lovely place.

SIMPLICITY

The primary value of these techniques is to *simplify* your life, to help you get rid of the vague, complicated activities that contribute nothing positive.

Arrange your life so that you don't have to spend every waking hour carrying out obligations, holding things together, trying not to rock the boat.

Make sure that every week has a specified time that's totally unplanned. Reserve that time so that you can decide—when it arrives—how you'll use it. Don't use it to catch up on unfinished business; use it to enjoy yourself, to do what you want most to do at that moment.

When you've accomplished that, arrange things so that every *day* has such a period of unplanned time. Make your life meaningful and tasty by enjoying happiness every day.

You'll have to make some long-term plans, of course. But periodically reappraise your routine to be sure those plans are still leading you toward rewarding goals.

I've been told so many times that freedom is just a fantasy, that you can't live that way in the real world, that there are too many daily commitments that have to be met, that in real life things are much too complicated to be able to do what you want and to enjoy yourself.

But who made your life complicated?

You did, of course. It wasn't society, the economic system, the people you consider to be nuisances, your parents, or anyone else.

Every complication in your life today is the result of something you've allowed to happen. You initiated it, or you consented to it, or you've allowed it to continue.

You are where you are today because you've chosen to be there.

And you can choose not to be there.

You'll have to pay for past mistakes, but no mistake warrants a life sentence. You can telescope those payments into the short term and get rid of them quickly.

You can get rid of bad relationships, meaningless obligations, negative commitments. You can do anything you want. You're free—if you'll only realize it.

Only you can choose to make things better for yourself. You can decide to stop "going along" with things that are handed to you. You can decide to live your life as the free person you are.

Don't tell me that it can't be done. There are too many people who've already done it.

No matter where you are now, you can unravel all the knots that you've woven into your life.

You can decide to be free. No one else has to be convinced—it requires only your decision and action.

30

A Fresh Start

NOW IT'S TIME to put many ideas together to create a practical plan with which you can transform your life from what it is to what you want it to be.

To do this in my own life, I've used a technique I call *Starting From Zero*. Its purpose is to clear your mind of the boxes, complications, and obligations that may be getting in the way of what you want to do.

The technique utilizes many of the ideas we've discussed already; it's a way of tying together everything we've seen. It has many uses—but its greatest value can be the creation of a new, freer life. It focuses attention on what you want and keeps you aimed toward it.

Even with the labeling techniques we saw in the last chapter, it's too easy to rationalize every part of your present existence as being necessary—if you use *it* as the starting point. So it's important to clear your mind of all present commitments; only then can you get a clear view of what you really need to be happy.

The starting-from-zero technique uses the life you dream of as the standard and compares everything with it, eliminating anything in your present routine that isn't part of the dream life. It provides the simplest way to determine which parts of your present life aren't what you really want—and to be able to visualize a way of getting to where you want to be.

There are seven steps in the technique:

1. Mentally step outside your present way of life. Start from zero by imagining yourself outside of your present routine. Expand upon the daydreams you've had before—imagine now that you're no longer entangled in *any* of your present responsibilities, obligations, or relationships. Envision yourself totally on your own—with none of your present possessions, family, career, social commitments, debts, or contracts.

In other words, you're completely free—starting from zero with a clean slate, a fresh start to go in any direction that you choose. Don't concern yourself now with the restrictions that presently exist in your life; don't even try to decide how you'll remove them. Just imagine that there's no one to restrict you or make any claims upon you.

2. What would you do? Ask yourself what you'd do with this totally free situation.

Where would you go? What would you like to do for a living? What have you always wanted to do that's been prevented by your old way of life? Whom would you like to see? What would you do with your time?

In this new life, would you be single? Would you want to live with the person you've always desired? Would you want a particular kind of home? What kind of work would you like to pursue? What material things would give you pleasure?

Only one restriction should be imposed upon your dreams: You can't make someone else be what you want him to be. It serves no purpose to imagine that your spouse has suddenly changed as you've wanted him to, or that your boss has finally given you that raise. Nor does it serve any purpose to dream that you're married to Sophia Loren.

However, you can dream that you're free to *pursue* Sophia Loren, and to apply your best efforts to the task of winning her love. In the same way, you can imagine that you're free to pursue any career you desire—but not to imagine that others will miraculously throw money at you in contradiction with their own natures.

But there are no other restrictions to prevent you from trying anything you want. So include in your fantasy anything you think you'd truly enjoy. Include parts of your present life—if they're sources of genuine pleasure to you. But don't include something simply because it seems necessary or irremovable.

Don't restrain your fantasies. Picture yourself actually doing the things involved. Act them out in your mind. See if they're really what you want for yourself.

After you've done this for a few days, your dream will begin to have more substance. You'll have a good idea what kind of work you'd like to try, where you'd like to go, who you'd like to be with, what would give you real pleasure. As you continue thinking about it, however, you might alter parts of the dream as other tasty ideas occur to you.

Do this for a couple of weeks—longer, if necessary. Continue building the dream until you no longer think of ways to improve upon it. Until then, retreat to your dream world every chance you get. Think about it, indulge it, live it mentally, change it, refine it, develop it. Get into the details of it so that you can see more clearly what you'd most enjoy.

After a while, the various fantasies should begin to settle into one basic dream. At that point, it would be very helpful to make a list of the elements in the ideal life you've pictured. Write down everything that occurs to you about it—the material things you want, the occupation, the new relationships, where you want to live, etc. It may take a couple of days to recall everything you've thought of that you want to be a part of your new life.

By writing down the elements of the dream, you can focus upon them more clearly—and make better use of the next step.

3. What is your present life like? Now take a close look at your present routine. What activities engage you now? What is your work? How do you spend your time? Whom are you required to associate with? Where does your money go? List the activities in your present life—if you haven't already compiled one for the techniques mentioned in the last chapter.

4. *Cross off everything in your present life that doesn't appear in your dream life.* If there's something in your present life that isn't part of the life you want for yourself, there's no reason to perpetuate it. All you need to find is a way out of it—and we're coming to that.

You might find that you'll cross off everything from your present life—that you're not doing anything now that conforms with your dream of an ideal life. If so, don't be discouraged by that discovery. Everything you cross off from your present life can be replaced with something new, something better, something more productive of happiness.

FINANCING THE NEW LIFE

The next part deals with the means of financing your new life.

5. *What do you need to make your dream life possible?* Estimate the requirements and costs of your imagined new life. How much time would be necessary to ready yourself for the profession you have in mind? How much money would you need to go where you want to be? How much time is required for the activities you crave? What other resources are necessary for the kind of existence you're dreaming of?

For the moment, don't worry about what you already have or how you'll get what you need; just determine the costs required. How much money would you need? How much time? Your knowledge will go with you anywhere—but you need to estimate the cost of adding any extra knowledge you might need to achieve your ends.

6. *What are your present assets and liabilities?* Set aside your dream world long enough to make an inventory of your present financial situation.

What are your present assets? How much money can you freely spend as you choose? What is the worth of your present property (home, land, furniture, savings, car, appliances, investments)?

Now list your present liabilities. How much money do you owe? What other monetary obligations have you incurred—family support, leases, business liabilities, charitable pledges? Make your list complete; you need to know exactly where you stand. Don't overlook any liabilities— you can't eliminate them until you recognize them.

If your assets are greater than your liabilities, the difference is your *usable net worth*—what you have available to meet the requirements of your new life.

If your net worth is very small—or even if your liabilities are greater than your assets—don't let that stop you. Don't decide that you can't make any changes until you're out of debt. The situation isn't likely to get any better as long as you continue your present way of life.

Losing businesses have been perpetuated for years in hopes that a few more sales would make them profitable. And in the same way, many hopeless routines are continued in the vain hope that things will be better tomorrow. Things will get better only when you make the changes that are necessary to make them better.

It's your present way of life that's piled debts and obligations on your shoulders. If you continue it, your debts will more likely increase. It's important to get to zero—to a free position—as soon as possible so that you can have a clean start to move in the direction you want to go. When you escape from your boxes, you'll have the opportunity to increase your net worth—if that's what you want.

In addition to monetary responsibilities, inventory your other commitments. Are you obligated to future social responsibilities? Are you married? Do you have children? What other commitments do you have?

Any burdensome commitments can be eliminated by paying some price; you can clear them with an expenditure of time or money. Add the monetary prices of eliminating unwanted commitments to your financial liabilities so that you can pay them off and be done with them.

And now we come to the best part:

7. Make changes. Eliminate present assets that aren't on your dream list. Turn into cash all the material possessions that aren't necessary to your dream life. Eliminate all the activities that consume time without contributing to the existence you really want.

Use the cash proceeds to pay off your liabilities. Try to eliminate every commitment in that way. If you wind up with nothing but a free life, you'll be way ahead. With a free life, you can acquire what you want much more easily, with no debts or obligations to eat up the money as you make it.

If you have cash left over after paying off the liabilities, use it to finance those parts of the dream world that require money. And use the time you save to indulge yourself in the dream activities you've previously denied yourself.

You should be able to create a workable plan on paper. You'll be able to see what can be eliminated, and how the proceeds in time and money can be used to pay off liabilities and buy the things you want.

But sometimes these matters are so complicated that it seems impossible to work them out on paper. If that's the case, the best alternative is to actually liquidate your present holdings. Sell everything—terminate all relationships, contracts, plans, programs. Sell *all* your property—whether or not any part of it is on your dream list—and pay off all your debts as far as the money will go.

That's a drastic step—and I don't advise it unless you absolutely can't work out a transition on paper. But if that's what's necessary, do it. When you've done it, you'll be free to move in any direction you want.

Don't be afraid to give up anything that's part of a basically unfree life. Anything you cherish can probably be reacquired later without any of the problems involved now. The important thing is to be free—and that may require a clean sweep.

TEMPORARY MEASURES

Part of your dream life may involve a period of time necessary to establish a new career or relationship, and it may be that you have nothing in reserve to finance such a period. If so, you might need to take an intermediate job or find an intermediate relationship to tide you over.

Be careful, however. Too often, "temporary" expedients turn into permanent ruts. Some of your present life may have been undertaken originally as a short-term means to an end that never materialized.

You might decide that your present job is suitable for your new life. Or there might be relationships you want to keep. If so, examine those things cautiously. They're part of your present situation—and they may be contributing to the rut from which you're trying to free yourself.

If you keep your present job to tide you over, use a miniature starting-from-zero technique to determine the absolute minimum you must contribute to it in order to be worth what you receive from it. Do what is necessary for you to be worth your income, but eliminate all other activities from your working routine—such as socializing, long-term investments in a distant promotion or increased skill, extra hours worked without pay, etc. Earn what you're paid but do nothing beyond that.

In the same way, apply the starting-from zero technique to any relationships you intend to keep. Don't start by considering what you do now to preserve such relationships. Instead, start from zero by determining what you truly need and want from the relationship, then determine what's necessary to make that possible, and eliminate from your present activities anything that exceeds that. You don't have to call friends daily or weekly to keep their friendship, nor do you have to visit your parents weekly to retain them as your parents.

BE HONEST

While you're in the process of thinking out these matters, someone may confront you with a question that seems to require a decision by you.

For example, while you're considering your career-plans, your employer might want to discuss a new position for you or a relocation to another city. Or while you're thinking about your marriage, your spouse might ask a question that indirectly concerns the future of your marriage (such as if you want to buy the new home you've discussed).

Don't allow such questions to pressure you into making a premature long-term decision. You don't have to sever the relationship on the spot; neither do you have to accept the new commitment, resign yourself to staying, and then pretend you had no thought of leaving.

The safest way to handle such a question is by being totally honest. And what *is* your honest position? It's probably that you don't know the answer—that you're in the process of reexamining your entire life, and that you're not sure yet what answers you'll find.

The person involved might be shocked to learn that you're even considering rocking the boat. He may accuse you of being selfish, thoughtless, disloyal, or irresponsible for suggesting that you might put your own life ahead of your relationships with other people.

But you know that you aren't going to be "irresponsible." You're facing your obligations and commitments—and you're considering what might be done to improve upon them.

As to your selfishness, *of course* you're going to put your own life first—as anyone with any sense would do—as each person *is* doing, each in his own way. And it's up to you to determine *your* way—regardless of structures, institutions, social pressures, moral codes, or relationships.

It's easy to be thrown off balance by a question for

which you have no immediate answer. "What are the poor children going to do?" "Won't this break your sick mother's heart?" "How are you going to satisfy your financial commitments?" etc.

Don't give up your dreams just because you can't answer every question yet. The only honest answer is that you're considering such matters now and you haven't resolved them yet. If you're not allowed to consider such things for yourself, you must be a slave.

If the person involved is reasonable and willing to discuss the matter with you, so much the better. His attitude may be helpful in discovering the price you might have to pay to eliminate a commitment to him.

It's also possible that someone will react negatively at first, but then become more agreeable when he's had time to think of the possible benefits to himself.

No matter what the reaction, I think the safest approach is to be honest in telling exactly where you stand—even if you stand at that moment in a state of indecision.

THE BIG DECISION

Throughout this book, we've considered many possibilities and alternatives that can enable you to live a freer life. Now we've finally come to the important question: What do you do about it?

The only sensible answer is to eliminate from your life whatever isn't suited to you, acquire the freedom you've craved, and start living your life as you want to live it.

The starting-from-zero technique can be a useful tool for getting from here to there. If you use your present life as the starting point, you have very little chance of getting what you want—you can find too many justifications for hanging on to each part of your present routine.

You have to go back to zero and start *there*, asking yourself what you'd do if you weren't involved as you are now. Only in that way can you create a clear, realistic picture of the life that would make you happy. Then you can determine the relevance of each of your present activities.

Once you know what is necessary to live the kind of life you want, bold action is required. Take your time *thinking* about these matters, but don't be slow in *acting* on them—once you've thought things out.

There may be other ways to be free, but I've never come across any that work. I've seen friends use various kinds of "gradualism" in their approaches, but years later they were still in the same boxes.

Freedom requires bold action. You may make mistakes in the process—and you may lose some of what you have—but anything you lose can be reacquired once you're free.

You don't *have* to remain in boxes. It's your choice. You can be free.

The worst thing one can do is not to try, to be aware of what one wants and not give in to it, to spend years in silent hurt wondering if something could have materialized—and never knowing.   —DAVID S. VISCOTT

There is a tide in the affairs of men,
Which, taken at the flood, leads on to fortune;
Omitted, all the voyage of their life
Is bound in shallows and in miseries.
                                    —SHAKESPEARE

31

A Fresh Start (Part II)

THE STARTING-FROM-ZERO TECHNIQUE can be used on a smaller scale to straighten out problems in any specific area of your life.

I've mentioned before the way I changed a business from an employee-employer structure to the use of independent contractors. The employees and myself all benefited from the tax advantages, the free time provided, and the lesser amount of supervision required.

This plan came about as a result of using the starting-from-zero technique. The business was operating at a loss and seemed helpless. Every time I tried to cut costs, I got nowhere—every expense seemed to be a necessity.

Finally, I cleared my mind of all preconceived notions and current arrangements. I took as the only given premise the amount of money the company received each month. Then I imagined what it would be like if we had to do nothing to receive that money.

Naturally, we couldn't continue receiving the income without providing something for it. So I listed the functions that would be absolutely necessary in order to maintain the income—without considering the existing expenses.

I didn't list employees or facilities necessary—only functions. If I thought of a function and then decided the income could continue without it, I didn't add it to the list.

When the list was completed, I could see that there were many functions I'd been taking for granted that didn't show up on the list.

Instead of assigning the necessary functions to employees, I asked for bids from the marketplace—inviting employees and outside businesses to submit prices for performing the necessary functions. The resulting costs were far less than the previous expenses.

The employees who continued to work with me became independent contractors. They performed specific serices—in their own ways and at their own speeds—for which they were paid a specific fee for each service. Rules were set only for the quality of the service and the delivery deadlines.

The new system changed the business into a profitable venture and made the work more profitable and enjoyable for every individual concerned. But I wouldn't have come to the system without using the starting-from-zero technique to eliminate all my preconceived notions regarding the expenses that were necessary.

The same technique can be used in any area of your life that requires changing but which seems too complicated to straighten out. Begin by imagining what it is you want—and then determine the minimum necessary to get it. Then compare that with what you're already doing and eliminate everything currently done that isn't part of the new system.

LIQUIDATION PROCEDURES

I've suggested that all relationships (marriage, business, friendships) will be more valuable if arranged so the individual sovereignty of each participant is maintained and respected. Each piece of property should be owned by one person who's responsible for it and has total control over it. Each decision should be the province of only one person.

Unfortunately, marriages and businesses are normally

arranged with communal ownership as the rule, so it may seem that my suggestion has come too late. But there are ways of unravelling any financial entanglements.

Here are three methods that can be used—either to convert an existing relationship to individual ownership, or to liquidate a relationship in which property is owned by more than one person.

The first method is the simplest. Sell everything that's jointly owned and split the cash proceeds according to the division of ownership. If the property was owned 50-50, split the cash 50-50. If several people have varying percentages of ownership, split the cash accordingly.

The drawback to this method is the reluctance to sell things you might want to keep. You'd have to sell them at wholesale and then use your share of the proceeds to buy back what you want at retail.

So let's move onto the second method. This one will work only when there are two participants and the ownership is divided 50-50. The object is to find a way to divide the property in such a way that neither party feels he's received the least valuable part of the split.

To avoid that, use an old trick. One person divides the property into what he considers to be two equal shares. Then the other person chooses which of the two parts he wants.

The second person can't complain that the split was unequal, for he had the privilege of choosing the best share. And the first person can't complain, for he was able to decide how the property would be split.

A variation of this method has been written into many business partnership contracts. The contract specifies that either partner can offer to buy out the other at any time—specifying the price he's willing to pay. The other partner must either accept the offer or buy out the first partner at the same price. In other words, one partner determines the price; the other then chooses whether he'll buy or sell at that price. Neither can complain that the price was unfair.

As you know, I don't think much of partnerships; there are much better ways of handling business arrangements. But if you ever decide you *must* form a partnership, I urge you to include that provision in the contract—no matter how sure you are that there'll never be any problems with your partner.

A BETTER WAY

There's a third method for dividing property that's the best way I know of. It was devised by a man named Wilmot Hunter. It will work no matter how many people are involved—and no matter what the divisions of ownership may be. It can be used in marriages, businesses, or any other type of relationship.

Let's use a marriage as an example. Suppose you and your spouse decide to convert your joint holdings to individual ownership. You may not be planning a divorce; it may be only that you agree with the principles of individual sovereignty expressed in Chapter 19 and want to implement them.

At first glance, it might seem to be a horrendous task. How are you going to divide equally such diverse items as the coffee table, the record collection, the gardening tools? But it really isn't difficult at all.

The answer is to hold an auction—an auction at which the two of you will bid against each other for the property that's been jointly owned.

First, eliminate from the auction any property or money that's already individually owned by either of you. You can also eliminate any personal items such as clothes, cosmetics, etc.—if both of you agree to it. Then split whatever money you have in joint savings or checking accounts.

Now place each item of jointly owned property on the auction block—one at a time. Each of you can bid as much money for each item as you think it's worth to you.

The highest bidder for each item gets it—and he then owes that amount of money to the proceeds.

When all the items have been auctioned, each thing will be owned by one person or the other. Total the winning bids to determine the proceeds of the auction and split that amount between the two of you—each of whom will use his share to pay off his winning bids.

If your winning bids exceed your share of the proceeds, you'll need to use your share of the cash that was split before the auction. You'll have to keep track of your bids and the proceeds as you go along—to be sure you're not bidding more than you can afford.

If there are so many small items that it would seem to take forever to auction them individually, you can group them to be auctioned as sets. That should only be done if both parties consent to it, however; if there's any disagreement over the handling of any item, it should go on the auction block by itself.

No one will get an item too cheaply just because it's of more value to him than the other person. There's always a *market price*—a price at which you can bid for the item, knowing you can sell it for more than that elsewhere. So no one is likely to obtain anything for less than what the other person considers to be a "fair" price.

If you aren't overly fond of some of your present property, you can invite others to attend the auction and bid. That should increase the proceeds, resulting in more cash for yourselves. It should be done only if both of you agree, however.

In a marriage, the normal division of proceeds is 50-50. But this plan can be used no matter how many people are involved—and no matter what the shares of ownership may be.

Suppose there are four partners liquidating a business. Let's say they have different-sized shares in the business— 40, 30, 20, and 10 percent respectively. They could argue forever over the way the property should be divided fairly.

Using the auction method, they can eliminate all the

bitterness. After the auction, the proceeds are split according to the percentages of the business each one owns.

In any kind of arrangement, no one can complain afterward that he was cheated by the auction. If anyone thinks that someone else is getting an item too cheaply, all he has to do is to bid more for it.

No one will be limited to bidding only his anticipated proceeds. Anyone can bid to obtain more than his share of the property—as long as he has the cash, or can borrow it, to cover his purchases.

This is a simple, clean way of untangling complicated affairs. There's no bitter aftermath; everyone can part friends without the recriminations and accusations that usually accompany property settlements.

A FRESH START

The techniques for getting out of boxes are by no means limited to those I've suggested in this book. More than anything else, my purpose has been to demonstrate that *there's always a way out.* Never feel that your life is frozen in its present routine and that it's hopeless to want anything better.

No matter how complicated your life has become, there's a way to unravel it. No matter how many boxes you may be in, there's always a way to pay a price and get out. No matter how alienated you may feel in your environment, there's always a way to find more compatible people.

You have only one life. If you resign yourself to living it in a hopeless situation, you're creating for yourself the greatest possible tragedy.

If that's what you do, it will be *you* who have caused it. What others want and demand is only *their* concern. What you choose to do will be your responsibility.

You have so much control in your hands. Why use it foolishly? Why not exercise the power you hold? Why not use it to make your life what you want it to be?

Why not get out of the boxes, the complications, the entanglements, the obligations?

Why not be free?

For of all sad words of tongue or pen,
The saddest are these: "It might have been!"
—JOHN GREENLEAF WHITTIER

32

Making Changes

THE SEVENTH STEP of the starting-from-zero technique is to make changes to bring about the life you desire. At that point, however, the changes may seem too difficult to carry out. You might be expecting strong opposition from the other people involved, and you may wonder how you'll ever get through the problems you face.

It will probably seem less difficult if you first think through the entire situation you face. If you do, you may find that there's nothing involved that you can't handle.

Let's go through it together. As you read this chapter, I'd like you to keep in mind the most important change you believe you should make. It may have to do with your job, your marriage, an important relationship. Whatever it is, everything I'm about to say will be directed at that change.

PRICES

There will be a price to pay, of course; any major change is bound to include one. The price may be in emotional upheaval, the admission of a mistake, the paying of a debt you haven't wanted to acknowledge, the loss of money or property you've thought was yours.

Whatever the price, identify it now. What will you have

to go through to get to where you want to be? The nice part of it is that there *is* a price you can pay to be free of the situation once and for all. It may be a fantastic price or a tiny one—but there is a price.

To find out what it is, determine who's involved. Who will you have to deal with? What will those people want? What have you told them they can expect? Maybe you know those people well enough to be able to estimate already what you must pay.

As you think about the price, it's important to decide *how much* you're willing to pay to be rid of the box. There's a point beyond which it would no longer be worth it to you to make the change. Decide now what that point is.

If it's a business arrangement, would you be willing to give up everything you've created to start over again—taking only your talent and knowledge with you? To be able to use them freely may be worth more in the long run than anything you might have to leave behind.

If it's a marriage, would you be willing to give up all the property, custody of the children, everything you own—if you have to? Determine now at what point it's not worth it to you to change.

Whatever you do, don't evade the price. Face up to everything that's involved. To ignore the price will only make it that much more difficult to handle when the time comes.

As you think about this, recognize any commitments you've made. Don't try to avoid responsibilities you've accepted. Each of them represents a price to be paid, and only when you've paid those prices can you be free.

Negotiate them if you can; maybe they can be minimized. But don't expect to avoid them entirely; if you do, you'll probably end up paying a higher price than you needed to.

If you've agreed to perform a certain job, talk to the person with whom you made the agreement. Maybe it's no longer important to him that you go through with it. But if he's counting on your work, deliver.

You might be able to subcontract the work to someone else—so that your time will be free. Even if the subcontracting would cost you more than you'll receive from the job, it might still be profitable to do it. The extra money you pay out of your pocket might be a small price to pay for your freedom.

In fact, you might be able to make more money doing something else with that time. If so, you're better off taking a loss on the original job by subcontracting it. Never be afraid to take a loss on a specific transaction; it will often help you to make more elsewhere.

The same principles apply to any other commitments you've made. Recognize them as prices to be paid in time or money for past mistakes. Often, however, you can negotiate a way of paying the price that is less expensive to you and just as satisfactory to the other person. Try to be imaginative in thinking of other alternatives that might work better for everyone concerned.

DON'T BE SIDETRACKED

If you're dealing with someone who wants to "punish" you or make you pay dearly for your selfishness, don't let it throw you. Understand that an emotionally distraught person might try every trick he can think of to make you feel guilty—moral recriminations, sympathy-seeking, "we need you" statements.

Don't get sidetracked trying to justify yourself or to prove someone else wrong. If he wants to teach you a lesson to satisfy his pride, let him.

Don't get caught in the "Who's right?" game. Each of you in the situation has made at least one mistake or you wouldn't be involved now. Maybe you think his mistakes were "worse" than yours. So what? Is proving that more important than your freedom?

No matter who's "at fault," recognize that you have mistakes of your own you'll have to pay for. Concern yourself with those prices; the other person will have to pay for his own mistakes in some other way. Don't make that your business; it will only tie you up further.

Be concerned with *your* commitments and try to satisfy them as quickly as possible.

The only commitments that can't be taken seriously are lifetime promises. It's unrealistic to promise lifelong love, devotion, loyalty, or presence. I'd be willing to break such promises. I wouldn't expect to get out without paying a price—my reputation would suffer, for one thing. But there's no reason to give up the one indispensable element to your happiness (your life) in order to honor a commitment. Obviously, the experience should demonstrate the importance of never again making such promises.

When the price is determined, try to pay it in as short a period as possible. The sooner you've satisfied the obligations, the sooner you'll be totally free.

If it's merely a confrontation you must go through, get it over with as soon as possible. If it involves money or time, arrange to pay the price in full as soon as you can.

PICTURE IT

Once you know what the price will be, *picture yourself paying that price*. Imagine yourself actually doing the things you'll have to do to finish this business. If it's painful, then do it again. Keep picturing yourself paying the price—the whole scene, every bit of dialogue—over and over again until it's no longer painful and terrifying.

Recognize everything that might go wrong and imagine yourself dealing with it. What will you say? How will you handle it? How will you respond if someone becomes hysterical?

If you do this, it won't be nearly so difficult to handle when you do it in reality. Your emotions will be calmer, you'll think more clearly, you'll be prepared for surprises and less likely to be thrown off balance.

It would be foolish to think you can handle in reality what is too painful and terrifying to imagine. So don't be mentally lazy and hope that everything will go well. Don't take the attitude that "things will work out" or "I can handle whatever develops." Positive thinking won't get you through this; only realistic preparation will.

CHILDREN

One of the prices may involve children. If you have children now, ask yourself if they were in the dream world you imagined when starting from zero. If not, you aren't likely to help them or yourself by taking them with you into your new life.

Children belong where they're really wanted, not where they're a burden. You don't do anyone a favor when you give up your happiness for him; that can lead too easily to a load of guilt for the beneficiary. You can't hide your sacrifice forever, and it can have very bad consequences when it's discovered.

Let the child be raised by someone who wants him dearly and who can give him genuine love and affection. Such things are vital to a child and they can't be faked.

If you choose to give up your children—either to your spouse or for adoption—you'll probably be condemned by some of the people around you now. But in your new life, those people may no longer be around you.

That won't eliminate all the prices, however. You may be required to support the child financially. Recognize that and determine how you can pay it with a minimum of discomfort to yourself.

Also, the price may be in disapproval from *new* friends when they learn what you've done. Recognize that now, too. How will that affect you? Imagine the disapproval and determine how you'll handle it.

Another form of the price may be a meeting with your child someday in the future. He may resent what you've done; be sure you can handle that when it happens. Are you really sure you're doing the right thing? Can you explain it?

Recognize all these possibilities *now*; don't ignore them and think you can handle them later. You have to know what you're doing—and why—and what the consequences will be. You can't be free by acting on a whim or on someone's advice; you have to be sure you know what you're doing.

I'm not presenting these challenges to talk you out of making big changes. Obviously, I believe that bold action is necessary to get out of a gray existence and into a sunny one. But it's essential that you know what's coming *before* you act.

You have to be convinced that you're acting in the best way. And that means you must realistically face up to every negative factor, every price you can think of—before you act.

When you've done that, you can act boldly, with confidence and conviction. Once *you* know what you're doing, nothing should be allowed to stand in your way. You can then face the censure that might come from those who'd prefer that you stay put and shut up.

WITHDRAWAL SYMPTOMS

One of the most important prices to be paid in dissolving a relationship is emotional. If you give up a child, a spouse, a lover, or a friend, you'll probably miss him. You might feel the urge to run back to where you were before.

These urges are *withdrawal symptoms*—temporary emotional reactions to relationships you've left. They're the emotional equivalents of the reactions you get when you give up smoking or some other habit.

It's important to recognize now that they will occur. Be prepared for them—imagine yourself living through them, cry about them. As with any other price, don't ignore them. Don't take the attitude that you'll worry about them when they happen.

If you face them now, you'll be better prepared to deal with them when they occur later. You won't be thrown off balance and tempted to run back to your old way of life, just to eliminate a temporary emotional discomfort.

THE BENEFITS

Just as you must be prepared for the negative aspects of your change, keep in mind the positive benefits that prompted you to make the change.

There's no sure way to keep your emotions under control as you go through the change. But if you keep reminding yourself of the benefits that await you, it will be easier.

You know why you want this, you know what you'll have to go through to get there, and you've made such decisions at times when your *intellect* was in control. Don't throw away your future when your emotions become intense.

If your emotions urge you to turn back, remind yourself of the important rule—*don't decide now*. Don't make important decisions when your emotions are strong; you can't see all the consequences at such a time. You'll have made your decision at the best possible time, when your intellect was in control; don't throw it away when your emotions become intense.

The strongest emotional pressure will be encouragement to turn back in order to avoid paying the price. Don't do it. Keep reminding yourself what you're paying for. Remember that you won't make things better by turning back now. Things will never be the same as they were before; the only way to better them is to continue forward to where you've decided to go.

Pay the price. Don't be so afraid of sudden, sharp, discomfort that you willingly tolerate chronic, continual, deadening pain the rest of your life. If you refuse to undergo temporary discomfort, you're resigning yourself to a lifetime with little happiness. The chronic pain can deaden your senses, destroy your love of life, and make you bitter.

You won't avoid the price by staying where you are. Instead, you'll pay it every day of your life as you stand on the sidelines and watch exciting alternatives pass you by. And the longer you put off the confrontation, the greater the price to be paid eventually.

The most important thing is to *act*, to do something to improve your life.

From where you stand now, you may be able to see *some* of the benefits of freedom. But only when you walk through that door will you see all the good things that can be yours on the other side.

Even if you can't be sure what awaits you, what's the value in continuing a wrong decision? Is that all your life is worth?

COURAGE

You may feel that you don't have the courage to make big changes in your life. But courage is too often thought of as being blind, thoughtless bravado. It usually isn't.

People who seem to act "courageously" usually have specific consequences in mind; they know the consequences both of acting and not acting. They've decided that the consequences of not acting are worse than the consequences of what we consider to be their courageous acts.

We don't necessarily know what their motivations are (they might be expectations of good things to come, fear of being thought a coward, desire for attention, etc.), but the person acting believes he knows.

When you're convinced you know the consequences of either course, you'll take action. If you have to walk through a dangerous mob to get to safety on the other

side of the street, you'll do so only when you're convinced
that the consequences of standing still are more dangerous
than moving. Until then, any talk of bravery is meaningless.

That's why it's important to think things out in advance.
Recognize the problems involved and how you'll cope with
them. And recognize the benefits that await you; focus on
them and remember them when things get difficult.

Once you can see and almost taste the good consequences of being free, once you know how to handle the
prices you'll have to pay to get there, you'll be impatient
to start. You won't lack the courage.

Certainly there will be many unknowns—and they can
be frightening. But they don't have to remain unknowns.
Identify the elements that are mysterious to you and then
try to get the information necessary to take the mystery
out of them.

If someone's attitude is an unknown factor, *ask him*
what his attitude is. If an unknown factor is the motivation of someone who's causing problems for you, go to
him and get it out into the open. Find out what he's trying
to accomplish. He may not be articulate enough to explain
it, so cultivate the art of asking enough questions to get
the answers you need.

It's amazing how many mysteries of life can be dissolved just by asking questions. Don't be afraid to ask
questions like "How would you feel if I were to make
some changes?" "What's the matter with our situation?"
"Are you upset with me?" Develop the technique of asking
for what you want to know.

Often someone will tell you that the answer will depend
upon circumstances. If so, find out *what* circumstances.
Keep asking until you know what standard he's using to
determine the circumstances.

For example, suppose you're considering changing jobs
but there's a possibility of a big raise coming soon—only
you don't know when or how big the raise will be. Find
out. Keep asking questions until you know what the circumstances must be in order to get your raise. "Do you

intend to give me a raise? . . . How much? . . . When? . . . *What* does it depend upon? . . . *What* must happen to permit the raise?"

Have him define such vague terms as "substantial raise," "increased business," "soon," "better quality work," etc. Then you can determine if it's worth your while to wait for it.

When you clear up all the mysteries, it will be much easier to act. You'll know *why* you're acting.

THE NEEDS OF OTHERS

It's easy to be influenced by the apparent needs of others—your spouse, children, employer, employees, friends, parents, relatives. They may seem to be dependent upon you. What will happen to them if you put your own freedom first?

Let's put your imagination to work one more time. This time take a few moments to imagine that you're going to die tonight. Yes—die. Pretend that you'll no longer be here to satisfy the needs of those who have been your responsibility.

After you think about it for a while, you'll probably come to a depressing conclusion—somehow, some way, by some miracle, *the world will survive without you.*

Somehow, your relatives will find someone else to borrow money from; the church will get someone else to arrange the flowers on the altar every Sunday; your friends will find new people to do favors for them. And your spouse may mourn for a suitable period—and then marry your best friend.

Your political crusades will succeed or fail—just as they would have if you were around to help. Your club will find someone else to do its fund-raising. And those who've leaned so heavily upon you for advice and sympathy will find other shoulders (and probably follow the new advice as infrequently as they did yours).

I'm not saying you won't be missed; that isn't the point.

The significance is that these people will find ways to survive without you. You're not as indispensable to others as you may have believed.

If they can survive without you, why couldn't you just disappear tonight without a trace, move a thousand miles away, and have a fresh start in an environment where no one knows you and depends upon you?

But why even do that? You don't have to move away. If others can survive if you died or moved away, why can't they survive without you while you stay here? Just remove yourself from the relationships and complications that don't add to your well-being.

In many ways, you'll be giving others *their* freedom, too. You might be surprised if you knew the discomforts others are suffering in their relationships with you. If a relationship is wrong for *you*, you can't possibly give to it everything a willing person would. Why not get out of the way and let others find better situations, too?

Even if they seem content with you, it may be that they, too, are afraid to speak up.

You can't know what's best for everyone else. Let nature take its course; let each person find his own place in the world—in accordance with his identity, his resources, and his desires.

You can't see inside of someone else. You can't decide what's good or bad for others. *You can only decide for yourself.*

SURPRISES

My own experience illustrates the impossibility of knowing what's good for others.

I tolerated an unhappy marriage for eight years. During the last few years of it, I knew I was dissatisfied but I wouldn't consider a divorce. My wife appeared to be physically and mentally helpless without me. I even feared that she might commit suicide if I left her.

When I decided to make the break, she resisted at first—but with much better control of herself than I'd ever seen before. And within two weeks she became a self-sufficient woman—doing many things neither of us had thought she could do.

I'd stayed with her for years, thinking it would be "unfair" for me to leave when she had so many problems. But *guess what her problem was.* As soon as *I* left, there were no more problems.

I never dreamed that could happen. Instead, I'd prepared for every dire possibility I could think of. When it turned out so well, it was a simple matter to adjust to my good fortune.[1]

MISTAKEN IDENTITIES

What else might be standing in the way of your making a change? Are you unwilling to give up the things you've acquired?

Perhaps those things aren't really yours. They may be cases of mistaken identities. Are you free to use them in any way your choose? If not, they aren't really yours.

If you're concerned about your wealth and property, ask yourself how much ownership you actually have. If you have to compromise your desires, if you can't use your wealth to live your life as *you* want to, why hang onto it so intensely?

Are you afraid of losing friends? If those people would turn against you because you've done something for yourself, maybe you don't really have their friendship. What would you lose if they turned away from you?

If it's your parents or children that you're afraid of losing, don't be awed by the powerful "family" mystique. Families *can* be wonderful, but not just because a group

---

[1] One of the most meaningful compliments I've received came years later when my wife thanked me for making her freedom possible.

of people happen to be of "common blood" or merely
bear the label "family." If a relationship—family or otherwise—isn't what it should be, why perpetuate it? The love
and closeness you need may be more plentiful elsewhere.

You can't lose anything that can't be reacquired later,
so don't focus on individuals and things. Recognize what it
is you desire from them and consider that you may be
able to get it more easily and richly elsewhere.

In my case, I decided in advance of the divorce what
I'd be willing to give up to gain my freedom—*everything*.
I knew that nothing was right the way it was. I had a
lovely house, nice furniture, some savings, a pretty wife, a
compromise relationship with my parents, and a lovely
daughter. But none of them satisfied what I really wanted.

When my wife said she wanted it all, including sole access to my daughter, I accepted those terms without fighting. I knew I could reacquire everything I really wanted
on a better basis.

I've since acquired far more property than I could have
earned where I was. The intellectual stimulation I'd always
missed is now mine. I have satisfying relationships now
that were out of reach where I was before.

My parents acted as you might expect parents to act.
At first, they took my wife's side and tried to influence me
to turn back. But they soon accepted the situation, acknowledged that I'd acted rightly, and are now much better friends than they were before.

I haven't seen my daughter since the divorce, nine years
ago, in accordance with the agreement. But that, too, was
a case of mistaken identity. I was fairly close to her and I
loved her. But it wasn't possible to have the kind of parent-child relationship I believe is right.

To keep the marriage intact, I had compromised my
own ideas about raising children; I went along with traditions of morality and religion that I didn't really believe. I
wasn't being myself; I wasn't giving her the things I have
to offer. What I *did* give her could have been had from
many other men.

What she lost by being separated from me has been replaced by someone else. What *I* lost was something I never really had—the opportunity to raise a child with enthusiasm, genuine rapport and mutual understanding, and the freedom to be the kind of example I'd like to set for a child.

I won't make those mistakes again. They couldn't be corrected where I was without someone having to sacrifice. Now that I'm free, I can find the right relationships in situations that are appropriate to what I want and need.

There were withdrawal symptoms, of course. But I was prepared for them. As it turned out, they were few—probably because I *was* prepared and because I was too busy making the most of my new life. All I missed was my daughter. But I could accept that temporary sadness and even cry about it—without any temptation to escape the sadness by jumping back into the box.

I was considerate and understanding of others, but I never thought that I should forfeit my free future for what others seemed to want. I knew that they would survive without me and that it was up to them to determine how.

YOUR PROBLEM

Everything I've said in this chapter has been intended to help you think through a major change you may be contemplating. The more you're prepared for what is to come, the easier it will be for you to act.

Recognize what you have to do. Anticipate all the prices and picture yourself paying them. Be straightforward with everyone concerned. And don't be ashamed of what you're doing.

Above all, recognize the prices in advance. Don't act whimsically, ignoring the consequences to come. Be prepared to have some of the unknown factors turn out negatively—and decide in advance how you'll handle them if they do.

Expect in advance the disapproval, the emotional difficulty, the withdrawal symptoms. And savor the good things that your freedom can bring you. Keep them in mind as you act; know *why* you're taking action.

If after thinking about these things you still feel unable to act, ask yourself what you'd do if you knew you were going to die next year. Once you knew you didn't have time to re-educate everyone and arrange things to everyone's satisfaction, what would you do?

You'd probably realize and accept the fact that *someone* will have to be displeased by your actions because you wouldn't have time to satisfy everyone. You'd probably get busy and settle your affairs on *some* basis in order to have some time left to live as you want to. You wouldn't let anything prevent you from being free to enjoy the time left.

Well, face it: You *are* going to die.

You're not going to live forever. You may live for decades or you may die in an accident tomorrow. But you *are* going to die someday. Are you going to wait until the last moment before you start living for yourself? You don't even know when the last moment will be.

What could be more important than getting a clean start *right now* so you can satisfy your dreams before it's too late?

They're your dreams; it's your life. No one else is going to make things right for you. Only your actions can provide the kind of life you want.

Your time has finally come. Make the most of it.

Certainly, if your spouse truly cannot change . . . he is entitled to be loved by someone for being the way he is. And, do you know, somewhere out in the world there *is* someone who can love him just the way he is, who can accept the shortcomings that you can not, who can appreciate things you don't even notice. What right have you to hold on to someone only to curse the dark side of his personality? —DAVID S. VISCOTT

The ultimate result of shielding men from the effects of folly is to fill the world with fools.

—HERBERT SPENCER

The first step is the hardest.

—MARIE DE VICHY-CHAMROND

He who hesitates is bossed. —DAVID SEABURY

Epilogue

33

Freedom in an Unfree World

WE'VE COME A LONG WAY, you and I, since we started in the first chapter. We've covered a great many matters and discussed a great many questions that affect your life.

It doesn't matter whether you've agreed with everything I've said—or even a large part of it. My main objective has been to get you thinking about yourself, to open up new avenues of freedom for you, to help you think of ways to use direct alternatives to build a better life for yourself.

The important thing is that you take yourself more seriously, that you respect your own view of the world and make sure that it really is *your* view, not something you've been told.

What I've said should never be considered to be the final answers to any of the questions raised—not even by me. For I'm growing daily. Today, I understand more about life and myself and my ways of living than I did when I began to write this book. There's no way that anything I write could be guaranteed to be my last words on the subject.

But that doesn't alter the usefulness of the ideas. What I say is a means of stimulating you to find ideas and rules for yourself—rules you can live by because they come from you. So whether you agree or disagree is unimportant. It's even unimportant if I've changed my mind about some point in the book since I wrote it.

I don't expect you to live by my code—anymore than *I* would live by someone else's code. I only hope you can find a way of life that fits your unique nature, one that will bring you the freedom and happiness that life has to offer.

Your life belongs wholly to you. Make it what *you* think it should be. Trust yourself. For you, your views are far more important than mine.

More than anything else, I've wanted to demonstrate that freedom *is* possible, that you can live your life as you want to live it—right here and now, without having to change the world. That may have seemed impossible when you first picked up this book; I hope it seems much more realistic now. And as you set to work at the task, the benefits you receive should make it seem even more realistic.

MY FREEDOM

In my own case, I've had several restrictions to eliminate in order to make freedom a reality.

The first was an uncomfortable marriage. But when I broke free of that, it became obvious to me that there were no restrictions that couldn't be surmounted.

The next restrictions to conquer were mostly philosophical. I had always thought highly of my own mind, but I too often ignored conclusions I'd reached. And it was too easy to submerge my own nature in an attempt to conform to whatever philosophical or intellectual set I found myself in.

Gradually, however, I discovered the benefits of acting upon my own ideas and desires. I stopped trying to enjoy the way of life I *should* live—and found ways to live as I *wanted* to live.

A big philosophical breakthrough for me was the realization that my own freedom was not only possible, but far more important than the establishment of a free society. I came to see how foolish it was to waste my precious life trying to make the world into what I'd thought it should be. I had always been intuitively partial toward direct alternatives, but now I was determined to build my whole life upon them.

The next step created a way of earning the money I wanted without being a slave to the treadmill. I never actually had that objective in mind, but the simple application of the principles I've expressed in this book brought it about.

Finally, the integration of all these principles into a single philosophy has made it possible for me to enjoy the blessings of freedom in all areas of my life. It has helped me understand myself, to understand those I deal with, to find valuable friendships, to understand what I crave in romantic relationships and to find that, and to keep myself out of boxes without any longer having to make a conscious effort to do so.

Now, freedom lets me enjoy each day as a new opportunity to discover new ways to taste life. Although I make more money than ever before, my work commitments are very few and always for brief periods. Most of each year is a free period in which I can pursue whatever I want.

My relationships with friends are on a very positive basis. They include no obligations, no duties, no claims to be presented for payment. I've learned how to say "no" and I've learned how to make it easy for others to say "no" to me when that's what they want to do.

When the telephone rings, I never have to fear that it represents a new burden I must cope with. Instead, the ringing of the telephone means a new opportunity that I can accept or turn down as I choose.

In the nine years since my divorce, I've enjoyed relationships with wonderful women who have added to my life. None of those situations has evolved into a lifetime relationship—but none of them had to in order to be of value. Each has provided a positive benefit, filling me with rich emotions and a sense of excitement about life.

Each relationship has been better than any before it because I've continued to learn more about what I need in order to be happy, and because I've continued to learn how to emphasize the positive benefits in each one.

In every area of my life, freedom has been to me like the sunshine—dispelling the gray shadows and spotlighting the beauties that life has to offer.

I don't believe I'll ever be 100 percent free or 100 percent happy or 100 percent knowledgeable. But that isn't necessary; life is a joyous experience as it is. Each new discovery and each new freedom brings its own rewards; there's no all-or-nothing reward way out in the distance that must be reached to justify the quest.

There are occasional moments of sadness or pain, but they're always short-lived. No setback can destroy me; there are too many good things in life—when one is denied to me, I have many other opportunities.

There are so many wonderful things to enjoy—good music, good food, good companionship, new discoveries, exciting sexual experiences, intellectual stimulation, challenging monetary opportunities. I've enjoyed too many of them to be willing to give them up for a fruitless crusade to change the world or any part of it.

YOUR FREEDOM

My way of life may be very different from what you want for yourself. So don't judge the value of freedom by what I've done with mine. Use the tremendous power you have to make your life what *you* dream it can be.

The examples I've used throughout the book were given to demonstrate that there are many practical ways by which you can improve your life and remove restrictions. They were never meant to suggest that you should do the same things I have done.

In the same way, the suggestions made were designed to

show you that *there's always a way*—as long as you're not looking for ways to change others. If I've written with passion and urgency, it's because the ideas were important to *me*. You will have to decide what's important to you.

You may have wished that some of the ideas were covered in more detail; there may have been questions raised in your mind for which you wanted answers. Let that be the stimulus for *you* to investigate and come up with answers that are suitable for you.

If you're determined to make things better, you'll probably find the answers you need. If one doesn't work, look for another. The problem for most people is that they *wish* things were better, but they're not determined to make them so.

The important thing is to concentrate upon what you can do—by yourself, upon your own initiative, without having to convince others of the rightness of your ideas. That's the common thread that unites all my suggestions; they are direct alternatives—none of them involves changing, educating, or forcing anyone to do what you want.

This is by far the easiest way to gain your freedom. It's always much, much harder to try to make other people do what you want them to do.

INCREASING REWARDS

There are rewards every step of the way. First, you can use direct alternatives to eliminate any restrictions that might have caused you to read this book. As you enjoy the benefits of that newly won freedom, you can apply the principles to broader areas of your life—to open up new hours, days, and opportunities for positive experiences.

Along the way, the sense of your own sovereignty will probably become more and more real to you. It's easy to accept intellectually that you make your own decisions and can choose to do what you want with your life. But emotionally you can find that hard to live by.

Slowly but inexorably, however, this realization that you

are the ruler of your own universe should become more vivid on new and deeper levels of your attitude. As that happens, you'll become more aware of your own power, you'll know that you can handle anything that comes. And you'll know that there's no reason to accept concepts and relationships that don't offer you what you want.

The rewards will be magnified as your sense of sovereignty underlies your way of life. You'll automatically avoid boxes and traps, you'll be ever alert for opportunities and new ways to experience happiness.

And you'll probably realize more deeply that you never need to change other people; you'll know that there are always easier ways to have what you want. And that's a greater reward than what you get from removing any single restriction from your life.

I'm sure that many people accept the abstract principle that you shouldn't try to change others or interfere with their lives. And yet the principle is rarely applied in practice.

An individual might say, "I don't want to change anyone." And yet, he might still spend a great deal of his time trying to get others to agree with his views, or trying to prevent someone from doing something he thinks will be bad for him, or trying to change people by participating in a movement over a burning issue, or voting to prevent others from doing what they want to do. In all these ways, he's trying to change others—to make them do other than what their natures lead them to do.

And he doesn't have to. Throughout this book, I've tried to demonstrate that there are always plenty of alternatives available to you that don't require that you take on the responsibility to make others see the light.

The recognition that you don't have to change others isn't the same as losing the *urge* to do so, however. The urge can remain long after you have accepted the superiority of direct alternatives. You may often find yourself tempted to intervene in the affairs of others in order to make things go your way.

But as you begin to enjoy the benefits of *non*-intervention, you'll probably find the urge fading away, slowly but surely. At first it may come only with strangers; you'll lose the desire to guide, suggest, change, or alter those who aren't immediately relevant to you.

Then, as this attitude permeates your way of life, the time may come when you'll no longer see any point in trying to influence your spouse, your lover, your close friends, your business associates.

You'll be so aware that each person must go his own way, *in* his own way, that you won't want the sour fruits of a victory that requires someone else to change his ways. What you get from trying to restrain someone's natural impulses is of little benefit to you. What you get from a person whose desires naturally benefit you is magnificent.

THE BREAKTHROUGH

And so one day you may discover that you've achieved a new freedom, an emotional freedom that's greater than any you've known before—*freedom from the urge to control others*.

When you have that freedom, you'll experience a wondrous sense of weightlessness, an absence of burdens, a freedom to let the world unfold as it will—adventurously, challengingly. You'll know that whatever happens isn't your problem because you no longer have the responsibility to see that others do what they should.

This freedom has only been completely mine for a year or two—so it's still new and awesome to me. I doubt that I could ever put into words the effect it has had upon my life. I know that it makes me feel lighter than air; I'm relieved of all the burdens that come from feeling that someone else must act in a way I want.

Even when the actions of others affect me directly, I know that there are many alternatives available to me; I don't have to feel that someone *must* act in one prescribed way. I can let each person be himself, do as he chooses, learn what he wants to learn, go where he wants to go. I have no duty to restrain him. *What a relief!*

Does a friend become angry with me because of something I've said or done? I can explain my position—in case he wants to understand. But I don't *have* to convince him of anything. There are always new, and probably more appropriate, friends.

Does my lover find someone else attractive? Let her. Let her find out for herself what's most important to her. I don't have to try to convince her that she "shouldn't" be attracted to others, that she shouldn't want to spend time with others, or that she should prefer me. That's for her to decide for herself—and in her own way. Let her be what she is, as she wants to be.

Does she want to leave me? Let her. Since every romance is better than those that preceded it, this only means that the time has come to find something better—to find someone more appropriate to what I understand of myself today.

Are there people who are polluting the atmosphere? Let them. There are plenty of ways I can make sure that doesn't affect me.

Do the politicians want to impose new restrictions? Let them. I'll find ways of avoiding them easily enough. I couldn't stop the restrictions anyway—and I have no urge to waste my precious time trying. I have no temptation to vote, to campaign, to try to stop a candidate who promises new follies. If he's elected, he'll probably do just what his opponent would have done—which means whatever he has to do to consolidate his power.

I'm free!—free of that awesome responsibility that once commanded me to worry about everything, that once caused me to continually try to make others see what I understand, that once made the actions of others my responsibility and concern.

Have I retired to a cave somewhere to live as a hermit? Obviously not.

It doesn't even mean that I'm continually switching friendships. Nearly all the friends I've made in the past nine years are still my friends—no matter how little or how much contact there may be between us.

Nor does it mean that I could never find a lifetime love relationship. It only means that I don't have to feel that any given romance (new or existing) *must* be made to last forever. I'm free to let my lover be totally free.

Nor does it mean that I never speak my mind about a difference of opinion with someone. I'm quite willing to state my views to persons who are important to me. But I'm not trying to change anyone. I use my view as a suggestion—a way to find out more about him, where he stands, and whether he's responsive to my thoughts.

If he finds my alternative attractive, it may provide a new opportunity for me. But I'm not dependent upon his acceptance; I'm fully prepared to go elsewhere, if necessary. I have everything to gain and nothing to lose except the small amount of time necessary to present the suggestion.

I feel this way whether the situation involves a personal relationship or a business proposition. Even when selling for a living, I never felt dependent upon any given prospect; I never felt that I *had* to convince anyone of anything. And that attitude has resulted in far more success and far less frustration than most people get when they feel they must be persuasive to get what they want.

When I lost the urge to control others, I also lost all need to hate or fear anyone. The world is no longer divided between the good guys and the bad guys. Now I can see that each person is seeking his own happiness, each in his own way (just as I am), and that there are some of those people with whom I have a conflict of interest.

But I don't have to hate or fear anyone. Those emotions come from a sense of vulnerability—from the feeling that someone *has* to act in a certain way to please you. When he doesn't, and you've depended upon him (or depended upon your ability to *make* him be as you want), you can easily respond with hate or fear. But when you're willing to let each person go his own way, you lose all need to hate anyone.

Neither do I have to worry whether anyone is "getting away" with anything. I'm not the world's policeman. I know that everyone will experience the consequences of his own acts. If his acts are right, he'll get good consequences; if they're not, he'll suffer for it. The consequences are the only standard that matters—and I'm certainly not needed to impose those consequences.

It isn't my concern to see that justice prevails; it automatically prevails—upon me and everyone else. *Justice is the natural, inevitable consequence that follows every act.* Any attempt to interfere with that natural justice will just bring about additional consequences that I might not like for myself.

So there is no reason for me to be concerned about anyone else's business—except as I decide how I will deal with that which affects me.

When you achieve freedom from the urge to control others, your life is truly your own—to make of it almost anything you might want. For you're no longer burdened by the need to make others understand; your time is no longer regulated by plans that depend upon your persuasive powers or your ability to dominate situations.

You're free—free to choose among thousands of direct alternatives—free to choose the ones that can make you happiest.

I don't think you can really be free until you're willing to let others be free. Only then are you relieved of that terrible responsibility for the way others act.

Then you can expose yourself as you really are, because you needn't be acceptable to any particular individuals. You can let the appropriate individuals come to you because of what you are—and you can disregard those who reject you.

This book is an example of that attitude. It should be obvious by now that I didn't write it in hopes of changing the world. I hope only to offer more ideas, more encouragement, and more alternatives to those who are receptive. My relationships with such people are mutually beneficial. I trade ideas for money—but I would never make my future dependent upon changing or controlling or persuading anyone.

There are many people to whom those ideas *are* important—and those people are the primary reason I've written this book. I'm letting those people know that they're not alone, that they have every reason to follow their own minds—regardless of the views of those around them.

Too, the book is a part of my personal advertising campaign—revealing what I am to those who would approve.

I know that there are plenty of people who see life in a way similar to mine. I've met many of them—and I know there must be many more. My life has been enriched by such people; their presence has brought me thousands of days of stimulation, excitement, and happiness.

With so many wonderful people alive, why should I focus on those with whom I have conflicts of interest? Why should I try to rally the kindred souls into a fruitless crusade to change the world? The world is already too beautiful, so full of wonderful opportunities that I couldn't possibly take advantage of all those already available to me. Why must I make the world better?

THE ULTIMATE FREEDOM

Freedom from the urge to control others has made my life more exciting than I could have imagined it could be nine years ago. But beyond that, there's a further freedom that I seek, a freedom that can come only after losing the urge to control others.

At that point, one is free to let *himself* be free; he's free to discover himself more intensely. He no longer needs to conform to *any* preconceived standard. He's free to let himself develop as his real nature dictates.

This, of course, means getting completely and permanently out of the Identity Trap.

It doesn't happen all at once, however; it develops in stages. There are constant discoveries to be made about oneself; there's no clear dividing line between being oneself and trying to be someone other than oneself.

You come to a point where you take yourself more and more seriously and begin to accept more and more of what you see in yourself. And then you come to another point where you feel you've never really seen yourself clearly before. And another point and another. You continually achieve new levels of awareness of yourself.

I call this *freedom from the urge to change yourself*. I don't feel I've fully earned this freedom, so there's little more I can say about it. But I know that every step closer to it provides its own benefits. As with the other freedoms, it doesn't have to be achieved *in toto* in order to be rewarding.

Every day I'm more and more willing to accept myself as I am; I regard my nature as a given fact and then work to satisfy myself as I am.

I can't say whether I will ever completely lose the urge to control my own nature. I only know that everything I do to move closer to that goal is of great benefit to me. And I know how valuable it has been to me to lose the urge to control others—so I expect to continue to benefit as I become less inclined to control myself.

THE FUTURE

Where you go with these ideas will be up to you. Wherever you go, it should be fun. Life is an adventure, not a burden.

So many people spend so much of their lives trying to unravel the mysteries of the universe, trying to understand the meaning and purpose of such things as wars, poverty, misery, complications, and boxes.

Others try to gain the upper hand over life through religion, astrology, ESP, positive thinking, or drugs. Why? All they need to do is to open their eyes and see what's in front of them—a beautiful world with every opportunity for freedom and happiness.

If others choose to make the world's ills their business, let them. If others choose to fight the politicians' wars, it's unfortunate but that's their choice. It doesn't have to be yours.

You can make a wonderful life for yourself; you have everything you need to do it. Let others fight their campaigns for themselves. Don't forfeit the only life you have; use it to make living everything you've ever wanted it to be.

Use the years ahead of you to advance the only really important cause that exists—your freedom and happiness. You can have it if you concentrate on yourself and what you need for happiness—instead of worrying about what others think and do.

You are the ruler of your world and no one can dethrone you—unless you choose to let him. No one can stop you from living as you want to live—unless you disregard your own sovereignty.

There is so much you can have—and it will be yours to keep, to cherish, and enjoy without guilt or insecurity. You won't be depending upon your ability to "hold things together"; you'll be enjoying what is easily and firmly yours. You'll be involved with people who want you to be what you are—and who will enthusiastically give you, without sacrifice, what you want to have.

I can't express how much I appreciate your spending this time with me. I hope that it has added something useful and beneficial to your knowledge and opportunities.

We'll probably never meet, but I want you to know that I'm on your side.

And I wish you the very best.

Live and let live. —FRIEDRICH VON SCHILLER

Appendix

Acknowledgments

IF YOU'VE FOUND the material in this book easy to follow and understand, a large share of the credit must go to two free individuals—Donna Rasnake and Mark Corske. They spent hundreds of hours working with me, clarifying the principles involved and editing my words. They understand the concepts very well, and so their suggestions were usually very helpful.

Our relationship was an excellent example of the use of the principles expressed in this book. Since the basic ideas and principles are mine, and since I'm responsible for everything said in the book, we were never involved in Group-Trap decisions. They provided numerous suggestions and examples, but the final decisions always remained with me.

Consequently, the ideas and writing style are still very much my own. But the clarity of presentation has been greatly improved by their help.

In addition, over the past several years, many people have helped me to better understand various principles that have led to the ideas expressed herein.

I'm particularly grateful for the help I've received in years past from Alvin Lowi and Marian Hall Landers, and from the writings of Murray Rothbard and Ayn Rand. Since there are significant philosophical disagreements between myself and these people, please don't assume that they endorse any specific viewpoints expressed in this book. There are also others whose past help is appreciated, but whose ideas are so different from mine that they have asked not to be named.

Dr. F. A. Harper and Stu Sanders made valuable suggestions after reading the manuscript.

I'm also grateful to The Macmillan Company for its willingness to publish controversial ideas, and to my editor, Eleanor Friede, for her encouragement, assistance, and patience.

Perhaps most of all, Jeannette Tromanhauser has been a valuable friend who encouraged and inspired me by her desire for me to write this book so that she could read it.

To take what there *is*, and use it, without waiting forever in vain for the preconceived—to dig deep into the actual and get something out of *that*—this doubtless is the right way to live. —HENRY JAMES

Glossary

Absolute morality: A morality to which an individual is expected to surrender his happiness.

Bad: That which brings you unhappiness.

Box: An uncomfortable situation that restricts your freedom.

Box Trap: The assumption that the cost of getting out of a bad situation is too great to consider.

Burning-Issue Trap: The belief that there are compelling social issues that require your participation.

Certainty Trap: The urge to act as if your information were totally certain.

Despair Trap: The belief that other people can prevent you from being free.

Direct alternative: A choice available to you that requires only direct action by yourself to get a desired result. (See also *indirect alternative.*)

Emotion: An involuntary response to something that happens.

Emotional Trap: The belief that you can make important decisions at a time when you're feeling strong emotions.

Empathy: The ability to understand and identify with someone else's situation.

Ends: Goals that provide happiness without necessarily being means to a greater end.

Feeling: An involuntary response to something that happens. (Synonymous with *emotion.*)

Freedom: Living your life as you want to live it.

General Market: The sum of all individual markets; the totality of all individual desires compared with the totality of products and services available.

Good: That which brings you happiness.

Government: An agency of coercion that's accepted as necessary by most people within its area of influence.

Government Traps: (1) The belief that governments perform socially useful functions that deserve your support. (2) The belief that you have a duty to obey laws. (3) The belief that the government can be counted upon to carry out a social reform you favor. (4) The fear that the government is so powerful that it can prevent you from being free.

Group Trap: The belief that you can accomplish more by sharing responsibilities, efforts and rewards with others than you can by acting on your own.

Happiness: The mental feeling of well-being.

Identity: The characteristics of a person (or thing) that determine what he (or it) is capable of. (Synonymous with *nature*.)

Identity Traps: (1) The attempt to be someone other than yourself. (2) The assumption that others will do things in the way that you would.

Indirect alternative: A choice available to you that requires that you induce someone else to do what is necessary to achieve your objective. (See also *direct alternative*.)

Integrity: Knowing yourself well enough to be able to mean what you say.

Intellect: The conscious, deliberate, volitional attempt to perceive identities and utilize them. (Synonymous with *thinking*.)

Intellectual Trap: The belief that your emotions should conform to a preconceived standard that has been intellectually determined.

Intuition: The unconscious use of previously recognized information.

Jealousy: The negative emotion caused by the fear of losing someone (or something) to someone else.

Justice: The natural, inevitable consequence that follows every act.

Liability: A price that must be paid if things don't turn out as you want them to turn out.

Market: A compatibility of interests that makes an exchange possible.

Means: A tool or course of action that doesn't provide happiness in itself, but is meant to lead to an end that will.

Moral decision: A decision that involves possible long-term consequences.

Morality: The attempt to consider all the relevant consequences of your actions. (Synonymous with *personal morality.* See also *absolute morality* and *universal morality.*)

Morality Trap: The belief that you must obey a moral code created by someone else.

Natural monopoly: A situation in which you are so appropriate to the needs and desires of your customers, friends, or lover that competition is relatively powerless to affect the relationship.

Nature: The characteristics of a person (or thing) that determine what he (or it) is capable of. (Synonymous with *identity.*)

Negative decision: A decision in which all known alternatives would leave you with less happiness than you had prior to the necessity of making the decision.

Non-marriage: A love relationship in which no attempt is made to merge property, uncommon interests, or decision-making authority.

Objective: (ADJECTIVE) Realistic; not colored by your own unique perception, knowledge, emotions and interpretation.

One-sided transaction: A relationship in which one party has used violence (or the threat of it) to force the other to participate.

Personal morality: The attempt to consider all the relevant consequences of your actions. (Used synonymously with *morality.* See also *absolute morality* and *universal morality.*)

Positive decision: A decision in which you can choose among two or more alternatives—any of which would increase your happiness.

Previous-Investment Trap: The belief that time, effort, and money spent in the past should be considered when making a decision in the present.

Price: Time, effort, money or property expended; or emotional or physical discomfort.

Relevant: That which has consequences that will affect you.

Resources: (1) *Natural resources:* land, minerals, vegetables, and animals. (2) *Human resources:* time, effort, and knowledge. (3) *Secondary resources:* property that is created by applying human resources to natural resources.

Responsibility: Vulnerability to consequences.

Right: That which brings you happiness. (Different from *rights*; see below.)

Rights (ADJECTIVE): That which you believe you're entitled to, despite the unwillingness of the person who must provide it.

Rights Trap: The belief that your rights will make you free.

Selfishness: Concern with your own happiness.

Sovereignty: The power to control your own life by deciding which information to accept and by making your own decisions.

Subjective: Colored by your own unique perception, knowledge, emotions, and interpretation.

Thinking: (NOUN) The conscious, deliberate, volitional attempt to perceive identities and utilize them. (Synonymous with *intellect*.)

Trap: A philosophical assumption that is accepted without challenge.

Truth: Information that leads to predictable results.

Two-sided transaction: A relationship in which both parties participate because they want to.

Unhappiness: The mental feeling of discomfort.

Universal morality: A code of conduct that is guaranteed to bring happiness to anyone who uses it.

Unselfishness Trap: The belief that you must put the happiness of others ahead of your own.

Utopia Trap: The belief that you must create better conditions in society before you can be free.

Value: The degree of happiness produced by an object, an idea, or a person.

Vulnerability: Exposure to consequences.

Withdrawal symptom: A negative emotion experienced after the end of a relationship.

Wrong: That which brings you unhappiness.

This above all: to thine own self be true,
And it must follow, as the night the day,
Thou canst not then be false to any man.
—SHAKESPEARE

Recommended Reading
(Bibliography)

THE BOOKS LISTED BELOW may be helpful in providing further elaboration on some of the areas covered in the text of this book. I have tried to provide some descriptive information so that you can know what you're getting into before you buy any of the books.

Obviously, I don't agree totally with any of the authors—any more than you would completely agree with what I've written.

FREEDOM

The Art of Selfishness by David Seabury. As the Foreword points out, this is "a manual for dealing with the problems of selfishness . . . *the selfishness of others.*" A very easy to read book that offers valuable suggestions for dealing with various kinds of problems in personal relationships. I highly recommend it. (Simon & Schuster, New York 10020. Hardcover $5.95; cardcover $1.45.)

Feel Free by David S. Viscott, M.D. Plenty of encouragement for the reader contemplating a major change—in his job, career, marriage, or whatever. The author also helps you anticipate the problems you'll face and suggests ways of dealing with them. Very easy to read. (Peter H. Wyden, New York 10017; $5.95.)

IDEAS ON LIVING

Return to Reason by Paul Lepanto. An unauthorized presentation of Ayn Rand's philosophy of Objectivism. In my view, Lepanto's book presents the best of Ayn Rand's philosophy with very few of its weaknesses. Consequently, it offers a great deal of insight into methods of clear thinking. Relatively easy to read and follow. (Exposition Press, Jericho, N.Y. 11753; $6.00.)

The Disowned Self by Nathaniel Branden. An excellent exposition of the problems caused by the Identity and Intellectual Traps—together with some non-psychotherapy suggestions. Although Branden is a psychologist, there is very little technical terminology, and the book is relatively easy to follow. (Nash Publishing Corp., Los Angeles 90069; $7.95.)

Walden by Henry David Thoreau. The ideas of Thoreau are always worth thinking about, even if the life-style he chose differs from your tastes. (Hardcover: Charles E. Merrill, Columbus, Ohio; $6.95. Paperback: Collier Books, New York 10022; $.95—includes essay "On the Duty of Civil Disobedience.")

MARRIAGE AND CHILDREN

Open Marriage by Nena O'Neill and George O'Neill. Many good ideas for improving a love relationship. Some of their ideas about love relationships are different from mine; but they also go into far greater detail in some important areas. (M. Evans & Co., New York 10017; $6.95.)

The Baby Trap by Ellen Peck. The first book-length presentation of reasons why children are *not* necessary or desirable in a marriage. Unfortunately, half the author's arguments are ecological (overpopulation, etc.), but the other half offers dramatic evidence of the personal drawbacks of having children. Also valuable, I think, for anyone already a parent —for it calls attention to the problems parenthood brings to a love relationship, and understanding those problems may help to suggest solutions. (Bernard Geis Associates, New York 10022; $5.95.)

"The Motherhood Myth" by Betty Rollins (an article published in *Look* magazine, September 22, 1970). Although *Look* is no longer published, you may be able to find this issue in a library. It contains the most concentrated stack of evidence I've seen for looking before you leap into parenthood.

GOVERNMENT

Power and Market by Murray N. Rothbard. Although this is a textbook with some heavy terminology in places, most of the book is relatively easy to read and follow. And it contains the most complete presentation of the evidence against government as an institution that I've seen. It refutes all the common claims of the necessity of government, and demonstrates the consequences of various kinds of government intervention. (Institute for Humane Studies, Menlo Park, Calif.; $8.00.)

Man Versus the State by Herbert Spencer. A non-textbook presentation of the case against government by a nineteenth-century English philosopher. Although the book is a hundred years old and deals with English laws, most of the examples match present-day laws and political problems. Fairly easy to read. (Peter Smith, Gloucester, Mass.; $3.75.)

No Treason by Lysander Spooner. A 70-page statement asserting that no individual is bound by the Constitution, written by a nineteenth-century maverick who operated his own postal company in competition with the government. A bit technical in places, but interesting reading. (Rampart College, Santa Ana, Calif.; $1.50.)

COMMUNICATION

Between Parent and Child by Dr. Haim G. Ginott. *The* manual for improving communication. Although its purpose is to improve relationships with children, the principles involved are valuable when dealing with *any* human being. (Hardcover: The Macmillan Company, New York 10022; $5.95. Paperback: Avon Books, New York 10019; $1.25.)

DIFFERENCES

You Are Extraordinary by Roger J. Williams. The chief value of this book is its semi-scientific presentation of evidence that all people are different; together with some of the resulting social implications. Easy to read; encumbered a bit by attempts to reconcile science and religion. (Hardcover: Random House, New York 10022; $6.95. Paperback: Pyramid Publications, New York 10022; $.95.)

PHILOSOPHY

For the New Intellectual by Ayn Rand. A thought-stimulating collection of excerpts from Ayn Rand's novels; very valuable, I think, for gaining new perspectives on age-old social issues. From this introduction, you may want to pursue her work further through her four novels. Not difficult reading. (Hardcover: Random House, New York 10022; $6.95. Paperback: New American Library, New York; $.75.)

SOVEREIGNTY

She Lives! by Paul Neimark (fiction). A realistic, heroic novel in a contemporary setting. The main characters demonstrate that their lives are not bound by the experts, the rules, or traditional limits. (Nash Publishing Corp., Los Angeles 90069; $6.95.)

FINANCIAL SECURITY

You Can Profit from a Monetary Crisis by Harry Browne. An explanation of the current monetary chaos and the difficulties in the U.S. economy—together with suggestions for approaching financial security in spite of the times. (Hardcover: The Macmillan Co., N.Y. 10022; $8.95; Paperback: Bantam Books, 666 Fifth Avenue, New York, N.Y. 10019; $2.25.)

How You Can Profit from the Coming Devaluation by Harry Browne. The predecessor to the above book, it is still relevant as it explains the value of gold as a form of financial security. (Hardcover: Arlington House, New Rochelle, N.Y. 10801; $5.95. Paperback: Avon Books, New York 10019; $1.25.)

Economic Research Counselors (1760 Marine Drive, West Vancouver, B.C., Canada) publishes information showing how to set up bank accounts in Switzerland and other foreign countries, as well as other information that may be helpful to you in beating the system.

Pacific Coast Coin Exchange (3713 Long Beach Blvd., Long Beach, Calif. 90807) also publishes information on ways to protect yourself against government economic policies.

OTHER BOOKS QUOTED OR MENTIONED IN THE TEXT

Selected Essays on Political Economy by Frederic Bastiat; Van Nostrand Reinhold Co., New York 10001; $7:50.

Fact Sheet, published by Willis E. Stone, Los Angeles 90028; $10.00 a year.

One Is a Crowd by Frank Chodorov; Devin-Adair Co., New York 10010; $6.50.

How to Keep Your Money and Freedom by Harry D. Schultz; Harry D. Schultz, 170 Sloane St., London S.W. 1., England; $8.00.

Index